DEAFNESS, DEVELOPMENT
AND LITERACY

ALEC WEBSTER

DEAFNESS, DEVELOPMENT AND LITERACY

METHUEN London and New York

To Richard, Joe, Lizzie and Anne

First published in 1986 by
Methuen & Co. Ltd
11 New Fetter Lane,
London EC4P 4EE

© 1986 Alec Webster

Typeset in Great Britain by
Scarborough Typesetting Services
and printed by
Richard Clay (The Chaucer Press),
Bungay, Suffolk

*British Library Cataloguing in
Publication Data*

Webster, Alec
Deafness, development and literacy.
1. Deaf – Education – Reading
I. Title
371.91' 24   HV2469.R4
ISBN 0-416-92050-0
ISBN 0-416-92060-8 Pbk

CONTENTS

TABLES

FIGURES

Their faces were alert and simple
Like faces of little animals, small night lemurs caught in
   the flashlight

Ted Hughes: 'Deafschool' from *Moortown*

(Faber & Faber, 1979)

PREFACE

This book represents the best part of a decade's research, thinking and discussion, about the special needs of hearing-impaired children, particularly in learning to read. Deafness is a 'hidden' handicap, not only in the sense that it cannot be seen, but also because there are few clearly visible solutions to the learning difficulties associated with it. In this book a number of things have been attempted. First, to broach the central issues simply and directly. All those professionally concerned with hearing-impaired children should find the book useful, and no specialist knowledge or experience is assumed. The developmental consequences of both mild and severe hearing losses are appraised straightforwardly. How these factors impinge on the child's language, reading and writing, has been the second major concern. Finally, the book provides a framework for thinking about the assessment and teaching of literacy, which should enable teachers themselves to explore further.

Many normally-hearing and hearing-impaired children took part in the studies reported here. Of the special schools and units visited, I would like to acknowledge my debt to the children and staff of the Royal Schools for the Deaf in Derby and Margate, Gatehouse School, Hamilton Lodge School, Heston School, Mill Hall School, Ovingdean Hall School, the Royal Cross School, St Thomas's School, Thomasson Memorial School, Whitebrook School, and the resources for hearing-impaired children in Berkshire and Buckinghamshire. I cannot pretend to have done other than trade off my goodwill in the local authority in which I work. Luckily, I have found myself amongst psychologists, doctors, academics, speech therapists and teachers, who all feel they have a lot to learn from each other, and from the children in their midst.

However, the main acknowledgement must be to the Deafness Research Group at Nottingham University. Without Dr David Wood's inspiration none of this would have been possible. To those who helped me sort out my ideas and this manuscript, I owe a special debt. Rosemary Ayles, Sylvia Baldwin, Margaret Davison, Dr Amanda Griffiths, Dr Rodney Maliphant, Cliff Moon, Dr Bridie Raban, Dr Philip Smith, and Rhona Stainthorpe, have all helped me greatly.

Deafness continues to pose some of the most tantalizing educational questions, more so, when taken together with another set of issues from reading research. For the sake of the children that this book is about, it is hoped that the work will bring a fresh perspective to some very old and complex problems.

ALEC WEBSTER
Kidmore Clinic, Reading, Berkshire

1
INTRODUCTION

This book has been written as a starting point rather than as a final statement. The reason for that lies in the nature of the exercise. On the one hand there are more research articles and books published about reading than any other topic, and yet our explanation of the reading process in ordinary children is far from complete. On the other hand teachers and researchers have been endeavouring to understand the developmental implications of a hearing-impairment for the child and the family, and here too, there is a great deal yet to uncover.

It is perhaps true that those involved in mainstream reading research have not offered much of any practical value to teachers working with hearing-impaired children. By the same token, the issue of reading and deafness has been a grossly neglected area, even by those who have specialized in working with the deaf. Quite simply, other much more contentious (and less profitable) issues have occupied the centre stage, such as whether to teach a child through sign language or speech.

The scope and purpose of the book

It is with some caution that psychologists write on and about teaching practice with hearing-impaired children, and it is only recently that teachers of the deaf have begun to work in close partnership with other professional groups in the United Kingdom. One purpose of this book is to draw attention to the special learning needs which children with only relatively mild hearing losses may encounter in the ordinary school. So, whilst this is a book which draws mainly on research findings from studies of more severely hearing-impaired children with highly specialized educational needs, it is intended to cover a broad spectrum of auditory difficulties.

The book has been written for a wide audience and not just the informed few. There are strong reasons, which we have addressed in some detail elsewhere (Webster and Ellwood, 1985), for expecting many more teachers to have contact with hearing-impaired children in schools, without necessarily having any specialist qualifications or experience with the deaf. This would arise, quite simply, if we widened the concept of what constituted an educationally significant hearing disability. One can argue that almost every primary classroom will have a child whose learning is affected by some degree of hearing loss, however transitory. To these children we owe a responsibility to raise the teacher's level of awareness and understanding, as well as to provide practical help. Where an initiative is taken to give a child with a known severe hearing loss some form of integrated learning opportunity within a mainstream school, there is a much wider and more difficult duty of providing in-service training to a range of teachers who will be directly involved in teaching that child.

As well as class-teachers in ordinary schools, the book should also be helpful to teachers who have a particular interest in reading, such as 'remedial' specialists. A very high proportion of children referred for extra help, for example, to reading centres or language support groups, have histories of mild hearing loss. Why this should be so, and what the implications for teaching are likely to be, are issues that the reading specialist will find addressed fairly and straightforwardly.

Those teachers who are professionally qualified to work with the hearing-impaired will find this book a useful update on current research. We have tried to provide a framework for language and reading which will enable teachers of the deaf to think out how to proceed, and to understand what the impact of any teaching programme is likely to be. There are, of course, no simple solutions. Teachers of the deaf will, however, find much that is stimulating and relevant to their central concerns: how best to foster language and literacy skills.

The book is also intended to address psychologists. Inexplicably, psychologists have tended to shy away from hearing-impaired children, despite the obvious significance deafness holds for understanding normal processes of language development. In the wake of the 1981 Education Act, educational psychologists are busy skilling themselves in order to contribute meaningfully to the multi-professional assessment of hearing-impaired children. Above all else, this book tries to warn professionals about the pitfalls ahead, when attempts are made to 'assess' children who are hearing-impaired.

Hopefully, too, the growing number of speech therapists who are widening their commitments to include written language difficulties, as well as hearing loss, will find this book of interest. Students, particularly teachers in training, and last, but not least, parents, will find accessible information on the relationships between deafness and the issues of language acquisition, reading and writing.

Our intention then, is to provide an introductory text for those who want to know about the implications of deafness and the learning difficulties associated with deafness in its varying degrees. Included, particularly for the ordinary class-teacher, are basic levels of information about conductive (as opposed to sensori-neural) hearing losses, which are highly prevalent in childhood. The major concern of the book has been to relate the implications of hearing loss to the processses of acquiring literacy. Essentially, the book will be judged on how well it succeeds in raising people's awareness about the hearing-impaired child, and on the practical spin-offs which it gives to those who are working at the coal face, with the children in the classroom.

The deficit model

This is a book then, for the practitioner. However, whilst we recognize that hearing-impaired children may have special educational needs, teachers have needs too. We tend to assume that the learning difficulties experienced by the child, lie *within* the child. O'Hagan and Swanson (1984) describe the ways in which this kind of thinking about children colours our expectations. This is sometimes called the deficit model. It may pre-occupy us to such an extent that we are diverted from the really important issues. Such a deficit model, for example, encourages teachers to exacerbate a child's handicap by attributing every problem which arises to the child's disability. Yet we know that teachers, classroom practice, and schools themselves, vary widely in their effectiveness. The hopeful side of the coin is that teachers and schools can help by changing the way they tackle things. In other words, it may be more effective to try and modify the learning situation, rather than the child.

One set of special needs we can identify, then, belong to the teacher. Teachers require a range of flexible, practical strategies. Some of these must be aimed at adult styles and the learning context. For example, one fundamental requirement is that teachers must be able to devise clearly stated objectives in their work so that the effectiveness of a teaching approach can be evaluated. Hopefully, this book will steer teachers towards clear objectives in language and literacy. But, as we have said, our present understanding of both deafness and the reading process gives only starting points.

To date, the deficit model has informed almost all of the existing research into the literacy skills of the hearing-impaired. Whilst we can recognize the flaws in this research, we cannot ignore its findings. Classic amongst the deficit studies is the book by Conrad (1979) which describes a range of verbal skills such as speech intelligibility, as well as reading comprehension, in school-leavers from units and special schools for the deaf in the United Kingdom. A universally depressing picture of the limited achievements of hearing-impaired children has been painted. A great deal of effort has gone into large-scale evaluative research to measure the relative standards of literacy in the hearing-impaired, compared with the normal peer group. The ironic point about this approach, as we shall later discover, is that its results are misleading and tend to obscure the much more interesting question of 'how?' the deaf child reads. Any light, however dim, that can be shone on the latter, will be of much greater practical value to the teacher.

Integration: speech or sign?

We have said that many more non-specialists, without specific training or experience with the deaf, will have some contact with children who have varying degrees of hearing loss in schools. There has always been a significant number of children with major hearing losses, who have enjoyed mainstream school situations. A survey of some ninety classes for hearing-impaired children in 'hearing' schools was carried out by the Department of Education and Science in the 1960s (DES,1967). About a third of the children in the survey, supported by units and teachers of the deaf in mainstream schools, had severe-to-profound hearing losses. This has been different from established practice with other groups of children with special educational needs who may have received some form of segregated provision.

It seems likely that there will be a growing trend to integrate more severely hearing-impaired children in ordinary schools. A stringent economic climate, pressure from parents, a concern for earlier diagnosis and intervention, developments in hearing-aid technology, such as radio aids, and changes in philosophy reflected in the 1981 Education Act have all increased the possibilities of integration for even the more profoundly impaired children.

In any book related to the education of the hearing-impaired it seems mandatory to declare one's position in relation to the 'oral' versus 'manual' debate. In the United Kingdom this debate is also inextricably linked with the question of special school versus mainstream school placement, since many special schools for the deaf have become identified with signing methods of teaching. There is a complex set of arguments on either side for the role of speech or sign language in the teaching of the severely hearing-impaired. It is important to broach this issue at the outset because claims have been made by both camps regarding the superiority of one method over the other in the child's acquisition of literacy.

On one side of the debate the strictly oral tradition places great emphasis on training the child to use residual hearing, make the best use of hearing-aids, and pay attention to lip-reading clues. Meadow (1980) suggests that practically all deaf children with hearing parents (which is more that 90 per cent of the total number) have had their initial exposure to language through spoken English, and the oral-only approach is the preferred parental choice. In an ordinary school situation, children who sign will be restricted in their social and linguistic interaction, unless other children and teachers are taught the system. Nevertheless, there are many hearing-impaired children who find speech, even with lip-reading and amplification, a most inaccessible code of communication which they find impossible to master.

On the other side of the debate, proponents of signing methods argue that children who are exposed to richer language experience, make quicker progress, are less frustrated and isolated, and are helped to acquire basic control of language structures, through the supportive use of a sign system. It is particularly important that terms describing a sign system are very carefully defined. In schools where 'total communication' is used, for example, the language environment usually includes normal speech, lip reading, a manual sign language, a method of spelling out some words by letters on the fingers, together with optimal use of the child's residual hearing and hearing-aids. One fairly predominant view amongst educationalists is that if a child's needs are so special that an esoteric means of communication is required, these needs will best be met in a special school where the *whole* community is fluent in a signing system. And so the debate continues. . . .

In the end, issues of 'where?' and 'how?' the deaf child should be educated are moral questions which cannot be decided by research. The evidence regarding the efficacy of one methodology over another is inconclusive (see summaries in Meadow, 1980; Mindel and Vernon, 1971; Quigley and Kretschmer, 1982). In other words, if we look at a child's functional mastery of the rules of *English* language, supportive sign systems have neither a positive nor a negative effect on a child's progress. (See also Bishop, 1983, who has recently collected data on the Paget-Gorman sign system.)

The collective evidence of several centuries of the history of deaf education has an important message for current practice. There has always been a bitter three-cornered struggle amongst those who advocate the use of the natural signs of the deaf community, those who propose a sign language which approximates to English grammar, and those who want the deaf to speak. For the majority of deaf people, none of these methods appears to *guarantee* the child sufficient language development to support high academic achievement. Sometimes the deaf experience of isolation and poor opportunity is blamed on sign language, or the lack of it. But it is deafness *itself* which isolates and the responsibility to respond differently to the deaf community lies in society's hands.

We have argued elsewhere (Webster *et al*, 1985) that we should seek to provide as wide a range of educational opportunities as possible: a flexible variety of options. There should not be a rigid and stereotyped response to the needs of hearing-impaired children as a whole. The stance taken in this book is essentially pragmatic, accepting that what works for one child may not work for another. Decisions regarding school placement will inevitably rest on the impact of deafness on the child's development, particularly in terms of language. The child's personality, confidence in relating to other children, ability and readiness to learn, whether the protection and security of small groups and the presence of other hearing-impaired children is required, are all important in determining what kind of educational demands the child will be able to cope with. Not least, the wishes of parents have priority.

It is hoped that the non-specialist teacher will be aware of these controversial issues and be able to keep them in perspective. In the present context the major focus is upon literacy and its relationship to hearing-impairment across a broad continuum, from mild middle-ear losses to severe sensori-neural impairments, in the developing child. The 'oral/manual' debate is not central to this discussion and will not be explored further.

Chapter outlines

In Chapter 2 the basic physical facts of deafness are introduced: aetiology, identification, incidence, diagnosis and treatment. We have assumed that many teachers and professionals may have no technical knowledge and so this chapter is pitched at the intelligent lay person. We shall be distinguishing between conductive and sensori-neural hearing losses in most of the terms listed above. Conductive deafness is much more prevalent in young children than is often realized, and yet less well-recognized or understood. The reason why most teachers find this unfamiliar territory is the predominantly medical orientation of the literature. However, teachers can play a part in recognizing some of the symptoms of middle-ear deafness, once they know what to look out for. Those who feel sufficiently well-informed may wish to skip over this part of the book.

In Chapter 3 some of the wider implications of deafness are charted. We begin this chapter with a discussion of some of the models which have guided people's thinking, such as the deficit research model, together with a more functional model derived from linguistics. We have used a framework of child language study throughout the book. This language model describes three important areas: phonology, syntax and semantics. This serves as a useful basis for putting research data into perspective and helps to relate theory with practice. No doubt some will find these divisions arbitrary and outmoded. However, teachers do find the model enables them to decide which aspect of language is under scrutiny at any point in time in a piece of research, when conclusions are drawn about a child's performance, and in making suggestions for remediation.

The literature on the implications of the milder conductive hearing losses is, unfortunately, not very accessible. The references gathered here are scattered amongst specialized paediatric or audiology journals. This body of work too, is largely evaluative. Research has usually revealed inevitable delays in development associated with a history of middle-ear disease in early childhood. There are, however, frequent problems of interpretation, particularly in relation to how far conductive hearing loss *causes* (as opposed to being simply associated with) developmental delay. We have, of course, devoted most space to studies concerned with language development and verbally dependent skills.

The effects of severe-to-profound deafness upon the course of normal child development are potentially devastating. Almost every developmental continuum known to psychologists shows an association of severe deafness with a dislocation in the normal processes of adjustment and achievement. Several recent summaries of this research literature are available (Fundudis *et al*, 1979; Meadow, 1980; Quigley and Kretschmer, 1982). These document comparisons which have been made between deaf and hearing populations on a wide range of variables, such as social maturity, egocentricity, peer-friendships, adaptivity, behaviour, levels of academic achievement, and most extensively in terms of linguistic and cognitive functioning.

Much of this chapter focuses upon existing commentary; for example, in relation to the reading and writing skills of deaf children. However, we have tried to shift the emphasis towards social-interactive processes. Could it be that we unwittingly make matters worse for the deaf child by trying to *teach* language and, in so doing, create less nurturing linguistic experiences? The whole point of this wide-ranging summary of the literature is to show that deafness is not simply the loss of sound. Complex factors in the social and language contexts in which children interact with adults must be taken into account when we assess the deaf child's achievements.

Chapter 4 addresses the second strand of enquiry in this book: what we know of the reading process. More than a decade ago a psychologist reviewing the literature on the acquisition of reading skills in normal children (Maliphant *et al*, 1974) remarked that, despite the plethora of experimental studies, reading was still not understood as a psychological process. That is still a fair reflection of current evidence. If we throw into the melting pot a significant sensory handicap like deafness, the situation becomes even more compounded. What we have tried to do is to relate findings from deafness studies to existing knowledge in mainstream reading research.

Wherever appropriate, then, we have borrowed existing experimental scaffolding constructed for the normal reading process, in order to help us understand the atypical group. It has been fashionable in the last decade to group reading studies into either 'bottom-up' or 'top-down' perspectives. Some people feel these terms are clumsy, but their directness outweighs their inelegance. 'Bottom-up' models begin at the level of the text on the page by identifying the elements which the reader is sensitive to, such as letter shapes. 'Top-down' models start with the reader and the strategies which are brought to the reading task. The two models are not mutually exclusive and, as it turns out, they do provide a useful way of understanding how the hearing-impaired child attempts the reading task.

We conclude Chapter 4 with a detailed examination of how we can set about appraising the reading process. One common fallacy is that reading tests somehow tell us how a child learns to read and what stage of reading has been reached. We shall be arguing that reading is a far more complex intellectual process than we are often led to believe, and reading tests sample an aspect of reading behaviour which may bear little relation to what children do when they read books for meaning. Furthermore, the research evidence cited here suggests that there may be a wide discrepancy between what researchers think reading tests measure and what they actually reveal. It is in the context of assessment that we have been most critical of the deficit model. We include here some recent work on the assessment of reading in severely hearing-impaired children.

One fundamental issue is whether traditional yardsticks, such as reading tests standardized on hearing children, can be applied to a group of deaf children. It is surprisingly the case that researchers have rarely gone beyond the desire to show how limited deaf children's achievements are, using traditional tests, whilst ignoring the much more pertinent question of 'how' the child approaches the reading task. In fact, paying attention to what children do when they tackle reading tests, attending to the strategies they adopt and the mistakes they make, gives a great deal of insight.

Chapter 5 examines the reading and writing development of

children with mild and severe hearing losses in relation to the language framework presented earlier. A major focus of this chapter concerns the possibility of *specific* auditory processing difficulties in the reading development of hearing-impaired children. Curiously enough, there are two quite contradictory assumptions at large. Firstly, it is commonly held that hearing-impaired children have problems in learning to read *because* of their inevitable difficulties in mastering the sound-symbol correspondences between the print on the page and the sounds of speech (Conrad, 1979). In some people's minds this inability to process the phonetic structure of the written language is shared by 'dyslexic' children (Russell, 1982). Similarly, the reading difficulties associated with children discovered to have the less severe conductive hearing losses have been ascribed to auditory discrimination factors: 'hearing the sounds in words'.

The second view, directly counterposed, is that hearing-impaired children have less access to the spoken word than hearing individuals and therefore depend on the visual patterns of the written word for learning language, gaining information and communicating with others. Indeed, a psychologist was overheard berating a teacher of the deaf for not spending more time on teaching reading to the children in her care, all of whom had poor language skills. Reading would be both a compensation and a way in. Not only is reading held up to be the 'window into knowledge', but also, it seems, the 'window into *linguistic* knowledge'.

We do not accept that a specific auditory deficit can explain the reading difficulties of hearing-impaired children. An important theme which runs through this book is that reading can never be explained by a single principle such as phonetic analysis. Reading can only be understood by clarifying what it is that the reader tries to do with a particular reading task, what strategies are adopted, and how children endeavour to use their skills and experience. If the child brings skills and experiences to reading which are different from normal, this will have an impact and must be taken into account. The likely source of reading difficulties in children with both minor and major hearing losses lies at an interface: where the child's language system and cognitive apparatus meet with the features of written text. So, we need a much broader, multi-faceted approach to the reading process, which encompasses a range of linguistic skills and learning strategies.

Indeed, the study of reading is captivating because at all stages of the process we have opportunities to study cognition: perception, thinking and understanding. The approach we have adopted is to discover how children use their intellects to make sense of the linguistic puzzles of reading. One of the essential differences between spoken language and written language is the level of awareness that the user requires. Children have an *implicit* awareness of the structure of oral language, in the sense that they can use it without being able to say how it is put together. Written language on the other hand, requires an *explicit* awareness, a knowledge of how the code is put together and how it works. An issue we shall be exploring at some length is whether, given that deaf children have less rich spoken language experiences, they can ever achieve the kind of explicit understanding of the language system required.

One other hypothesis we shall be making is that reading and writing are related to the child's capacity to handle complex sequences of ideas. Actually, the real question for the deaf child is whether poor 'inner' language limits the child's auditory memory. How powerful is this idea in explaining some of the idiosyncracies of the deaf child's reading and writing behaviour?

In the final chapter we consider the different approaches which could be made towards remediating the literacy problems of hearing-impaired children. It is important for teachers to be aware of the likely impact of their intervention and which aspects of the child's abilities and skills are involved. It is commonplace, more so in mainstream remedial work, to teach poor readers 'bottom-up' skills, such as grapheme–phoneme rules. Yet such a 'phonic' programme is only one aspect of the language model we have adopted, and not the central aspect. For many children, including the hearing-impaired, it may be of much greater relevance to devise a programme which is aimed at improving the child's control of the grammar of the language. We discuss some of the materials which have been designed to do just that, and point out some of the possible drawbacks of this approach.

The most recent thinking suggests that reading cannot be considered in isolation from the child's wider discovery of language. Spoken language arises in a communication context which surrounds the child. The child learns to speak because of its functional importance. There is an urgent momentum to piece together the rules of the system, to test out rules and try out language forms. The adult's role in this is as facilitator, not teacher. Parents provide the stimulus and opportunity for interaction, through which the child organizes and makes sense of the language experience. Such learning is active, has purpose and is rich in meaning.

One of the conclusions which we have drawn from the background literature is that hearing-impaired children may be exposed to less nurturing experiences which interfere with the social context in which language is learned. A legacy of this might be less effective learning styles and strategies. It may be more productive, in considering remedial work, to provide opportunities which will help the child to become a more active learner, modify the style of coping with written materials, and develop strategies of interacting with text in order to derive meaning. Essentially, this approach aims at using the child's existing skills more effectively. It has the broad intention of drawing the reader's attention to the rich sources of information available within most written materials.

Those who come to this book looking for solutions to the language and literacy problems of hearing-impaired children will be disappointed. Professionals who work with this fascinating group of children do not expect to stumble across a magic key which will somehow unlock a child's learning potential. The book will have achieved what it sets out to, if it stimulates teachers into thinking clearly, flexibly and imaginatively, about how they can help. Whatever teaching level or approach is adopted, we have one plea: that teachers state the objectives of their work with sufficient clarity to know, at the end of the day, whether the targets have been achieved.

2

THE BASIC FACTS OF
HEARING IMPAIRMENT

The implications of a child's hearing loss for learning are the major concern. However, hearing-impaired children are not a homogeneous group and great care must be taken to define the characteristics of the children to whom reference is made. One problem in conducting research into deafness is finding subjects who can be collected together. If children are grouped together simply because they are 'deaf' then the results of research will be impossible to interpret. The reason for that is because there are likely to be as many differences *within* the deaf group as there are between the 'deaf' group and the hearing controls with whom comparisons are made.

Where might some of these differences lie? Some of the questions we need to ask about a hearing-impaired child include: What is the nature of a child's hearing loss? How was it caused? How severe is it? Did it occur at birth or in infancy, when the child had already begun to talk? When was it identified? How much benefit is gained from hearing aids? How has the child been educated? Are there any confounding variables, such as English as a second language in the home? Does the child have any additional handicaps, such as a visual disability? This is by no means an exhaustive list. However, if attention is not paid to these variables it can be hard to assess how far deafness itself is responsible for what the child is able or unable to learn.

We set out in this chapter to account for the varying ways in which deafness can arise, how these are identified and diagnosed, what treatments are available and what the significance of a hearing loss in auditory terms may be to the child. For those coming to the field of hearing-impairment anew, it will be necessary to understand the distinctions which are drawn between hearing losses of sensori-neural and conductive origin, and to have some insight into the parameters by which hearing losses are defined and described. A brief overview of the basic facts is presented. For those who want to gain more technical knowledge there are several good textbooks on the audiological aspects of deafness, such as Martin (1978) or Tucker and Nolan (1984).

The normal ear

The mechanisms of the ear are highly complex and it is surprising that this delicate system is trouble-free for the majority of people, most of the time. It is easier to appreciate this complexity, and to understand what can go wrong, if we look first at the normal healthy ear and how it functions. In Figure 2.1 a diagram of the main features of the ear is given, divided into three sections. It is useful to bear these separate sections in mind, since the breakdown of the hearing system will involve one or more of these parts of the ear, and sometimes there is malfunction involving different parts of the system concurrently. The healthy hearing system depends on the three separate areas working normally.

The function of the ear is to pick up sound signals from the air and, ultimately, to pass on this information to the brain where it can be interpreted or given meaning. The ear is designed exclusively to pick up signals transmitted from a vibrating sound source through the air by means of variations in air pressure. Every object which produces a sound, whether that be a guitar

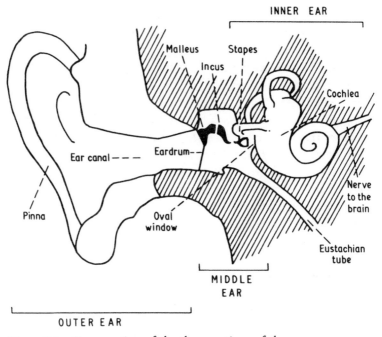

Figure 2.1   Cross-section of the three sections of the ear

string, fire alarm or human vocal chord, does so by causing the air to vibrate in a certain way. The *pinna,* or outer ear which is visible on the side of our heads, is shaped the way it is in order to collect sound vibrations from the air. The presence of two outer ears enables the brain to make judgements about where the sound source is located, since the transmitted signals are being collected at different points in space and time. The pinna traps and then feeds the sound vibrations into and along the outer *ear canal* where they meet the *eardrum* or tympanic membrane.

Using an instrument known as an auroscope a doctor can see the eardrum by looking into the ear canal. The middle part of the ear beyond the eardrum cannot be examined routinely in this way. The middle-ear cavity is an air-filled space in the bone of the skull. It houses three tiny bones which are linked one to another across the air space. Sound vibrations meeting the eardrum in turn cause the thin membrane of the 'drum' to vibrate. The function of the three bones is to conduct the incoming sound vibrations from the eardrum across the middle ear. The *ossicular chain*, as it is known, consists of the *malleus, incus* and *stapes*. The stapes delivers sound vibrations which have been intensified *en route*, to a structure known as the *oval window*. The oval window is the last stop on the way to the inner ear.

It is important to be aware of one particular aspect of the middle section of the ear and that is the *eustachian tube* which ventilates it. The eustachian tube connects the middle-ear cavity to the nose and throat. When we swallow the tube normally opens up to allow air into the middle ear. We may find ourselves doing just that in an aeroplane because of changes in air pressure. There has to be an equal air pressure on both sides of the eardrum in order for it to work properly. If there are differences of pressure on one side from the other, the tympanic membrane would be unable to move and vibrate freely, and therefore not function as a 'drum'. We shall be reiterating this fact when we consider the ways in which a conductive hearing loss may arise.

The inner ear, or the section labelled *cochlea* on Figure 2.1, is by far the most complex. The cochlea is a coiled tube like the shell of a snail. Its function is to convert information transmitted through the oval window into electrical impulses. The cochlea tube contains, at its centre, the hair cells which are sensitive to different sound frequencies. The neurones which innervate these hair cells pass nerve impulses along the *auditory tract* to the brain. We can consider this to be the last, but most complicated stage of the journey which sound vibrations make across the hearing system. It is at this point, when information reaches the brain through the auditory pathway, that an individual may decide to do something about the auditory message just received and made sense of.

Conductive hearing problems

Hearing difficulties can arise if any one of the three sections of the ear we have outlined is not working properly. A major distinction is usually drawn between hearing losses which arise in the conductive mechanisms of the ear, and those which arise in the inner ear as a result of damage to the nerves in the cochlea or auditory tract.

However, as we shall see, it is not uncommon for a conductive loss to exacerbate a hearing loss caused by sensori-neural impairment.

Generally speaking, a conductive loss is less-severe in its effects although it may have significant implications, particularly for a child in early infancy. Any difficulty which affects the passing or conducting of sound into the ear and across the middle-ear canal may be referred to as a conductive hearing problem. Fortunately, many kinds of conductive difficulties are amenable to medical or surgical treatment which will improve or restore hearing. Not so fortunately, the more severe effects on hearing caused by sensori-neural difficulties are not often able to be remedied. When the nerves of a child's hearing system are damaged there is no medical treatment which can restore hearing; the damage is permanent.

A few conductive hearing difficulties originate at the pinna or outer ear, the very first structure in the three sections of the hearing system. Occasionally, a child may be born with a malformed ear, no outer ear at all, or no ear canal for the sound to pass along. Some thalidomide-affected babies suffered in this way. The problem for hearing sensitivity, when a child is born without external ears or ear canals, is that the sound waves are not channelled efficiently into the inner mechanisms of the ear. If the inner mechanisms are perfectly normal, as they may be, a surgeon might be able to help by creating an outer ear, canal or drum. However, problems with the external features of the ear are frequently associated with malformations of other parts of the system.

Any obstacle or blockage in the outer ear may cause conductive hearing problems. Wax is a normal secretion which is usually soft enough to find its own way out of the ear canal. However, wax can become compacted into a hard plug, especially when over-zealous parents have attempted to remove it with special cotton implements bought for the purpose. Compacted wax has the effect of dampening sense of hearing, and is often likened to the effect of plugging one's fingers tightly into one's ears. Some children have been known to put marbles, aniseed balls, pebbles, beads, even sweet wrappers into their ears. The problem then may be not so much the obstacle *in situ* as the damage which could be done in removing it.

By far the most common cause of an acquired conductive impairment in children is *otitis media*. The overall effect of this condition is a mechanical one. The efficient transmission of sound waves across the middle-ear space is affected because the eardrum and ossicles are prevented from vibrating freely.

In many cases, otitis media is associated with an infection of the upper respiratory tract when a child has the symptoms of a 'catarrhal cold', runny nose, sinus or a chest infection. The child's adenoids may become enlarged. There are important consequences of this because the adenoids lie at the base of the eustachian tube which is short and more horizontal in a child and therefore more susceptible to infection than in adults. The eustachian tube has an important ventilating function in the middle ear. We have said that the effects of the eustachian tube in operation can be felt when we swallow, since this opens up the tube and allows air into the middle ear cavity from the throat. We need to do this periodically in order to equalize the air pressure on both sides of the eardrum.

If the eustachian tube is prevented from working as it should, a chain of events may follow. In the first stage, air already in the middle-ear cavity is absorbed by surrounding tissue. The air pressure within the cavity gradually becomes negative relative to the air outside. This has the effect of sucking the eardrum tightly inwards. Stretched and taut, the eardrum is no longer elastic enough to vibrate freely in response to sound waves. If the eustachian tube dysfunction persists and the middle ear remains unventilated, a watery fluid is produced in the middle-ear space. We can describe this middle-ear effusion as a second stage of otitis media. Hearing sensitivity will be affected because the presence of fluid in the middle ear affects the free movement of the tiny bones in the sound-conducting ossicular chain.

It is the increased stiffness of the system, then, which impedes transmission of sound energy to the inner ear. The suspected presence of middle-ear effusion is the most common reason for referral to ENT departments, but if often escapes detection since the hearing loss is usually mild and transitory. A hearing loss caused by thin fluid can come and go within a few days. This makes it disconcerting for parents and teachers to decide whether a child really does have a hearing loss, when the evidence for it seems to fluctuate so much. Very often children are more affected in winter months when there are more infections about, than in the summer.

A third and more severe stage of the condition may arise when otitis media goes untreated for long periods. It has been said that every middle-ear infection suffered predisposes a child to yet another. If the child has frequent attacks, further infections and unresolved middle-ear effusion over a long period, then the fluid becomes mucoid in consistency. The eardrum and ossicular vibrations are severely dampened by the presence of a thick exudate. It is sometimes suggested that antibiotic treatment may maintain the disease in a sub-acute form, leading to further complications such as adhesion and scarring. This could happen if parents were careless in administering a prescribed course of treatment or if they were not asked to return the child to their GP to check the outcome.

There are different forms of otitis media in children. In some cases, children may have fluid in the middle ear without any earache or infection. Otitis media without any symptoms of inflammation is sometimes described as *secretory otitis media*, or more often by the term 'glue ear'. In many cases the condition clears spontaneously over a period of one to three months and does not recur, but in a number of cases the condition is persistent.

We have given here the traditionally accepted view of eustachian tube dysfunction as being responsible for middle-ear effusion. Very recently, some researchers have suggested that allegies and other kinds of immunity reactions in the body may play a part in the cause and persistence of middle-ear disease. (Smyth and Hall, 1983)

Sensori-neural hearing problems

Sensori-neural hearing losses are usually associated with damage to the inner ear: the third section outlined in Figure 2.1. Conditions which affect the inner ear usually have serious implications for hearing sensitivity. Unlike conductive hearing losses where the cause is usually mechanical, there is little or nothing that can be done to repair damage to the nerves of the cochlea or auditory pathway. There are many ways in which a child's hearing can be irreversibly and permanently affected and we shall be describing some of the main causes. It should be noted that for a very large group of children who suffer sensori-neural deafness, the exact cause may never be ascertained. When a hearing loss is identified, factors affecting the mother's pregnancy, the child's birth, or events in early infancy, have then to be examined in retrospect. More often than not, all that can be given is a *probable* reason for a sensori-neural hearing loss.

Pre-natal causes

Many children with sensori-neural hearing-impairment inherit the condition, even where there has been no deafness in earlier generations. That may seem contradictory. However, it is possible for an individual to carry the particular chromosome within his or her genetic make-up, which could produce a hearing-impaired child if the other parent was also a carrier. Such a couple would have a one-in-four chance of having a hearing-impaired child with every pregnancy. This process is known as a 'recessive' genetic tendency. There are children, of course, who inherit deafness directly from one or both parents. It is perfectly possible for the same couple to produce normally-hearing and hearing-impaired offspring. Two parents with inherited sensori-neural deafness could produce a normally-hearing family. The only way in which the numbers of children born with inherited deafness can be reduced is by genetic counselling.

There is still a sizeable proportion of children whose hearing is damaged before birth by a viral infection. An expectant mother who gets German measles (rubella) between the sixth and twelfth week of her pregnancy is at risk of having a damaged baby. The first trimester of pregnancy is the time when the embryo's delicate organs are forming, including the cochlea. A baby affected by the rubella virus before birth could have serious heart defects, visual disabilities and brain damage, together with a hearing-impairment. In some cases it is thought that the embryo can still be attacked by the virus even if the mother has immunity to the disease. Nevertheless, there is a national rubella immunization programme for young girls and this has reduced the number of affected babies. Many doctors offer abortions to mothers who are known to have contracted rubella at a critical time in pregnancy. Therapeutic abortion is perhaps the main reason why the numbers of multiply handicapped, hearing-impaired children are falling. A few years ago a rubella epidemic meant a certain increase in severely hearing-handicapped children, and it is possible for there to be future outbreaks of the disease if people become complacent about immunization.

Many other viral infections contracted at important stages of pregnancy can cause damage to the inner ear, such as chicken pox, measles or influenza. Deafness resulting from causes such as cytomegalo virus is usually much more complicated than hereditary deafness. Although some forms of inherited deafness have associated anomalies, there is less chance of additional damage to the central nervous system than there is when deafness is caused by a viral agent.

Peri-natal causes

A difficult labour or a long, complicated birth could result in the baby being short of oxygen. Lack of oxygen (anoxia) can result in damage to the nerve cells in the auditory pathway. Both peri-natal anoxia and insults caused through the use of instruments during birth, are associated with multiple handicaps together with deafness. Hospitals, however, take great care to monitor the baby during birth if the labour is not straightforward and if the baby is 'distressed'.

Prematurity is also associated with a high risk of hearing-impairment, usually because the premature baby also suffers anoxia. An infant born before having spent the allotted forty weeks in the womb is described as premature. Sometimes this term is used of any baby which weighs less than 2½ kg (5½ lb) at birth. There are many risks for premature babies, including damage to the nerve cells of the ear. Premature infants are more likely to be injured during birth or to contract infections. They are less robust and therefore more vulnerable than full-term babies.

Whilst improved maternal care during delivery is a good reason for hoping that fewer handicapped babies may be born, there is the possibility that some infants will survive in special care facilities who may otherwise have died, and this is a group at risk of severe hearing-impairment and other forms of handicap.

Post-natal causes

There are some conditions, such as jaundice, which can affect the newly-born child. Jaundice is a blood condition which sometimes arises because of a mismatch between the blood groups of the mother and child. Severe jaundice can cause damage to the nerve cells in the auditory pathway. Fortunately, it is another problem which is better understood and better controlled in modern hospitals and far fewer children suffer deafness as a consequence of jaundice than used to.

Meningitis is probably the commonest post-natal cause of deafness in young children. It is an acute inflammation of the covering of the brain which can lead to mental handicap and spasticity, as well as hearing-impairment. The commonly occurring illnesses of childhood can very occasionally be suffered so severely as to lead to inner-ear damage. Mumps, measles, scarlet fever and whooping cough have all been reported as causing hearing-impairment.

Adventitious deafness due to inflammatory diseases has shown the most marked decrease of all the factors which cause a severe sensori-neural hearing loss. Vaccination has helped to eliminate some of the viral diseases thought to cause deafness, whilst antibiotics have also lessened the impact of many childhood illnesses.

Identifying a hearing loss

The sooner a hearing loss is discovered, the sooner something can be done to help reduce the impact of deafness at source. Unfortunately, some children with severe hearing losses escape detection for several years. We now know that even a mild degree of hearing loss in the early stages of infancy, well before the child actually begins to talk, can have serious consequences for the child's development. For the child with a severe sensori-neural loss the prospects of developing useful language are crucially dependent upon early diagnosis and provision of hearing-aids; if possible, within the first year of life. There are some sensori-neural hearing problems, such as a high-frequency loss, which may only come to light much later, perhaps when the child's hearing is screened in school.

There is a much greater recognition of the problems which intermittent conductive hearing losses may bring. Yet this is a condition which may be undetected throughout childhood. To the unsuspecting teacher, such children may appear 'lazy' or 'uncooperative' when in fact there are periods when they cannot *listen* very easily.

There are many grounds for suspecting a hearing problem and we shall be examining these, together with the more formal assessments which can be made to identify a loss. It is helpful to distinguish between the processes of identification and diagnosis. The former establishes the fact that a child's sensitivity for hearing is abnormal, the latter attempts to explain why.

Some children are known in advance to be at risk of having a sensori-neural hearing problem. Parents, relatives, or other siblings in the family may be known to have suffered hearing disabilities. Similarly, factors in a mother's pregnancy, or the delivery of a baby, may be known which predispose a child to having a hearing loss. A premature or small-for-dates child, or a child known to have a syndrome usually associated with a hearing-impairment, would be carefully monitored for hearing loss from an early time onwards.

In the United Kingdom the community health services organize screening and testing procedures, to try and pick out children who may have hearing difficulties as soon as possible. Health visitors usually endeavour to screen every baby either at home or in a child health clinic. They use simple but carefully prepared techniques to see whether the baby responds to everyday sounds. This screening procedure is not failsafe and is often criticized. There are many reasons why babies fail or pass the screen, apart from a hearing loss. Other, more 'objective' methods of screening babies for hearing loss are being developed. In some health services health visitors also ask parents to complete a questionnaire which gives an opportunity for parents to register any concerns they might have about their child's hearing. Concerns about a child's hearing at this stage would usually be passed on to a community medical officer whose special concern is audiology. Alternatively, the family doctor might refer a child directly to a hospital ENT department.

Health visitors normally visit the families of pre-school children and are vigilant to problems of speech and hearing. At age 5 years another hearing screen is given in school by a school nurse or audiology technician. Again, if concern is expressed about a child's hearing in school at any time, the school nurse can follow this up and refer on to the community medical officer. The next step may be for the child to be referred to hospital for treatment and advice. An alternative referral route for the school-age child would be via the family doctor direct to the audiology or ENT department of a hospital. One possibility, given that there are bound to be difficulties in co-ordinating all the various services at large in the community, is that a child will slip through the net. For a discussion of how the various agencies can work together, see Webster *et al,* (1985).

Irrespective of whether a child has passed a screen test or whether the medical records declare hearing within normal limits, there are two sources of evidence about a child's hearing which should always be taken seriously and acted upon. Firstly, parents often *know* there is something amiss with their child's hearing. A father may sense that his baby of a few months old does not seem to react to sudden loud sounds or to hear his voice. The baby may have been visually startled as the mother approached the cot, although the mother had signalled her presence by voice. A parent's worries should always lead to a thorough assessment, and as often as not are found to be justified.

Secondly, for the child in school, the onset of a hearing problem may produce symptoms such as poor concentration, tiredness in class, inattention and a fall off in performance. A child may frequently seem to be daydreaming, forget to bring equipment or misunderstand instructions through having mis-heard. Requests

Table 2.1 Warning signs of a hearing loss

1   Verbal reports or medical records give a history of ear infections or failed screening tests, particularly in winter months.
    NB Passing an audiology screen does not rule out the presence of a hearing loss.
2   Child appears 'catarrhal', has frequent absences with coughs and colds, or is a mouth-breather.
3   Child complains of earache, 'popping ears', fullness in the ear, or has a visible discharge from the ear.
4   Appears to daydream and drift off, or is more alert when positioned close to the teacher.
5   Watches the speaker's face for clues and has difficulty listening to a message where there are no situational or speaker clues, such as a tape-recorded message.
6   Child's speech may be limited in structure or vocabulary, with immature or confused speech sounds.
7   Slowness in responding to verbal instructions, asks for repetition or watches other children's lead.
8   Misunderstands or gives inappropriate responses, particularly if a sequence of spoken instructions is given.
9   Child may need to sit nearer a TV than usual or ask for the volume on a record player or tape deck to be turned up.
10 Child may need to search visually for the source of a sound or is unable to locate a sound quickly.
11 Speech may seem softer or fuzzier than normal.
12 Appears inattentive or restless or distracts others, and is much more responsive in quiet conditions or small groups.
13 Some irritability, atypical aggression, bad-tempered behaviour or more frequent upsets in school.
14 Little interest in following a story, especially in noisy conditions.
15 Child may not turn immediately when called by name, unless other visible signals are given.
16 Pace of learning falls away periodically and attention span shortens or child tires much more quickly than usual.
17 Asks for much more individual help and explanation than usual but may withdraw from social contact with other children.
18 Discrepancies between verbal and practical skills.
19 Particular academic difficulties in verbally-related skills such as reading, particularly in establishing sound–symbol associations, sound-blends or in discriminating between sounds.
20 Periodically seems short of energy, listless, poorly-motivated and difficult to reach or involve.

may have to repeated several times. A child may not turn immediately when called by name. The teacher may have noticed a tendency to 'mess about' in class, and problems in listening. The child with a conductive loss may have started to mouth-breathe and have frequent absences with catarrh and colds. Earache itself is obviously a clear sign that something is amiss and may need treatment.

The ordinary class-teacher is in a good position to observe the child's hearing behaviour once the warning signs and symptoms have been highlighted. In Table 2.1 a list of features which could signal a hearing loss is given, and every class-teacher should be alert to them. Follow-up of a child with such symptoms is imperative. The school medical services may then want to investigate the child through some kind of audiometric test. Different techniques have been devised to suit children of different ages and capabilities. Each ear is usually checked separately because it is possible for one ear to be affected and not the other. All audiometric tests try to give us accurate and reliable information about two separate aspects of hearing which are then recorded on a graph called an audiogram. (See Figure 2.2.)

The audiogram

The first aspect of a child's hearing sensitivity which we need to know about concerns sound *frequency*. The axis across the top of the audiogram represents the normal frequency range of sounds from low to high pitch. Frequency refers to the speed of vibration of sound waves measured in Hertz. Slow vibrating sound waves give rise to low sounds. Sound waves vibrating very rapidly produce high tone sounds. Speech is produced partly by our vocal chords causing the air to vibrate. It contains a complex mixture of high- and low-frequency sounds. Some of the sounds in speech are not made by the vocal chords but by the tongue and lips, such as 's', 't' or 'p'.

It is possible to have defective hearing for high sounds and normal hearing for low sounds. A child with a high-frequency hearing loss would have some difficulty in hearing the beginnings

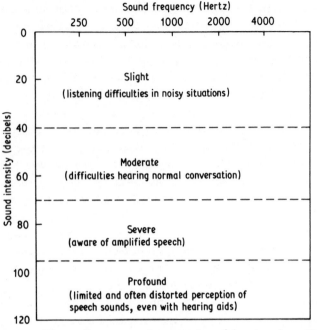

Figure 2.2 The audiogram and categories of hearing loss (British Association of Teachers of the Deaf, 1981)

and endings of words which are mainly consonants, such as 't', 's', or 'f'. On the other hand, the middle bits of many words, usually vowels such as 'a', 'e', 'i', 'o' and 'u', have mostly low-frequency components. The most important frequencies for understanding speech are in the middle of the range shown on the audiogram at 500, 1000 and 2000 Hertz.

For a child with a conductive hearing problem the loss of hearing sensitivity commonly affects all frequencies by a similar amount, or, unlike most sensori-neural losses, it may be worse in lower frequencies. A child with a mild hearing loss across all the frequency range is going to miss the sounds of speech which are weakest in intensity. These include consonant sounds, fricative sounds such as 's' and 'f', nasal sounds like 'm' or 'n', plural endings on words, and the weaker, briefer, or unstressed components of speech. In a noisy environment, such as a busy classroom, the child's sensitivity to speech sounds is reduced even further.

This leads us to the second aspect of a child's hearing sensitivity which we need to know about: *intensity*. The axis down the side of the audiogram records the loudness of the sounds which the child can hear. It is essential to know the loudness levels at which the child detects sounds across the frequency range. Sound intensity is measured in decibels. Zero decibels on the audiogram represents the softest sound that can be heard by most young adults with normal hearing. Whispered speech is at a level of about 20 decibels. So a child with a 20-decibel hearing loss would just be able to detect the presence of a whisper. Normal conversation is at the level of about 50 to 60 decibels. So a child with a 50-decibel hearing loss would just be able to detect the sounds of conversation. The noise of a vacuum cleaner is around 70 decibels, busy traffic is around 80 decibels and a pneumatic drill is about 100 decibels. Sounds above 100 decibels are extremely loud and can be painful to people with normal hearing. A child with a 120-decibel loss would be unable to detect the presence of a jet aeroplane taking off at close quarters.

It is important to understand that the intervals in the decibel scale are not equal. Because the scale is logarithmic, the actual difference between 100 and 120 decibels is many times greater than the actual difference between 20 and 40 decibels. The audiogram charts the discrepancy from normal in the child's hearing. The further down the graph the child's thresholds for hearing are recorded, the greater that sounds have to be made louder in order for the child to detect them, compared with a person of normal hearing. In testing hearing we need to know the level of loss at every separate frequency, because of the different implications which different audiogram configurations have for the child's speech perception.

In Figure 2.2 several broad categories of hearing loss are shown on the audiogram. One method often used to summarize the information given in an audiogram is to average the decibel hearing levels over the five frequencies shown (British Association of Teachers of the Deaf, 1981). It has been estimated that a mild conductive loss would produce an average hearing loss of about 15 decibels across the frequency range whilst a more serious 'glue' ear condition could give a sensitivity loss of about 35 decibels, occasionally up to 50 decibels. It should be remembered that the audiogram for a child with a sensori-neural hearing loss is unlikely to show an even configuration. A typical configuration is the 'ski-slope' with an increasing fall of hearing sensitivity, the higher the frequency. So the figure given as an average hearing loss may obscure important information. Nevertheless, a sensori-neural loss which averages more than 60 decibels will mean that a child will be unable to hear the normal sounds of conversation without hearing-aids.

Hearing tests

We have to be very sure with tests of all kinds, but particularly with tests of hearing, that we are absolutely clear what the test is revealing. A child who is anxious, or who does not understand what to do, or who is uncooperative, may fail a hearing test for reasons other than a hearing loss *per se*.

Traditional tests of hearing are often subjective. The audiologist gives the child some form of sound signal in one ear and has to interpret the response which the child makes to the stimulus. Efforts are being made to devise more objective measures of hearing. It would be extremely useful to have a test of hearing which cut out human interpretation and error, and which could be used from early infancy. Whilst there have been some important developments using computer technology, these are still in the experimental stage. For the majority of children, traditional testing will be the norm for some years to come.

Distraction tests

The hearing of babies from about 7 to 18 months of age is often tested using the distraction technique (Ewing and Ewing, 1944). The test cannot be performed until a baby can sit up, with good back and head control, and is able to turn to locate a sound made out of the field of vision. Health visitors are trained to use this test in their screening of babies at about 8 or 9 months of age. The baby is usually sat on the mother's knee, supported at the waist and in a slightly forward position. One of the examiners attracts the baby's attention, using something like a cuddly toy or ball. A second examiner presents a sound stimulus behind the child's line of vision. High- and low-frequency sounds are presented separately at about 35 decibels in quiet conditions. If the baby does not respond to these sounds, they are made louder until the baby shows a definite response. A baby who did not begin to turn to high and low sounds until they were presented at a 65-decibel level may be suspected of having a 65-decibel hearing loss. The test would normally be repeated several times, using different stimuli, at both sides of the child.

The distraction technique is difficult to carry out properly. Conditions have to be quiet, the baby must be contented but alert and not too absorbed in the examiner's efforts to attract the baby's attention. The examiner has to be scrupulously careful not to move into the child's line of sight when presenting the sounds. Many babies with normal hearing do not respond to the sounds for a variety of reasons. Conversely, a hearing-impaired child may respond to the smallest visual clue and persuade the tester that the sound has been heard. There are added difficulties in babies who show developmental delay, although the incidence of hearing loss in babies with other handicaps is much higher than in the general population.

Despite the widespread recognition that distraction testing is not easy to carry out in practice, it remains the recommended procedure (DHSS Advisory Committee on Services for Hearing-Impaired People, 1981). It has been reported that as many as 41 per cent of babies with significant hearing losses are not identified in this screening programme (National Deaf Children's Society, 1983).

Co-operative testing

Children from 18 months to 2½ years of age are often tested for hearing loss using a co-operative technique. The key principle here, which many parents would dispute, is that at this age most children can follow instructions and make appropriate responses. So, the tester asks the child in a voice of carefully controlled intensity (around 35-40 decibels) to 'give the car to daddy', or 'put the dolly on the chair'. If a child begins to respond appropriately only when a louder voice is used this may suggest a hearing loss. It may also suggest that the child does not understand instructions easily, is unused to doing things when asked, or is simply inhibited.

The major drawback of this approach to testing the hearing of infants is the limited specificity of the information gained. It is not possible, using co-operative testing, to tell whether the child has hearing difficulties in high as opposed to low, frequencies, and other testing would have to be done to find this out.

Visual reinforcement audiometry

In visual reinforcement audiometry a child is trained to look in a certain direction wherever a sound stimulus is heard. The looking response is usually rewarded with the sight of an animated toy, attractive picture, or illuminated puppet. This procedure can be used with children from about 6 months to 3 years. The child is usually seated at a small table and occupied with a toy. A sound stimulus is presented through loudspeakers placed to the left or right of the child. As the child turns in response to the sound, a reward is given by briefly presenting a puppet, toy or flashing light, usually close to the sound source.

This technique may overcome some of the limitations of distraction and co-operative testing. The child has to be contented, alert and interested, but when successful, the procedure provides fairly precise information about the child's hearing sensitivity to sounds across several frequencies.

Performance tests

In a performance test the child is trained to respond to a stimulus (such as 'go') by dropping a brick in a box, or fitting a peg in a board. This should be possible with children at about a 2½-year developmental level. The test proceeds with the child continuing to respond to other signals, such as a high-frequency 's' sound, or to sounds produced by an instrument at controlled levels of pitch and frequency in free field. If the child does not respond to a sound signal at the level given, it is made louder until the child begins to indicate that it has been detected.

Pure tone audiometry

By the age of 3 or 3½ years most children are capable of completing a pure tone audiogram, and this is the test which is favoured from then on because of the much more detailed information it reveals. An audiometer is used which is an instrument capable of producing sounds at specific intensities and specific frequencies across the range of normal hearing. Sounds are delivered to the child's ears via headphones and the child is trained, or asked, to listen and wait for a sound before making a response. The results of the test are displayed on the audiogram chart.

An example of an audiogram showing a sensori-neural hearing loss in both ears is given in Figure 2.3. Convention is followed

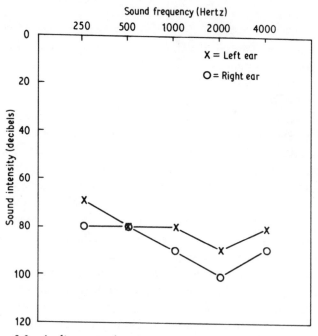

Figure 2.3 Audiogram showing a severe bilateral sensori-neural hearing loss

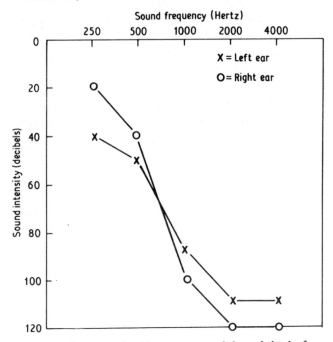

Figure 2.4 Audiogram showing a severe bilateral high frequency sensori-neural hearing loss

and an 'x' is used to indicate results for the left ear, and 'O' to denote results for the right ear. Remember, when interpreting the scale showing hearing threshold along the vertical axis, that it is logarithmic. The further down the intensity scale from 0 decibels the child's threshold appears, the greater the hearing loss. A child with an audiogram like this would be felt to have a severe loss averaging 80 decibels in the better ear. There is much useful residual hearing in both ears. There is a measurable response to sound across the frequency range important for speech, and with appropriate hearing-aids fitted, the child's sensitivity for hearing could expect to be improved by about 30 decibels, perhaps more. So wearing aids, such a child may have access to the speech sounds of conversation in good acoustic conditions.

In Figure 2.4 an example of an audiogram showing a severe bilateral high-frequency sensori-neural hearing loss is given. The sound frequencies sampled during the test are plotted along the horizontal axis from low to high. The right ear shows a response at 20 decibels in the low frequency of 250 Hertz. The hearing loss increases in both ears, the higher the frequencies sampled, to give a 'ski-slope' configuration. This child would have considerable awareness of sound but may miss a lot of the nuances of speech. A hearing-aid which amplified high-frequency sounds greater than low frequencies would need to be prescribed. Interestingly, this audiogram also shows an average hearing loss of 80 decibels.

Bone conduction

When an attempt is made to diagnose the underlying reason for a hearing loss, the information revealed by a bone-conduction test can be very useful. This test enables the hearing difficulty to be located either in the middle ear or the inner ear. When a pure tone is presented to the child through headphones, the signal travels down the ear canal where it vibrates the eardrum and ossicular chain. The sound waves are converted into electrical impulses at the cochlea and eventually perceived by the brain. In order for the pure-tone test to be passed the whole hearing system has to be in working order.

Instead of pure tones through headphones, sounds can be presented to the child through a small vibrator placed on the skull, usually the mastoid bone behind the ear. The signals produced in this way stimulate the inner ear directly through the skull. The mechanisms of the middle ear are effectively by-passed. A normally-hearing person will hear the signals conducted through the air and through the bone at about the same levels of intensity.

In Figure 2.5 the audiogram shows the results of pure-tone audiometry and bone conduction for a child's right ear. In order to achieve that, the left ear has to be masked off by noise input. If the left ear were not masked off it would be impossible to say whether the results for bone conduction derived from the left or the right ear. That is because the vibrator placed on the skull will stimulate both inner ears. It can be seen that the bone-transmitted signals (marked by C) are within normal limits across the frequency range. However, the pure-tone results through headphones indicate up to a 40-decibel loss. Since the pathway through

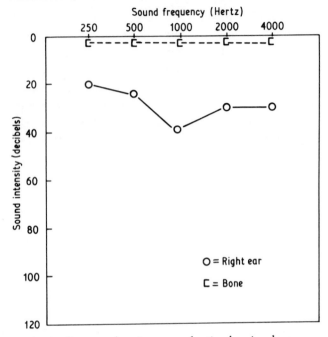

Figure 2.5   Audiogram showing a conductive hearing loss

the bone to the inner ear is normal, the loss must lie in the mechanisms of the middle or outer ear before the sound reaches the cochlea. The loss is therefore conductive in nature.

If a child's audiogram showed a loss for both air *and* conducted signals then the results of the bone-conduction test and pure-tone audiometry would look very similar. A loss through bone as well as air would indicate a sensori-neural loss. It is possible that a child has a mixed hearing loss involving both the middle ear and the inner ear. In such a case the bone-conduction levels would be depressed with an additional loss of sensitivity for air-conducted signals. It is important to realize that children with sensori-neural hearing loss are just as susceptible as anyone else to middle-ear disorders causing conductive loss. For such a child the effect could be temporarily very serious, reducing the residual hearing of the child even further.

Impedance audiometry

Another test which gives important diagnostic information is impedance audiometry. This is not strictly a test of hearing, but it is a technique which assesses the functioning of the middle ear. In simple terms, it measures the amount of sound reflected by the eardrum when a sound wave reaches it.

It will be recalled that a hearing loss may arise because of negative air pressure and fluid or 'glue' in the middle-ear cavity. When these conditions are present the eardrum is unable to vibrate as freely as it should in response to the incoming sound signal. Sound transmission is dampened because of the increased stiffness of the system.

Impedance audiometry uses a simple but clever technique. A small plastic probe is placed in the child's ear canal for a few seconds. A tube in the probe feeds sounds into the ear. A second tube has a microphone which picks up the sound being reflected from the eardrum. A third tube allows the examiner to control the air pressure on the outside of the eardrum. In a normal ear the sound travels down the ear canal, through the eardrum and across the middle-ear cavity. Very little sound is reflected back from the eardrum because of the flexibility of the middle-ear system. Normally, sound is conducted very efficiently.

Inefficiency in the sound-conducting mechanism will arise if a child has a middle-ear problem such as otitis media: the system becomes stiff. The result is that less sound is conducted across the middle-ear cavity, and more sound is reflected back by the drum. This is picked up by the probe and recorded on a chart. Because this test is less subjective than others and enables the examiner to tell whether or not a conductive disorder is present, a number of people have advocated the use of impedance audiometry for screening. (For a review of this literature, see Webster *et al*, 1984.)

Speech audiometry

An audiogram may give fairly precise information about a child's ability to hear pure tones. However, it is also useful to know something of the child's ability to hear spoken language, and this is not always straightforwardly determined from the child's audiogram. Speech sounds are very complex and cannot easily be broken down into pure frequencies. We can hazard a guess as to some of the components of speech which a child might have difficulty hearing, such as 's' and 'f' sounds for a child with a high-frequency loss. However, there are tests which reveal what a child can hear of spoken language. When children come to be fitted with hearing-aids to help them use and understand speech, information from speech audiometry is very important.

In speech audiometry the child listens to a voice presented free-field, or alternatively through loudspeakers or headphones, listing phonetically balanced words. More recently, children have been asked to listen to especially constructed sentences which contain representative proportions of the different speech sounds and familiar vocabulary (Bench and Bamford, 1979). A judgement is made about how clearly the child can discriminate between different sounds in speech at different loudness levels. This technique can also measure the extent to which a child can follow normal conversation and how this changes with the intensity of the signals.

The auditory cradle

This survey of hearing tests would be incomplete without some mention of the newer developments in audiology. One of the major problems we have noted regarding the testing of very young infants is the difficulty in getting reliable responses to sound. The child has to be actively involved and the tester has to be absolutely sure that the child is not responding to clues *other than* the sound signal. And yet it is crucial that a hearing loss is diagnosed as early as possible in infancy.

The auditory cradle has been developed to test the hearing of new-born babies in maternity hospitals. It uses a computer to present sounds to the baby in a cradle, and then measures changes in breathing and body movements in response to the sounds. The computer works out whether these physical changes are real indications of hearing loss, compared with the response patterns of a normal infant. The auditory cradle is being evaluated at this experimental stage; although it is not yet in general use, results are encouraging.

Electric response audiometry

Another recent development is electric response audiometry. It is known that very small electrical changes occur in the auditory nerve and the auditory pathways in the brain when a sound signal is presented to a normal ear. Over the last decade or so, tests have been devised using computers which can measure these minute electrical changes in or near the brain. Electric response audiometry can be used to confirm a suspected severe hearing-impairment with children who are handicapped or uncooperative, and therefore unable to participate in conventional testing.

The scope of these specialized test techniques is limited by expense and availability. There are only a few centres where such specialized testing can be performed in the United Kingdom. The process may involve the child having a general anaesthetic so that an electrode can be passed through the eardrum to the covering of the cochlea. More often the test is conducted using non-invasive electrode placement when the child is asleep. The information derived from this kind of testing is not very specific. Severity of hearing loss may be indicated, but not the pattern of frequencies involved. Electric response audiometry is an important *supportive* means of identifying hearing-impairment.

Incidence of hearing-impairment

Conductive losses

The incidence of middle-ear deafness in infants and children is very much higher than generally recognized. It is a surprise to many teachers to know that approximately 1 in 5 children will have a mild hearing disability at some point in their school careers (Murphy, 1976). Otitis media occurs most frequently in children under 10 years of age and it has been estimated that some 30 per cent of children will suffer middle-ear disease in the first two years of life (Reichman and Healey, 1983). A worrying aspect of this figure is the importance of these early years for normal child development. A child suffering conductive hearing loss at this critical stage is much more likely to be affected than an older child. Perhaps even more worrying is the fact that mild hearing losses of a conductive nature are often undetected. In a survey of London children in ordinary nurseries, Shah (1981) found that more than 35 per cent of his sample of pre-schoolers had evidence of fluid in their middle ears, which no one had suspected.

There are groups of children with other primary handicaps who are very susceptible to conductive hearing loss. Two such groups are those with Down's syndrome and those with cleft palate. Down's children often have small outer ears and narrow ear canals which are prone to wax blockage. These children are also very vulnerable to chest infections and repeated bouts of otitis media.

The majority of children with cleft palate are vulnerable to conductive hearing loss. The source of the problem in this group is probably the deficiency in palate musculature which gives rise to a dysfunction in the working of the eustachian tube. We have seen that where the eustachian tube fails to allow air into the middle ear, a chain of events may follow, such as negative middle-ear pressure, fluid in the middle ear and consequent hearing loss. Any child with an abnormality of the ear, nose or throat, should be considered at risk of conductive hearing disorder.

Some very interesting figures have been reported by researchers for the incidence of middle-ear problems in children categorized as being 'poor achievers' or having 'learning difficulties'. In several studies, children referred for extra help because of poor school performance, especially in reading, were examined for middle-ear disorder. Some researchers report as many as 46 per cent of children referred for learning problems, who also have histories of otitis media (Gottlieb et al, 1980).

In subsequent chapters we shall be examining the nature of the relationship between poor school performance and conductive hearing loss. The assumption is sometimes made that difficulties in learning to read are *caused* by deficits in auditory perception and auditory processing. We shall be passing a critical eye over this evidence, particularly the claims for specific reading disability in children with otitis media.

Sensori-neural loss

Figures for the incidence of hearing-impairments caused by sensori-neural damage are more systematically recorded than middle-ear losses, largely because of their severity and permanence. In 1983 local education authorities in England reported that there were 4040 moderately hearing-impaired children receiving or awaiting special education. This gives a prevalence rate of 4.88 per 10,000 of the total school population (approximately 0.05 per cent). There were 3268 children reported as having more severe hearing losses, a prevalence of about 4 per 10,000 (approximately 0.04 per cent) (DES 1983).

These statistics do not take into account children who are fully integrated into mainstream classes and children whose principal handicap is not hearing-impairment. Medical intervention such as rubella immunization of teenage girls, therapeutic abortion for rubella-exposed pregnant women, and general improvements in the care of mothers and babies, should be reflected in a diminishing population of severely hearing-impaired children. This would appear to be the trend.

We have said that children with sensori-neural losses are just as susceptible to middle-ear disorders as anyone else. A study of 8-year-olds in the European Community with a hearing loss of 50 decibels or more, shows that 3.8 per cent of children have both sensori-neural and conductive losses, with otitis media the largest contributing factor (Commission of the European Community, 1979).

Treatment

It is the range of treatment options which is one distinguishing feature between hearing disorders of a conductive and a sensori-neural origin. In both conditions the sooner a hearing loss is identified and diagnosed, the sooner that the impact of deafness on the child's development can be reduced *at source*. However, whilst middle-ear disorders are usually amenable to medical treatment, there is often little that can be done in terms of medical intervention for sensori-neural hearing damage. For the latter the most significant treatment option may be the provision of hearing-aids.

Medical and surgical management of otitis media

Early treatment of otitis media is important not only to minimize the consequences of a hearing loss, but also to prevent more serious complications developing, such as perforation of the eardrum, or damage to the ossicular chain. In short-term cases of otitis media, the first course of action may be to prescribe a course of antibiotics to clear up the middle-ear infection. It has been suggested that the widespread use of this approach is a possible explanation for the increase of non-infected 'glue' ear cases in recent years. In many children otitis media occurs acutely. Inflammation arises suddenly and causes much discomfort. It is at this point that a caring parent will take the child to the doctor, when earache is complained of. The child's discomfort, given antibiotics, may disappear quickly. Some parents may be inclined not to finish the course of antibiotics in the mistaken belief that the infection has cleared. Certainly, many parents never return to their GP to check, nor are they asked to do so. An infection which remains in a subacute state may not be painful, but have insidious effects. In any case, antibiotics by themselves will not necessarily help middle-ear fluid to disperse.

Conservative medical treatment would include the prescription of decongestant medication to dry up the sinuses and the lining of the middle-ear cavity, with inflation of the eustachian tube. The aim of this treatment is to reverse the changes brought about by the middle-ear infection, to allow the fluid to drain off down the eustachian tube, leaving an aerated cavity.

There is also surgical treatment for middle-ear problems if other methods have failed. The surgeon may remove tonsils and/or adenoids if they are blocking the eustachian tube or contributing to repeated infections. Myringotomy may be performed, in which the eardrum is pierced and any fluid present is sucked out. Frequently this procedure is linked with the insertion of a plastic grommet through the eardrum. A grommet is a tiny tube which allows air to pass into the middle ear, which in a sense replaces the function of the inoperative eustachian tube. The grommet allows the mucosal linings of the middle ear to return to normal, by which time the eustachian tube recovers its normal function and normal hearing is restored. This treatment has been likened to opening a window in a damp bathroom in order to dry it out.

Until recently, grommets did not remain in the eardrum for very long, perhaps several weeks or months, and usually came out of their own accord while the hole in the eardrum healed over. A new T-shaped grommet is now in use, designed to stay permanently in the drum until removed by the surgeon. In the past it was not unknown for children particularly prone to fluid in the middle ear to have grommets inserted several times during childhood. It has been estimated that this surgical treatment can improve hearing thresholds by as much as 25 decibels (Richards *et al.*, 1971). While there is no doubt about the efficacy of the treatment, there is still some controversy about possible side effects and the long-term benefits.

It is highly important that parents and professionals do not assume that once a child has been treated for a middle-ear problem, then he or she is necessarily cured. Conductive hearing difficulties of this kind may well recur. We have already highlighted some of the signs and symptoms which might indicate possible hearing loss (see Table 2.1), and these are applicable even when a child has had treatment. It has been said that every middle-ear infection predisposes the child to yet another.

Hearing-aids

We conclude this chapter with a brief discussion of the most significant and in some cases, *only* 'treatment' available for a child with a severe sensori-neural hearing-impairment: the provision of hearing-aids. Most authorities would agree that the whole purpose of early identification and diagnosis of severe deafness is towards providing meaningful auditory experience for the child by using residual hearing to the full through appropriate amplification. Sensori-neural deafness is very rarely total. There are very few children who derive no benefit at all from hearing-aids, and some who benefit a great deal. The human baby responds to sound in the womb and continues to be receptive to the human voice in early infancy, before starting to talk. We shall be examining recent findings which show that deafness interrupts the developmental process from the early months of life. Any steps that can be taken to lessen the impact of deafness should be delayed as little as is humanly possible.

We must begin by outlining what hearing-aids *cannot* do for a child with a sensori-neural loss. They cannot *restore* the child's hearing to normal. In the vast majority of cases the hearing mechanism is permanently damaged. What hearing-aids do is to make sounds louder. The increase in amplification, or gain, from a hearing-aid is usually about 30 decibels, but can be as much as 50 decibels. How well a child uses hearing-aids will depend on: the age at which they were introduced; the configuration and nature of the hearing-impairment; the kind of hearing-aids prescribed; and a complex interplay of factors within the child, including social, intellectual and educational factors.

One of the most important variables will be the degree of hearing loss. The child with a profound loss, even with very powerful amplification, may not receive very much useful auditory information. Most importantly, the child may not have access to the sounds of natural speech. In some cases the child with a very uneven audiogram configuration may be difficult to fit with aids. A high-frequency loss (see Figure 2.4) requires the higher sound frequencies to be amplified by larger amounts than others to reach threshold perception. There may also be further discrepancies between the two ears. So there can be technical problems in providing hearing-aids which do not distort sound input to the child by amplifying the already better-perceived frequencies greater than others. There are several ways of evaluating the improved auditory sensitivity which wearing aids brings to the individual. Measures such as pure-tone audiometry or speech audiometry can be completed whilst the child is wearing aids, thus giving an indication of the benefits of aided listening compared with unaided.

Types of conventional hearing-aids

In simple terms a hearing-aid picks up sound, amplifies it and then delivers the louder signals into the ear canal. The basic components of *conventional* aids are a microphone, amplifier and receiver (or speaker). Conventional aids fall into two categories: those worn on the body and those worn behind the ear. Within these two basic designs there are many models available, each with different qualities and characteristics. Whether a particular aid is selected depends on the age of the child, the nature of the hearing loss, the degree of amplification required, and the effectiveness of the aid for the individual user.

Behind-the-ear (post-aural) aids are more acceptable cosmetically, less inconvenient to wear, and replicate some of the normal ear's capacity for detecting direction, since they are worn at the normal location for perceiving sounds. On the other hand, post-aural aids are more easily lost or damaged, can be difficult to adjust, and give feedback problems because the components of the system are close together. Notwithstanding their drawbacks, post-aural aids are prescribed for the majority of children, including small infants.

Body-worn aids are sturdy, the controls are easy to handle, the batteries have a long life, and they are capable of giving good-quality, powerful amplification across a wide frequency range. In the body aid, the case worn on the child's chest houses batteries, microphone and amplifier. The receiver which delivers sound into the ear canal is separated from the amplifying system by a long cord. The most important advantage of the body-worn aid is that feedback is less of a problem. Feedback occurs when amplified sound leaks out around the ear-mould in the child's ear, and is picked up by the microphone of the aid again, giving a disturbing high-pitched whistle. Because of the greater distance between the microphone (on the body) and the receiver (at the ear), the feedback cycle is less likely to occur than it does with post-aural aids. The main disadvantages of body-worn aids are their bulk, keeping the microphone clean and the cords out of the way, and the fact that the speech signal is not detected at the normal ear position.

Both kinds of conventional aids are selected and adjusted within sympathetic acoustic conditions to give as good an amplification of sound as possible. Children usually find advantages in listening when two aids are prescribed. It is much easier to locate a sound source and focus attention on it, with binaural listening: a common misconception is that children fitted with two hearing-aids are necessarily more severely handicapped than a child who wears only one. One other important fact to highlight, is that hearing-aids do not *select* the sounds which are most meaningful to the child. Most situations in which aids are actually used are unsympathetic in acoustic terms. This means that the aids pick up and amplify every detail of sound, irrespective of its relevance. The noisier the environment, the more likely it is that unwanted noise will be amplified to the detriment of important sounds, such as the teacher's voice. Attention to sound details is controlled by central mechanisms in the brain. In normally-hearing children, these mechanisms are very sensitive to fine auditory details. Such details may be lost with the imperfect auditory information available to a deaf child, even with good hearing-aids. Also, technical problems such as 'recruitment' lead to sounds that are highly amplified being blurred and less easily discriminated from their backgrounds. (Recruitment is the condition whereby a relatively slight increase in sound intensity results in a much greater increase in the sensation of loudness perceived by the child.)

Radio aids

Radio aids have been designed to eliminate some of the problems associated with conventional hearing-aid systems. A microphone and transmitter unit are worn by the speaker, whilst the child wears the radio receiver. There are several variations available. However, the basic process involves, at one end of the system, a microphone attached to within 20 cm of the speaker's mouth. What the speaker says is picked up by the microphone, converted into a radio signal and then broadcast on a permitted radio frequency range. The child's radio receiver is tuned to the transmitting frequency and picks up the radio signal. At the other end of the system, the output from the receiver is amplified by the child's hearing-aids and fed into the child's ears.

Since what the speaker says is transmitted via radio waves to the child's hearing-aids, the speaker's voice may be heard just as well across distances of many metres, without any interruption to the signal, or reduction in clarity. The most important aspect of radio-aid systems is that the speaker can be sure that what is said

will be clearly transmitted to the child, regardless of other inter-
fering sound sources and the general level of background noise.
Radio aids cannot improve the child's hearing thresholds. But
they do ensure that a clear speaker signal is received by the child.
They are, undoubtedly, a major factor in the successful integration of hearing-impaired children into normal classrooms where
acoustic conditions may be appalling.

Radio aids, like conventional hearing-aids, are only one aspect
of helping to maximize communication with a hearing-impaired
child and the book by Webster and Ellwood (1985) gives much
more detailed discussion of possible strategies which can be used
in school. Hearing-aids are an indispensable part of the resources
available to try and enable children and their caretakers to overcome the obstacles which deafness presents to learning. But they
are not a panacea. That point becomes abundantly clear when we
turn to examine the wide range of developmental difficulties
which deafness leaves in its wake.

Chapter summary

1   This chapter sets out the physical aspects of deafness which
may differ widely from child to child. A major distinction is
drawn between hearing losses arising from conductive dysfunction and sensori-neural damage. Otitis media is described as the
commonest cause of middle-ear problems. Several of the leading
known causes of sensori-neural deafness, such as maternal rubella,
prematurity and meningitis, are also associated with additional
handicaps.

2   The identification of a hearing loss should be made as early
as possible. Risk factors, screening, together with some warning
signs of a hearing loss, are discussed. Methods of testing hearing
sensitivity are given. Young children are difficult to assess. In distraction tests the examiner has to be certain the child's responses
are to sound rather that visual stimuli. Audiometric testing gives
more useful information about the frequency range and intensity
levels of a child's hearing profile.

3   The implications of various kinds and degrees of hearing
loss are discussed in terms of access to speech sounds. Conductive

losses may reduce a child's hearing thresholds intermittently by upwards of 15 decibels across the frequency range. Sensori-neural losses usually show uneven configurations, whilst a severe loss averaging more than 70 decibels will mean conversation will not be heard without hearing-aids. Techniques are described which permit the diagnosis of conductive problems, such as bone conduction and impedance audiometry. The role of speech audiometry and objective testing is acknowledged.

4   The incidence of sensori-neural deafness is much lower than conductive impairment, whilst a minority suffer both. Twenty per cent of primary-age children will suffer a middle-ear problem; other handicapped groups are more susceptible. Otitis media is commonly associated with learning difficulties such as reading, but the cause is uncertain. Approximately 0.04 per cent of the total school population has a severe sensori-neural loss.

5   Otitis media can usually be treated medically by antibiotics and decongestants. Surgical treatment may involve myringotomy and insertion of grommets to compensate for eustachian tube dysfunction. Middle-ear disease tends to recur and treatment may have to be repeated. Hearing-aids may be the only 'treatment' for sensori-neural losses. Various types of aid, both conventional and radio are described, together with their strengths and weaknesses. Hearing-aids do not *restore* hearing, they make sounds louder. All aids require effective management strategies to be of maximum benefit to the user.

3

DEAFNESS AND CHILD DEVELOPMENT

In this chapter we shall be drawing on the research literature to make several points about deafness, its impact on the course of child development and the characteristic approach which has been made to its study. First and foremost, deafness is not simply the deprivation of sound. We would do better to describe deafness as the deprivation of language. But even that view is too narrow. We cannot agree with Wolff (1973), when he says in his book that deafness is just a problem of auditory experience:

> The problem of deafness is simply stated: if a child cannot hear the difference between phonemes, morphemes, words and larger syntactic patterns, he cannot learn to recognise these patterns and to associate them with meanings. (p. 154)

We now know that hearing-impairments of a very mild and episodic kind do much more than interfere with what children can hear of the language around them. As well as language, many aspects of the child's social, emotional and educational development can be affected. Where a child suffers a more severe sensori-neural hearing loss, we know that very early social interactions between parent and child are disrupted. These early stages may be crucial to later language development. The point is that the effects of deafness are felt in parent–child contexts well before the child begins to talk. These broader implications of deafness are important for our understanding of the less obvious obstacles to learning which deafness presents.

The second major point is that almost all of the research evidence regarding both conductive and sensori-neural deafness, is either descriptive or evaluative. The typical approach is to use tests of verbal comprehension, word knowledge, or reading, and then compare respective levels of test performance between deaf and hearing groups of children. Many so-called language and intelligence scales rely on normative data. This tells us how children of different ages in the 'normal' population tend to score on the test materials. We can relate any individual's score to the test norms and make a judgement about how far above or below the norm, the individual falls. Researchers have largely been content to demonstrate how less well-adjusted, less independent, more egocentric, more immature, more limited in academic achievements and linguistic competence, hearing-impaired children are when comparisons are made with their normally-hearing peers.

Evaluative research tells us very little about the processes involved when a child is learning language, tackling intelligence tests, or attempting to read. For that reason it is difficult to use normative data in order to learn more about the child's learning strategies, or to plan a teaching programme. Piaget recognized this some years ago when he rejected traditional cognitive testing in favour of a form of observation which attempted to unravel how children make sense of the intellectual problems they meet.

We can align evaluative research with the deficit model described earlier. As we have seen, the underlying philosophy of this approach is that children fail to achieve because of their disabilities. The failure is felt to lie within the child, rather than with the adult caretakers or the way the child has been taught. The deficit model has several influences on people's thinking.

Firstly, it diverts attention away from some of the marked achievements of hearing-impaired children in overcoming obstacles to learning. Secondly, it discourages researchers from finding out how children learn what they do. The reason for that is because it focuses on measuring outcomes, rather than processes of learning. Finally, it makes no demands on adults to adapt their own practice to the child's unique efforts to learn. These points are clearly illustrated when we come to consider the attempts which have been made to assess the reading skills of the severely hearing-impaired.

Linguistic approaches

The acquisition of language is perhaps the most critical achievement of childhood. Language, thinking and conceptual growth are intimately conjoined. Language both shapes, and is shaped by, our experience of the world. Social relationships and emotional well-being depend on communication. For the child with a severe hearing loss, learning to speak tends to be the focus of much educational effort and directly affects the nature of the child's acceptance by a hearing society. It is not surprising therefore, that the linguistic skills of hearing-impaired children (or their linguistic limitations, to use the terms of the deficit model) have frequently come under scrutiny. It is helpful, before turning to the details of the main features of language, to see how they are interrelated, and how they may be studied.

The sounds of language

Figure 3.1 shows some of the main branches of linguistics from a model provided by Crystal (1976). The left-hand side of the diagram, under the heading 'pronunciation', is concerned with the *sounds* of language. Phonetics is the study of the range of sounds which the human being is able to produce with the vocal apparatus. Only a small set of sounds is used in any particular language and the 'phonology' of the sound system of English refers to the forty or so distinctive sound units which we use in

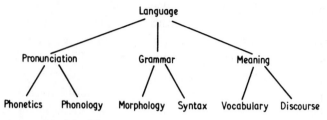

Figure 3.1   Model of language structure

the pronunciation of the English language, and which are known as phonemes.

One interesting aspect of the phonological system is that children move through a series of stages in their acquisition of sounds. The first crying, cooing and babble sounds are felt to be independent of the speech environment of the child and it has been noticed that the vocalizations of hearing-impaired babies at 6 months of age are similar to those of hearing infants. This early period is a kind of practice phase prior to the production of speech sounds proper. From around 9 months to 7 years the child learns the sound contrasts which signify meaning and builds up the production of sounds step by step. For example the consonant sounds produced at the front of the mouth, such as 'b' or 'm', generally appear before back consonants, such as 'k' or 'g'. Accounts of the development of speech sounds are given in Ingram (1976) and Dale (1976). The process is long and not fully understood. By 5 years of age most children use the majority of sounds correctly but may still have problems with certain features, such as the complex cluster of sounds in a word like 'toothbrush', or 'twelfth'. Knowledge of the normal stages of development of phonological skills enables a judgement to be made on the relative maturity of one child's sound system compared with the norm. Just as the sounds of a language can be described, so too, a corresponding approach can be made to its written features. The study of the spelling and punctuation patterns of a specific language has been called 'graphology' (Crystal 1976, p. 27). In the same way as each language has a distinctive phonology, each language also has its own range of 'graphemes': the particular units of writing which are used in setting the language down on paper.

The learning of reading has sometimes been described in terms of establishing grapheme–phoneme correspondences. This 'phonic' approach emphasizes the links which exist between some of the printed symbols of the alphabet and the sounds of speech. The child's attention is drawn to distinctive letter sounds, so that the process of reading is one of decoding print into sound. It is sufficient at this point to note that the significance of phonemic or phonological aspects of reading are the subject of some dispute. In terms of the language model given in Figure 3.1 the study of grapheme–phoneme features is restricted entirely to the left-hand side of the diagram and ignores the rest. For very good reasons, the central part of this language model is taken by grammar and it may well be that a child's control and understanding of the grammar of language, particularly for the hearing-impaired child, will be more important in determining the child's progress, particularly in reading.

The grammar of language

In recent years a great deal more attention has been given to the child's acquisition of the grammar of language. Grammar can be studied in two respects. First, the study of changes in word structure (such as word endings: 'go', 'going', 'gone') is known as morphology. Secondly, and more importantly, the way in which words are fitted together in an organized sequence, such as phrase, clause and sentence patterns, is accounted for by the study of syntax.

Linguists often describe the development of syntax in early childhood by a stage analysis (See Crystal et al., 1976). All normal children are felt to pass through similar stages of language growth towards the adult language. However, some children will do this more or less quickly than others, and there may be considerable overlaps between different stages. The stages are simply a convenient way to describe the particular features associated with a child's use of syntax at a particular point in development.

Table 3.1 Examples of sentence patterns at different stages of grammatical development

Stage	Approximate age of child	Examples of sentence structures
1 (single words)	9 – 18 mths	Mummy, car, biccy, hot, gone, more, teddy
2 (two elements)	18 – 24 mths	dolly bed, naughty baby, where Daddy, Mummy wash, give teddy
3 (three elements)	24 – 30 mths	Mummy rided car, where my doggy, I eated my din din, Nana going now
4 (four elements)	30 – 36 mths	We going to the swimming bath today. You give Daddy a sweetie. I got a new dress for the party.
5 (complex sentences)	36 – 42 mths	We had our tea and then we watched telly and then we went to bed. I can come out when I've put my toys away. That boy who was in the car opened the door.

For a more detailed analysis, see Crystal *et al.* (1976), or de Villiers and de Villiers (1978).

At the most primitive stage, between about 9 and 18 months of age, most children can be described as using single element sentences, such as 'baby', 'more', 'bye-bye', 'drink'. Sentence patterns at the second stage, between about 18 and 24 months, begin to have two elements of structure, such as 'daddy car', 'dolly drink', 'give teddy'. At the third stage, between about 24 and 30 months, children begin to use sentences which contain three elements of structure such as 'dolly want drink', 'Daddy gone car', 'where my Mummy?'. By the fourth stage, about 2½ to 3 years, most children have acquired all the main elements of sentence structure and are able to use simple questions, commands and clauses of four elements or more, such as 'Daddy give teddy to doggie', 'where my Daddy going?', 'where my dolly's hat gone?'.

Stages beyond these levels account for the structures the child has to learn in order to be able to connect sentences together, to embed one within another, and to produce longer, interrelated sequences. This is often felt to be the most exciting and creative period of language growth. Once the child has learnt to extend sentence patterns using devices such as 'because', 'but', or 'and', the range of expression available to the child is limitless. It is often forgotten that this mastery of the basic patterns of syntax and the ability to generate long and complex sentence sequences is achieved well before the child arrives at school and normally by the age of 3½ years. As with phonology, knowledge of the normal developmental stages enables a judgement to be made about the relative maturity of a child's grasp of syntax in comparison with other children of the same age.

Language and meaning

On the far right of the tree diagram in Figure 3.1 can be found the study of meaning or *semantics*. This is a more complex area of language study, if only because meaning has to be inferred rather that observed. How does meaning develop and what does it involve? Obviously, a child's mastery of meaning must include knowledge of individual words as well as sentence structures. We can study the way in which meaning is distributed in a sentence and how it arises from the interrelation of its different elements. Crystal (1976, p.28), in his model of language study, refers to this as 'discourse'. How in fact, meaning does develop from the child's competence in using words and sentences is difficult to determine. This is not simply because meaning is covert, unlike sounds and grammar; the main problem is that we cannot approach meaning *in isolation*.

Meaning can be described as the sense, significance or intention of language. It requires a social context where people are trying to understand each other. This is not a passive process. In conversation, meaning requires the collaboration of a listener and a speaker, actively creating and searching a context for communication clues. To discover how meaning develops in infancy we have to pay attention to how the child interacts with caretakers, the strategies both parties adopt in managing early conversations, and the 'negotiations' which take place by which one receives the intended message of the other. There are important implications of this 'interactive' view of language learning for hearing-impaired children and we shall be examining them in some detail.

It is also important that the limitations of earlier, 'static' views of meaning development are known. It used to be thought that a person's inner understanding of a word was simply what it referred to 'out there'; in other words, its *referent*. So that the meaning of the word 'baby' is learned by hearing 'baby' spoken in the presence of a baby. The word then becomes a symbol for the real object in concrete experience. There are some problems with this explanation since a lot of words, such as 'and', 'but', 'if', do not have referents. Similarly, words that have referents may be used to convey different meanings by different individuals. An ambiguous word like 'dig' requires a sentence context: 'dig in your pocket', 'dig the garden', 'dig the music', or the Cockney rhyming slang 'dig in the grave', in order to particularize its meaning. It is part of the richness of language in use that words can have a multiplicity of meanings.

One way in which earlier researchers have sought to chart the development of meaning in child language studies is through vocabulary growth: counting how many words the average child at a particular stage is likely to have. Various estimates have been made, such as 20 words at 18 months of age, 300 words at 2 years, and so on. In one study, Davis (1974) showed that over a range of word concepts relating to time, quantity, space and others, hearing-impaired children were far less likely to have as broad a grasp of everyday concepts as hearing children. The meaning of words such as 'least', 'equal', 'always', 'between', were particularly confusing because, presumably, of their lack of concreteness. This study highlights several problems in the static counting of vocabulary growth in children. It is very hard to differentiate between words that a child understands, but may not actively use, and vice versa: words which are used, but not fully understood. We have said that the majority of common words in English, such as 'have', 'go', 'do', 'come', have many senses (they are *polysemic*). So counting the number of separate items in a child's vocabulary, or assessing understanding of a word in a test item, will be far less revealing than discovering the range and flexibility of a child's comprehension of words in use.

The crucial point is the social context of language use. How do children learn the rules by which conversations are conducted, such as when to listen and when to contribute? How do they learn the rules of the language game whereby messages are given, received, confirmed and agreed upon? In fact the moves of this language game do seem to be designed around a triangle: what the speaker intends to say, how the message relates to the situation, and how the listener interprets the message. What enables an infant with only primitive language mastery to become engaged in this language triangle is the special skill of adult caretakers. The skill can be observed in linguistic interactions where the adult appears to mediate on behalf of the child. In the study of interactive learning by Wells (1981), he describes adults as 'negotiating' meaning with the child. The adult is an active collaborator in conversation, especially tuned to the child's needs as a language novice.

In the following conversation, recorded between a 2½-year-old and her mother, we can see a range of adult strategies:

Child: I'm a Mummy.
Adult: Lizzie's not a Mummy, is she?
Child (holding doll): Gotta baby, I'm a Mummy.
Adult: Lizzie's got a pretend baby, so she's a pretend Mummy.
Child: I'm a Mummy, yes.

The child opens up with a simple declaration. However, the adult's move is to query what the child says. The child is thus prompted to enlarge on what she said earlier, to clarify what she means. So, she shows the adult her doll. After this second attempt the adult gives more positive feedback. The adult expands the child's utterance and provides a better sentence model. The adult also introduces some missing information to develop what the child is intending to say (she is a *pretend* Mummy). The special skill of the adult lies in the way responses are finely tuned to the child's. The child's level of understanding is gauged accurately. The child's intended meaning in the play context is both interpreted and made explicit. We can only understand how meaning arises from this conversation by looking at the intentions of both child and adult as they 'negotiate' an acceptable interpretation of the doll's play context.

Some interesting features have been identified which characterize the different stages of emerging semantic development as children interact with adults. In the early stages, the language context is strongly dependent on the 'here and now'. Talk arises out of practical activities such as shopping or making the dinner. Contrast this with many of the teaching contexts in school which demand more formal and abstract language use. How well a child copes with language related to more formal tasks will depend to some extent on the nature of early experiences and the kind of linguistic encounters shared with parents.

Early word meanings tend to be very fluid. There are several accounts of children either 'under-extending' or 'over-extending' word meanings. These processes show that children may have only a partial grasp of what a word signifies to the adult. For example, a child may use the word 'doggie' to refer to one specific dog: the family pet. Later on, the child may extend the word to other dogs and animals. One of the author's children started off using 'hot' for an apple juice drink (which she preferred warm). It was some time later before she adjusted the word's initial meaning to match the adult's.

The same child went through a phase of calling all meat on her dinner plate, 'chicken'. This word had a wider range of application than is usual, until the child narrowed down its use. This is an example of a word being over-extended. The child has picked out just a few of the salient features of the word which are criterial for its use, from an adult point of view. Development seems to consist of adding to, or redefining, the salient semantic features. Eventually, the meaning which the child attaches to the word will overlap with the adult's. Mothers are said to be frequently embarrassed when their young children begin to call every male adult, including the milkman, 'Daddy'. Later on the child may redefine the use of 'Daddy' to include only dark-haired men wearing glasses and beards; and it may be some time before the word is used selectively to apply to father figures, including those of other children. It is inappropriate, then, to describe words as being acquired one by one.

A memorable example of the development of a word's meaning and the different features which are salient for the child over a period of time has been given by Ferrier (1978). On entering her daughter's bedroom each morning to encounter an offensive smell, she would exclaim 'Phew!'. Subsequently, the child produced this word in the same setting, but when the smell was absent, as a kind of greeting. Some time later, when 'Phew!' had been used by the mother in a nappy-changing context, the child began to use the word to refer to nappies, both clean and dirty, as well as to the nappy bucket. Ferrier suggests that the important features of contexts such as these may be very different for adult and child. For the infant in her cot, the dominant feature captured by 'Phew!' was the social event rather than the smell. But the instability of the child's concepts is shown in the range of meanings the word acquired.

In the study of language interaction by Wells (1981) attention is drawn to some of the devices and strategies the child has to learn to become a communicator, to join in language interchange. The very basic strategies include: turn-taking (each listening while the other speaks); collaboration (agreeing on the topic of discussion); and cohesion (using devices such as repetition and pronouns to link one response with another). For example:

Child: Gotta baby, *I'm* a Mummy.
Adult: Lizzie's got a pretend baby, so *she's* a pretend Mummy.

We mention two other kinds of strategies which children may use in order to interpret a language interchange, and which have important implications for hearing-impaired children later on. The first can be described as a word-order strategy. Using this strategy, young children assume that all sentences follow a

Subject-Verb-Object (SVO) rule, which many sentences do. This is fine for understanding simple, active, declarative sentences such as 'Richard loves the pussycat', but quickly gets the child into trouble when applied to sentences where the surface word order does not reflect the underlying 'deep' meaning: 'Richard was bitten by the cat'. In more complex sentence patterns where the subject of a phrase may be deleted ('Richard hit the cat and went out'), young children up to the ages of 6 or 7 years are likely to assume that the cat, and not Richard, went out. This strategy, whereby the noun closest to the verb in the surface structure is interpreted as the subject, is known as the 'minimum distance principle'.

Some of the semantic features of language are not fully mastered until much later in childhood. Clark (1978) working with hearing children describes the different stages children go through in their use of pronouns. Children begin by referring to themselves by name, later using 'I', and later still appreciating that 'I' can be used by other speakers. Contrasts such as 'here' and 'there' in relation to 'you' and 'I', precede contrasts such as 'bring' and 'take', which may not be acquired until 11 or 12 years. Children have to learn the kinds of words that can go together, how to substitute words for others, how particular words modify emphasis, and how the different relationships between words in sequence serve to define meanings in subtly different ways. It is only possible to arrive at a full understanding of the meanings of words and the systematic ways in which meanings can be varied, by *using* language in a wide range of contexts and situations. We have stressed, particularly, the interactive role of the 'to and fro' of conversation in providing a joint and active experience through which the changing language forms are experienced and meaning negotiated.

We have deliberately spent some time on the semantic aspect of language development in children because of its importance in the present context of hearing-impaired children learning language and literacy. We will have more to say about the way in which language emerges as a process of hypothesis-testing through which the child attempts to make sense of his world. One central issue is how semantic development in language shapes a child's thinking. We shall be returning to this point later in the book, but it is important to be aware that word meanings help the child to organize experience, and the question of *where* children get their ideas from, is not easily separated from the question of *how* children put their ideas into words.

Early development and conductive hearing loss

We begin by considering the less serious but far more commonly occcurring condition of middle-ear deafness. There is widespread agreement that an association exists between repeated attacks of otitis media in early infancy and delays in development. We have defined delays in development in terms of the criteria drawn from knowledge of normal children in the different areas of language study described in Figure 3.1. The child who is not hearing the sounds of speech clearly and consistently in early infancy seems likely to show marked delays in the maturity of the sound system, in the use of more complex sentence patterns in speech, and understanding language forms. Subsequently the child may be described as having learning difficulties in school and show poorly on measures of auditory processing, verbally-dependent skills and academic achievement.

Why should a hearing loss of only 20 decibels, for example, produce such significant effects? After all, conductive loss due to otitis media is rarely present from birth. The hearing loss is not usually continuous, so that there are periods when the child has normal hearing. Furthermore, in the rare case where hearing sensitivity is depressed by up to 50 decibels, the loss is likely to be *consistent* across the frequency range. This contrasts with a sensori-neural hearing loss where the child's sensitivity to sound is likely to be *uneven* across the frequency range. A sensori-neural loss usually leads to a severe distortion of sound input. But the effect of a middle-ear loss is to dampen. It has been likened to listening with fingers tightly plugged in one's ears. Why should this effect be so difficult to compensate for? Why do research studies pick up such dire consequences of middle-ear disease?

Research studies: problems of interpretation

We can respond to the questions which have just been posed in several ways. One important fact to realize is that children subject to repeated attacks of otitis media may be at risk of developmental delay due to other factors. So when it is said that children with conductive hearing loss show marked lags in their learning and development, care must be exercised over interpretation. How far middle-ear disease actually *causes* language problems is unclear. We can identify some of the factors which contribute to developmental delay and also predispose children to otitis media: poverty, general ill health and poor nutrition, inadequate housing and overcrowding, quality of parenting and family circumstances, low birth weight. Of course, in some children with middle-ear disease, none of these factors may be relevant. We are talking about a general tendency. Where these factors do apply, any one of them may contribute towards a child's learning problems, as

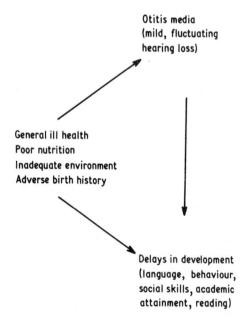

Figure 3.2 Relationship between otitis media, developmental delay and other factors

well as increasing the risk of middle-ear disease. The fact that there is a high association between the two should not be interpreted causally, as the one bringing into being the other.

One other point about this body of research is that it tends to have a lot of flaws in experimental design. A good design should make comparisons between two matched groups of children: one known to have otitis media, the other free from the disease. Unfortunately, many of the existing research studies have been careless about this. Children have sometimes been selected on a very imprecise basis. For example, children have been included in the otitis media group with very diverse histories. In some cases, the middle-ear problems began before the child began to talk (before about 18 months). In other cases, the onset of hearing problems was much later in childhood. Some children have been included in studies on the basis that the parents could recall earlier attacks of otitis media. Other children were much more thoroughly examined by doctors and audiologists. So, we have a great variety of children taking part in research. Otitis media may have started early in infancy or much later. It may have lasted short periods, or persisted through childhood. In some instances the condition will have responded to treatment; in others, maybe not. Often neglected in the research design is whether the child had a current hearing loss on the day any psychological or language tests were given.

Similarly, control-group subjects are just as badly selected, and, in many studies, the way children are matched leaves a lot to be desired. Ideally, subjects in both the otitis media group and the control group should be matched for age, sex, and intelligence, as well as for other factors which we know contribute to individual differences in learning, such as home background and school environment. The children should be matched in every important respect apart from hearing loss. Where this is not carried out adequately, it is impossible to say definitely that any difference between the two groups, on, say, a test of vocabulary, is due to hearing loss, or some other factor such as home background.

In some studies children have been used as control subjects, supposedly with normal hearing, without a hearing test being done. Usually, the parents are simply asked if the child has ever had any hearing problems. It is possible that some of these children have had unnoticed and untreated, middle-ear episodes. Perhaps the most important thing is to check that none of the control children have hearing losses on the day any tests are given, but this is rarely done. All of these issues have been discussed in some detail in the book by Bamford and Saunders (1985), whilst a recent study (Webster and Bamford, in press) attempts to avoid some of the pitfalls.

The effects of otitis media on speech and language

We have noted that many of the research studies have design flaws. Despite this, some researchers are convinced that a mild hearing loss can seriously affect the child's processing of speech and language. What kind of arguments have been put forward to account for the serious effects of only relatively mild hearing losses?

It is the *fluctuating* nature of the condition which is felt to confuse the child at a critical time. A very mild but constant hearing loss might not have such an adverse effect as a loss which is intermittent and inconsistent. What the child hears of the sound patterns of the language undergoes slight changes. It is this that makes it difficult for the child to build up a memory bank of meaningful sounds. The child is unable to build up a store of the important sound contrasts in speech. Instead of periods of good hearing when the child 'catches up', a fluctuating loss confuses the child's speech perception. (For a more detailed discussion of these ideas, see Bamford and Saunders, 1985; and Webster *et al.,* 1984.)

We do not know exactly how speech is perceived or how the child learns which sound contrasts are more important than others. How speech perception relates to the development of other areas of language is also unclear. Obviously, the acquisition of sentence structures does depend on the child's experience of the sound patterns of speech. In Chapter 2 we referred to the units of speech which would be susceptible to the effects of a conductive loss, such as fricatives, plurals, and the weaker or briefer consonant sounds. It follows, therefore, that such auditory processing problems will lead to delays in the acquisition of sentence structures.

Some authors, such as Downs (1977), have gone so far as to suggest that intermittent hearing losses in the first 3 years of life may lead to a long-term and irreversible deficit. The child's ability to process sounds and language might be permanently damaged. This is a view which derives partly from studies of animals. It has been shown in animals that if auditory input is reduced at a critical time then the nerve pathways to the brain seem to develop abnormally (Webster and Webster, 1979). We shall be returning to this notion of irreversible auditory disabilities when we come to consider sensori-neural hearing losses, where this view is more commonly expressed.

What kind of auditory processing problems have been highlighted? One of the earliest and best-known studies was carried out by Holm and Kunze (1969). They collected together a group of 16 children, aged from 5 to 9 years, who had been attending a hospital clinic for treatment of chronic otitis media. These were compared with a control group of children who had no history of middle-ear disease. The control group were matched for age, sex, and home background. The otitis media group had suffered hearing problems since before the age of 2 years. The researchers assessed the speech and language skills of the children using three standardized language measures. These were: the Illinois Test of Psycholinguistic Abilities, the Peabody Picture Vocabulary Test, and the Templin-Darley Articulation Screen. On the day of testing, the otitis media group were not felt to have any current hearing loss which could have affected performance on the tests. It is important, as we have said, that such a check is made on current hearing levels, so that we can be sure that any differences in test scores are the result of earlier hearing problems.

Some of the details of the language measures used, together with the main findings, are given in Table 3.2. On all of the tests which were related (however loosely) to verbal skills, the otitis media group performed more poorly than the controls. The Templin-Darley test is a check on the number of speech sounds the child can pronounce correctly. Actually, the child has to say words aloud, so the test does rely on the child's knowledge of

Table 3.2 Test findings for otitis media and control group children on measures of language (Holm and Kunze, 1969)

Name of test	Test description	Control scores better than otitis scores*
Templin-Darley Articulation Screen	Child has to pronounce sounds in words	yes ($p < 0.05$)
Peabody Picture Vocabulary Test	Identifying a picture to match a spoken word	yes ($p < 0.05$)
Illinois Test of Psycholinguistic Abilities		
1 Auditory decoding	Simple questions (do dogs eat?)	yes (NS)
2 Auditory association	Verbal analogies (soup is hot, ice cream is . . .)	yes ($p < 0.05$)
3 Visual decoding	Matching pictures which belong to the same category (shoes)	yes ($p < 0.05$)
4 Visual association	Relating pictures (hammer with nail)	yes (NS)
5 Vocal encoding	Expressing ideas in speech (child has to talk about pictures showing ball, brick, etc.)	yes ($p < 0.05$)
6 Motor encoding	Miming appropriate actions to pictures (guitar, telephone)	yes (NS)
7 Grammatical closure	Grammatical skills (tenses, plurals, superlatives)	yes ($p < 0.05$)
8 Auditory memory	Recalling a series of numbers in the order given	yes ($p < 0.05$)
9 Visual memory	A series of picture designs has to be reproduced	yes (NS)

* On all tests, control children score better than otitis media group, but where marked 'NS' differences are not significant

words as well. The otitis media group had significantly poorer scores ($p < 0.05$) than controls on this test of speech articulation.

The Peabody test is a measure of the child's understanding of vocabulary. The child is shown four pictures. One of the pictures represents a word spoken by the examiner. The child has to identify the correct picture to match the spoken word. On this test also, it was found that the otitis media group scored significantly poorer ($p < 0.05$) than the controls. In other words the children with histories of hearing loss understood a more limited range of vocabulary compared with controls.

The Illinois test samples a number of different processes in both understanding and use of language. These include simple comprehension questions and tests of grammatical skills using plurals, tenses and comparatives. In one task the child has to describe a series of objects, and the ability to express ideas in words is assessed. In another task the child has to remember a series of numbers as a measure of auditory memory. Other tasks require the child to complete an analogy, or to relate pictures on the basis of similar meaning (for example, two unlike shoes are matched because they belong to the category 'shoe'). On almost all of these test items there were significant differences between the otitis media children and the controls. However, where the tasks seem to be less heavily dependent on verbal skills, the difference in scores between the two groups was much smaller. Some tests of visual or motor skills are obviously less reliant on language. The motor encoding task requires the child to mime how an object like a telephone is used. Differences between the two groups on this test, where the child uses gestures rather than speech, were not significant.

This study has been criticized on a number of counts. No effort was made to make sure the subjects were matched for intelligence. It could be argued that the control children were more able than the others. Inferior ability, and not otitis media, could have led to poorer scores on the tests. Perhaps more importantly, there are some misgivings about the auditory processing deficits which this study is said to highlight. We shall be returning to the nature of this auditory processing deficit later. However, it seems clear that all of the tests which were used in this study depend on *word* skills.

The child has to show knowledge of word sounds, word endings, word associations, word meanings, or to remember word sequences. In these terms, the children suffering repeated middle-ear attacks from infancy did seem to be delayed in their language development. Whether that can be considered to be an auditory processing deficit is another matter.

Recently, there have been many more studies which support the negative effects of persistent conductive hearing loss. This is thought to be the most damaging to language growth when onset of the disease is within the first 3 years of life (Howie *et al.*, 1979; Needleman, 1977; Zinkus *et al.*, 1978; Sak and Ruben, 1981). Several authors have reported on the very high prevalence of middle-ear disorders in children with speech articulation problems. Something like two-thirds of children with immature speech sounds are said to have middle-ear disease (Djupesland *et al.*, 1981; Lehmann *et al.*, 1979). We have already noted that most of this research is evaluative. What that means is that researchers give various test batteries of language skill to children, with and without the disease, and then look for differences in scores between the two groups.

One other influential study was carried out on Aborigine children by Lewis (1976). He devised tests of auditory discrimination and listening. In both quiet and noisy conditions children had to listen to speech sounds and were then asked to say whether they were the same or different. Children were also given a sound blending task where they had to join phonemes together. Aborigine children with histories of otitis media were much more likely to score poorly on the sound discrimination and blending tasks, when compared with children without the disease. Lewis argues that this evidence does support the idea of an underlying auditory disability affecting the child's central processing of sound. In other words, fluctuating hearing levels in infancy do, somehow, prevent the child from developing the auditory mechanisms necessary for handling and processing the sounds of language. It follows, of course, that such an auditory deficit will give rise to wider learning problems when the child starts school. More specific problems might be predicted in learning skills such as reading, where ability to make sound discriminations may be felt by some to be an important aspect.

Specific auditory processing deficits?

What, then, should we make of the evidence for an underlying auditory processing deficit in children with early, persistent middle-ear disease? How convincing are the research claims? We have seen that children with long histories of middle-ear trouble do seem to have problems in discriminating between sounds and in blending sounds together. They find tasks involving listening to sounds, sequencing and remembering sounds, much more difficult than do children who have always had good hearing. There are other, more general language problems, too. The child's understanding of words and use of more complex sentence patterns may also be affected. However, the fact that most of these tests are presented *to the child's ear* does not necessarily mean that they are tapping fundamental auditory processes *necessary for* learning language.

Almost all of the tests of auditory processing used in research, such as sound blending or memory, rely on the child's knowledge of words. So, a child who is delayed in language development is likely to do less well on such tests, anyway. The child's poor performance reflects a general language delay. It does not have to mean that there is an underlying deficit, as Downs (1977) proposes. The commonsense view of the pooled findings of this body of research is that a *strong link* exists between early middle-ear disease and delays in language skills. If there are any longer-term disabilities in processing speech and language these will be more evident in difficult listening conditions. They will be highlighted in situations where the child is expected to listen for long periods and where there is competing sound stimuli. The best example of that is a busy, noisy classroom replete with distractions. For a more detailed discussion of these issues, see Bamford and Saunders (1985).

Otitis media and educational achievement

Several questions can be asked about children who have suffered from otitis media as they enter school. Obviously, disruptions to speech and language associated with early hearing loss will affect the child's learning in school. But are school difficulties a *result* of delayed language, which in turn causes problems in reading and writing? After all, in primary classrooms language is the raw material of learning, the process and the product. One could predict that any gaps in the child's linguistic skills would have consequences for school learning. On the other hand, the question has been raised steadfastly by researchers, whether fluctuating hearing loss actually causes learning problems, particularly in listening and reading.

Downs (1977) goes so far as to suggest that middle-ear disease results in a syndrome: a set of clear symptoms. This she called the 'irreversible auditory learning disaster'. At the heart of the condition we are likely to find that reference is made to the child's 'phonological system'. Needleman (1977), for example, suggests that the central learning problem for the child is an inability to process sounds in words. Since this ability is felt to be crucial to reading, we have a ready explanation for failure in school.

The sequelae to conductive hearing loss (the symptoms which follow in its wake) have been looked for by researchers in three different ways. Firstly, by studying groups of children known to have an early history of chronic middle-ear disease, but no current hearing loss. The question which has been asked of this group is whether there are long-term, irreversible effects on academic progress. The second source of evidence comes from children with *current* middle-ear problems. This group of children have persistent episodes of otitis media where the hearing loss is unresolved. Evidence of poor achievement has been looked for in this group of children. Finally, studies have been made of children identified by separate criteria as being learning-disabled. Children in need of remedial help in school and those referred to remedial reading centres, have been examined to see whether there is any associated middle-ear disease.

These studies have not gone uncriticized. Almost all of them are open to the same criticisms which were levelled at the research comparing speech and language development in children with otitis media and controls. We simply cannot tell whether it is the hearing loss which is the root cause of any differences found between the two groups of children. Evidence of causality does not emerge cleanly from the data. Factors which predispose children to middle-ear disease are also implicated in learning disability. We have mentioned some of these factors already. They include low birth weight, anoxia at birth, poor-quality family environment and low socio-economic status. Every condition which affects a child's overall health and well-being will increase the risk of *both* conductive hearing loss *and* poor performance in school.

With these reservations in mind, what kind of conclusions have been drawn about children in the first research category? These are the children who had otitis media in infancy, but no current hearing loss. A fairly typical study was done by Brandes and Ehinger (1981). They gave a battery of test materials to 7- to 9-year-old children, including auditory processing tests, as well as measures of intelligence and school attainments. There were no significant differences between children with otitis histories and controls on the non-verbal tests. One such test is the Ravens Matrices Test, designed to assess reasoning skills without the need to use language. All the children have to do is select a coloured design from several given, to complete a gap in a large geometric display. No differences were found, either, on tests of reading or mathematics given to the two groups. The significant differences which were found, were confined to measures of verbal processing, such as sound blending and analysis.

In another representative study, Sak and Ruben (1981) looked at children with histories of early conductive hearing loss, in comparison with their siblings. Again, a number of tests were given, including the Wechsler Intelligence Scale for Children–Revised. It is worth looking at this study in some detail because the WISC–R is an intelligence battery very commonly used by psychologists in schools. It taps a wide range of skills in both verbal and non-verbal areas. A description of some of these tests is given in Table 3.3. The non-verbal (or performance) tests revealed no significant differences between the two groups. The child might be asked to look at a picture and spot a missing detail, or have to put a jigsaw together. Tests involving the sorting and arranging of pictures or shapes obviously depend far less on language in order to do them.

There were, however, large differences in the scores achieved

Table 3.3   Subtests of the Wechsler Intelligence Scale for Children and main differences between severe and mild otitis media children

Significant differences (p < 0.05) between severe and mild otitis media groups are marked* (Zinkus *et al.*, 1978)

Verbal subtests

Information	(child has to answer a series of general knowledge questions, e.g. month names)
Comprehension	(social reasoning, e.g. child has to explain what to do in a particular emergency)
Arithmetic*	(mental arithmetic: addition, subtraction, division questions, such as a simple money problem)
Similarities*	(language concepts, e.g. identifying how two objects are alike)
Vocabulary*	(child has to explain the meaning of individual words)
Digit span	(recalling a sequence of numbers)

Performance subtests

Picture completion	(visual awareness for missing details in pictures of everyday objects)
Picture arrangement*	(sequencing a series of pictures to tell a story)
Block design	(child has to match block models to a picture template)
Object assembly	(child has to fit jigsaw pieces together)
Coding	(child has to write a series of coded symbols)

Verbal scale IQ (summary of verbal subtests)*
Performance scale IQ (summary of performance subtests)*
Full scale IQ (summary of verbal and performance subtests)*

---

by the two groups on the verbal tests. The WISC–R verbal scale samples the child's general knowledge of the world, the ability to use verbal concepts, mental arithmetic, understanding of word meanings, as well as facts learned in school. To do well a child needs good expressive language in order to put ideas into words. Good short-term memory is helpful, as well as good recall for facts. Children who have missed a lot of school are unlikely to do so well. It is in these verbal areas that the otitis media children made poor scores. Other tests of mathematics, sight-reading and reading comprehension showed no deficits.

Taken together, this area of research suggests that there are some pervasive effects of early conductive hearing loss which can be identified in older children. These are likely to be highlighted in verbal processing and language-dependent skills. However, they are unlikely to be insurmountable. They may not even last throughout a child's school career. In support of this, one study gave a battery of language tests to children with conductive hearing-impairment and examined the same children again five years later. At the earlier assessment all the children compared very badly with normally-hearing peers on the verbal tests. By the time of the later assessment, besides showing improvements in their hearing, the children had caught up with their peers in overall school performance and no longer gained poorer test scores (Hamilton and Owrid, 1974; Dalzell and Owrid, 1976).

Let us turn now to the second research category. These are children who suffer ongoing and unresolved middle-ear disease. Researchers have tried to identify the learning difficulties experienced by this group. Kaplan et al. (1973) looked at the long-term effects of otitis media in Eskimo children, who seem to be particularly prone to middle-ear disease. This study reported much lower achievements in reading, mathematics and language, as measured by the Metropolitan Achievement Tests. They also found significant deficits on the verbal scale of the WISC.

Similarly, Burgener and Mouw (1982) examined children aged 9 to 11 years who had current, long-standing hearing losses because of middle-ear disease. These children were given a whole host of tests to assess spelling, sight word recognition, reading comprehension and arithmetic, as well as abstract reasoning. What the authors then did was to make correlations between all the test scores and measures of the children's hearing sensitivity. In other words, they were trying to find out the extent to which hearing loss was related to school achievement. They found, as might be expected, that good hearing was not necessarily related to good academic performance. However, even very minor hearing losses showed a consistent association with lower IQ scores and poor attainment.

What is the smallest degree of hearing loss which can affect children's progress in school? This question has been addressed by Quigley (1978). He says that children with hearing losses of only 15 decibels (which is a level that may not be detected by school screening audiometry) are found to underachieve. There can be less argument about this group of children. An ongoing, persistent hearing loss of only a minimal degree presents a considerable hindrance to learning in school and shows a strong link with poor achievement. Many authors pinpoint the source of learning difficulty in poor listening skills. Classrooms are often busy, noisy places. A child with a minor hearing loss may suffer lapses of attention or concentration and be unable to listen for long periods. This may be especially difficult where there is competing and distracting auditory stimuli. When we come to consider remedial strategies, listening skills are an important starting point.

The third and final research category concerns children classified by other criteria as having learning difficulties. Researchers have looked, for example, at children referred to centres for the teaching of remedial readers. The aim of these studies is to determine how many children have unsuspected middle-ear problems. If so, what is their profile of abilities and weaknesses like, and how might a hearing loss account for some of the difficulties experienced? Some estimates of the incidence of middle-ear disease in groups of children with reading difficulties were given in Chapter 2. Broadly speaking, a current or earlier conductive hearing loss is reported to be more than twice as common in children with reading difficulties. Indeed, some studies put the figure even higher than this.

There is a large body of evidence on this topic. Most researchers are content to describe the characteristics of the children who are discovered to have middle-ear problems, without jumping to conclusions (Freeman and Parkins, 1979; Glass, 1981; Masters and Marsh, 1978; Tweedie, 1983). Most of these authors, too, are content to accept that otitis media may be one of a nexus of factors which tend to go together with language delay, poor listening skills and poor achievement. Two studies by Zinkus *et al.* (1978) and Burgener and Mouw (1982) give a detailed breakdown of the child's strengths and weaknesses, where otitis media was known to play a part.

In the Zinkus study two groups of children were collected together from a number referred for investigation because of poor progress. The children selected had to be of average IQ, from middle-class backgrounds, and with no other handicaps. Children were assigned to one group if they had suffered multiple episodes of otitis media during the first 3 years of life, according to medical records. In fact, all of the eighteen children in the group had undergone middle-ear surgery. Thirteen of the children had current hearing losses. Children were assigned to a second group if they had documented histories of relatively mild otitis media in infancy, not requiring surgery. Only 2 out of 22 of these subjects had mild current hearing losses. So, there were two groups: one severe, one mild. Without knowing which children belonged to which group, psychologists administered a battery of intelligence and achievement tests.

The main findings of this study are shown in Table 3.3. This also describes some of the subtests from the Wechsler Intelligence Scale for Children. Differences in test scores between severe and mild otitis media groups which reach statistical significance, are identified in the table. Zinkus says that the severe otitis children did less well than their counterparts on all those subtests which depend heavily on auditory processing skills. In other words, where the child has to listen to complicated instructions, remember spoken items, such as in the mental arithmetic task, or cope with verbal sequences, such as in picture arrangement, then differences are marked.

In terms of the language model outlined in Figure 3.1, it should be said that the WISC taps abilities across the three areas of language skill. One subtest designed specifically to assess concept development (the right hand 'semantic' side of the model) clearly discriminated between the severe and mild otitis groups. Some of the performance subtests carry a high verbal loading, others do not. What that means is that some of these practical tests also tap language skills, whilst others appear to depend less on language.

Picture completion, for example, asks the child to spot a missing detail in a picture, such as the strap on a wristwatch. Instructions can be mimed to the child, whilst the main faculty required is good visual awareness. The picture completion subtest is one of several that did not differentiate between the two groups.

The Zinkus study shows fairly clearly that early, persistent middle-ear disease is associated with poor verbal skills as measured by the WISC. The poorer the child's verbal scores, the more difficulties were found in learning to read. Zinkus claims that his study shows the importance of auditory processing for reading. It should be remembered, however, that we have taken a very much wider view of the auditory processing skills assessed by the WISC, than does Zinkus. We mention Burgener and Mouw's (1982) study to highlight the fact that these authors also gave the WISC to poor readers found to have otitis media. They discovered that *all* the subtests on the verbal scale of the WISC, together with the more verbally-loaded performance items, showed significant differences between otitis media children and controls.

Some investigators have been tempted to say that middle-ear disease actually *causes* reading and spelling disability (Nowell and Eaton, 1982). In our view, this is going beyond the limits of the evidence and into the realms of speculation. The specific reading deficit is felt to be located in the child's mastery of phonological skills: the rules which relate the sounds of speech to the written features of print. As we have said, these aspects of language occupy the left-hand side of our language model and ignore the rest. When we come to discuss normal reading development, we shall not be trying to explain the reading process in terms of a single factor. Phonological skills may well be important to beginning reading, but they are not the whole explanation.

From the evidence so far, broad aspects of language comprehension, awareness and use, seem to be implicated in hearing loss and academic achievement. At present we have a high association of reading difficulties with conductive hearing loss. But that is as far as it goes. We would argue that a much more diffuse relationship exists between otitis media and particular verbal skills such as reading. There is no firm evidence that it is because children have middle-ear problems that they are unable to read. This presumes that what children have to be able to do, in order to read, is to distinguish the sounds in words. If children with middle-ear problems struggle to read, this is likely to be due to a spectrum of language factors.

It follows that a much more acceptable model of the reading process will be multi-factorial. Indeed, in Chapter 4 we put forward a view of reading where the child derives meaning from many information sources: letter shapes, sounds, words, syntax, story context, as well as picture clues and sensible guesswork. This is an approach to reading as a highly complex intellectual task which makes demands on the whole of the child's linguistic and cognitive competence, as the child interacts with text.

Behavioural and social consequences of otitis media

Very little attention has been given in the literature to effects of recurrent otitis media on a child's behaviour and social adjustment. Yet we know from experience of normal children in schools that behaviour, adjustment and learning usually go hand in hand. Unhappy and poorly adjusted children often fail to learn. Children with otitis media and associated communication problems may be perceived as being unwilling or of limited ability, especially if the condition is undetected and the child does not draw attention to a hearing difficulty. The hidden and inconsistent nature of the condition simply reinforces the problems, because parents may be less likely to compensate for the child's difficulties. One plausible suggestion is that otitis media may interfere with social interaction between adults and other children in a way that has only recently been brought to prominence for the more severely hearing-impaired.

In a five-year study of several hundred children from urban areas, Bax *et al.* (1983) found several patterns of adjustment subsequent to upper respiratory tract illnesses and middle-ear infections. These children were much more likely to be difficult to manage and have temper tantrums than children without high incidence of such illness. Similarly, there was a strong relationship between speech and language delay and behaviour problems, a finding also reported by Richman *et al.* (1982). A group of forty-seven 5-year-olds with otitis media (mean loss 20.2 decibels) studied by Silva *et al.* (1983) showed much more maladaptive behaviour than controls, such as short concentration span, high dependence on adults, and poor motivation. Mothers of these children described them as being restless, fidgety, destructive, disobedient and socially isolated. Other clinical observations suggest that otitis media may lead to a listless, shy and withdrawing personality (Rapin, 1979). The important point about all these findings is that there are secondary consequences of even very mild hearing losses, which could contribute to a child's learning difficulties, over and above hearing loss *per se.*

Child development and severe sensori-neural hearing loss

The effects of the more severe sensori-neural hearing-impairments upon the course of normal child development are unpredictable, not fully understood, but certainly potentially devastating. Much of the available research evidence relates to children with severe or profound hearing loss. However, we should say from the outset that there is no straightforward dichotomy between children with mild conductive and severe sensori-neural deafness. It would also be a mistake to assume that there is a unitary dimension along which 'man-minus-hearing' can be distinguished from 'man-plus-hearing'. Indeed, in any group of hearing-impaired children a sense of homogeneity will be largely superficial and unjustified. In Chapter 2 attention was drawn to the many causes of deafness, the widely varying effects on a child's auditory experience, and large discrepancies in the *functional* impact deafness has on individual development. Of course, the problems encountered by children with severe or profound impairments are very different in kind and degree from the less heavily impaired, and there will be many 'in-between' children who share characteristics of both. We have highlighted these contrasts in order to make some important points about the process of development towards literacy. In the end it is a teaching response geared to *individual* needs which we advocate.

Given that the numbers of severely hearing-impaired children are relatively small, and yet it is a group whose development is differentiated by so many varied factors, we should therefore be cautious in making general pronouncements about the deaf population. Meadow (1980) in her summary, points out that deaf children of deaf parents (approximately 10 per cent of deaf children) are likely to encounter fewer behavioural or emotional problems, and may do better academically, than deaf children of hearing parents. In the latter situation every family has to rediscover all the obstacles and how they can be negotiated, completely anew. It is also well known that children whose deafness was caused by maternal rubella are much more likely to suffer additional handicap such as heart disorder, visual defect and intellectual impairment (Murdoch, 1984).

Such children run a high risk of social, emotional and learning difficulties. Wood (1984) points out that in addition to degree and cause of deafness, we must also consider a range of socioeconomic factors associated with child development and achievement. Factors which have been found to relate to differences in achievement in normal children, such as income level and parental occupation, will apply to the deaf child's performance. Wood also makes the point that some very profoundly deaf children achieve language and academic levels up to and beyond normal children of the same age. We have noted that a deficit model approach tends to steer researchers away from the marked achievements of such children and the strategies or circumstances through which they were fostered.

Early interaction

It has been assumed until fairly recently that the fundamental problem for the deaf child is one of being cut off from the ordinary speech environment. For the child who cannot hear speech, even with the provision of powerful hearing-aids, there are bound to be enormous difficulties in acquiring basic language skills because of the limited and distorted nature of the child's auditory experience. However, research evidence has begun to show that deafness does not simply restrict what the child can hear. Deafness also disrupts some of the social-interactive processes which take place between children and adults, and which are felt to be crucial stages in normal language development before the child begins to talk.

In our earlier discussion of the social interactive processes involved in the development of meaning we asked how the child learned to take part in the language triangle whereby adults and children 'negotiate' understanding. Studies by Bruner (1975) and Schaffer (1977) have shown that the games which mothers play with their babies, such as 'peek-a-boo' or 'this little piggy went to market' have an important function. They are the first shared dialogues in which the child takes part; the first 'conversations' about a shared experience; the first exchanges involving turn-taking, when the mother and then the baby, responds; and the earliest means by which the mother uses language, gesture and tone of voice, to signal coming events. It has been argued that these processes are the roots of communication.

Gregory and Mogford (1981) made a study of mothers inter-acting with their hearing-impaired babies. They looked at such precursors to speech as turn-taking, mutual eye-gazing and mother-infant voicing. All these early interactions were felt to be interfered with and in some cases, missing altogether. If it is true that deafness interferes with processes such as the sharing of attention between mother and baby, then the very foundations of language may be damaged. Deafness seems to affect the very basic way in which the mother integrates her vocalizations, gestures and expressions, with the experience shared with her child.

It may also be true that parental expectations of a hearing-impaired child are affected. Parents may feel it is not worth talking to the child if the child cannot hear. Or it may be that parents will try and flood the child with talk. Some parents end up deliberately teaching the child words. They may attempt to draw the child's attention to new things and contrive to bring new vocabulary and language forms to the child. Certainly, the intuitive skills of adult caretakers in negotiating meaning with the child, may be lost. We have mentioned other skills which parents intuitively possess, such as tuning the complexity of language used to the child's own, and paraphrasing or expanding on the child's contributions. These too, may be lost.

In Gregory's (1983) recordings of mothers' speech to their 3-year-olds, mothers of hearing children were observed *discussing* a set task with their hearing child, such as how to go about shutting the door. Mothers of deaf children tended simply to *command* the child. In Gregory's study the more profoundly deaf children had less than ten words by the age of 4 years. Language delay is attributed not merely to the children's limited auditory experience, but also to factors such as less nurturing adult–child interactions. Whilst these may be evoked by the child's deafness, they are not dependent on deafness *perse.*

The teaching environment

Several recent studies have looked at factors in the nursery and school environment which have a significant effect on the child's development. One possibility is that some teachers are unwittingly not very good at providing children with a language environment which fosters their development. In the study of pre-school hearing children by Wood *et al.* (1980), some interesting conclusions have been drawn about the way in which adults behave and the effect this has on productive language interaction between adult and child. Some of Wood's nursery staff behaved as managers and verbal exchanges with children reflected the adult's concern to organize resources and materials: '. . . I hope you're going to put that apron on if you want to paint. Not so much noise, please. . . ' Other staff were much more genuinely interested in what the child had to say and fostered the kind of conversational interaction which we described earlier as being important for the development of shared meaning in language. Less effective of Wood's nursery staff were those who controlled conversations by asking many questions, particularly open questions ('What did you do at the weekend?'); or questions designed to test the child ('How many fingers am I holding up?'). Strategies which were the very least effective in sustaining interaction included enforced repetition ('Say "I went", not "I goed"'), and demands for restatement ('Tell me that again, slowly this time').

Similar kinds of both productive and unproductive strategies have been identified in teachers working with the hearing-impaired. It may be that when teachers are faced with the problem of understanding a deaf child's speech, or when a breakdown in understanding occurs, then the teacher reacts in a way which is non-facilitative. Characteristically, some teachers of the deaf control conversation through questions: they may ask a child to repeat a well-formed sentence model, and the intention of the adult may be principally to 'teach' language. In the following extract from a primary classroom recording, the sense of language being a process of negotiation between adult and child is absent, the style is directive, the teacher's aim is to hand over information:

Adult: Today we are going to talk about furniture. What's furniture? Brian, have you any furniture in your house?
Child: No.
Adult: Everyone has furniture! Here is a picture of some . . .

In one experiment teachers of the deaf were asked to change their styles of conversation with hearing-impaired children, in order to foster more productive interaction (Wood and Wood, 1984). It did prove possible to avoid an overquestioning, controlling kind of conversation. The successful ingredients included the teacher finding a mutual experience or activity around which a commentary could be shared: a social context. The teacher needed to give something from personal experience, to hand the conversation back to the child and allow time for a reply. The adult and the child had to be able to enter the dialogue as equal partners and this needed to be reaffirmed with 'phatic' comments from the teacher, otherwise known as 'social oil' ('Well I never!', 'Ooh, that sounds nice!'). Modified styles of conversation are described in terms of greater success because they lead to an increase in *spontaneous* language contributions from the children: they become more active participants in using language.

This kind of research touches upon some fundamental issues: can language be systematically trained or programmed? There is a view that children who are language-delayed can be *drilled* on specific points of language. Indeed, there are many commercial language programmes on the market which claim to do just that. Earlier on in this chapter we put forward a more recent view of language learning whereby children learn through interaction. Children contribute to their own development by actively creating an understanding and mastery of language in use. How the child interacts with caretakers, the strategies that adults and children adopt, and the 'negotiations' which arise in a communication context, are all important facets. A review of twenty-four language-training programmes which focus on the early production and comprehension of specific features of spoken language has been provided by Harris (1984). He expresses the view that language cannot be dispensed bit by bit from a teaching package. It is the quality of the child's linguistic interactions with others which is the most effective teaching tool.

The focus of interest then, has shifted to the conditions which surround language activity. These include the intentions of the speaker and the social context in which a conversation arises. If we reject the idea that the child is a passive assimilator of language, we must also reject the idea that the teacher's role is one of handing over, rehearsing or drilling, linguistic structures. Similarly, if we accept that the child's part in constructing the language system is central, then the teacher's best efforts will go into providing and facilitating opportunities for meaningful language use. What Halliday (1973) said raises some interesting questions about the teaching of language:

> the child knows what language is because he knows what
> language does. (p. 10)

It has been argued that deliberate efforts to teach language directly simply usurp the child's central role. Such efforts are less facilitative because the child is not able to learn language by discovering what it can do.

There may well be secondary consequences for the child's overall approach to learning, if an increase in adult control appears early on and persists for a long time. Brennan (1976) has considered this in some detail. She says that most teaching of the deaf is based upon three processes: imitation, repetition and reinforcement. She looks at each one of these teaching processes in turn. Imitating an adult model sentence is not a strategy which is observed in normal language development. Sentences such as 'allgone biccy', 'nomore car', and 'where my daddy?', show children creating language patterns according to the sophistication of the language under their control. So there are problems in accepting that children learn by copying adult models. Children are not normally exposed to the kind of language patterns which they themselves produce in the early stages.

By the same token, when a hearing child is requested to listen to an adult model in order to imitate it correctly, a kind of filtering may be observed:

Child: Nobody don't like me.
Mother: No, say 'Nobody likes me'.
Child: Nobody don't like me.
(8 repetitions of this dialogue)
Mother: No, listen carefully, say 'Nobody likes me.'
Child: Oh, Nobody don't likes me.

(McNeill, 1966, p. 69)

In this dialogue the adult model is reduced to a sentence form within the child's own control. Imitations can only be made within the constraints of the child's own language system. Repeating a correct sentence model, particularly if this includes structures of a complexity *beyond* the child's control, is likely to be unproductive in terms of the child's language growth.

According to Brennan (1976), the degree of exposure, practice and repetition of 'correct' language, is irrelevant to the child's basic learning task, which is to abstract rules from an experience of language in use. The two other teaching processes which Brennan looks at are those of repetition and reinforcement. These occur when the teacher steps into normal conversation. Teachers of children with poor language may feel this is justified if it gives the chance to practise and reinforce an aspect of language. This is sometimes described as *repair*. The teacher deliberately halts the dialogue in order to patch over a breakdown in understanding, check a word, or make a teaching point.

It is, of course, highly likely that repair occurs more often in conversation with the poorer oral communicators. These are likely to be the children with profound hearing losses or more limited speech intelligibility. In the following extract, a teacher of the deaf is giving a language lesson:

Teacher: Why do you like nice weather?
Alice: Because . . . because father and mother . . . father and mother, brother and I go swim.
Teacher: Say it better.
Alice: Because father and mother, brother
Teacher (interrupting): brother*sss* . . .
Alice: Brothers and I . . . go for a swim.
Teacher: That is right . . .

(Van Uden, 1977, p. 265)

Clearly, the teacher's main concern lies with the grammatical correctness of the child's sentences. This is at the expense of disrupting the conversational flow, and with some disregard of what the child wants to convey.

We have said that there are a number of children with severe hearing impairments who do overcome the obstacles to learning associated with deafness. Some severely deaf children, in fact, develop 'normal' speech and language. One possibility is that some teachers and schools do provide exactly what is needed for the deaf child to succeed. We will have to speculate about what this entails. However, it may be that success is associated with the degree to which schools can provide learning experiences which transcend the linguistic limitations of deaf children. We have said that the question of where children get their ideas from, is not easily separated from the question of how children put their ideas into words. For the deaf child limitations in language experience may result in diminished cognitive demands and fewer opportunities to develop reflective awareness. Donaldson (1978) has said that the pursuit of education in our society is towards 'disembedded thinking': the ability to reason about events which have no immediate context. Children's thinking may start off by being constrained to 'here and now' situations. Thinking moves beyond these bounds to manipulate ideas, and to infer relationships between events in the abstract. Developmentally, this could be described as a turning of attention from what is *without*, to an awareness of events *within*. Growth of language and growth of disembedded thinking are closely enmeshed.

We shall be pursuing some of these ideas further in Chapter 5. So far as deafness is concerned, it seems likely that there are secondary consequences which may constrain the linguistic and cognitive demands made upon the child. We have characterized interactions between adult and deaf child in terms of greater adult control, greater use of questioning, and efforts to teach language directly. Strategies such as imitation and repetition arise which treat the child as a passive assimilator of language. The deaf child is not exposed to the same complexity of speech or language in the classroom as a hearing child. It may be difficult to move beyond the 'here and now', to talk about events which are not simply the banal features of present experience. In order to move children forward in their linguistic development the teacher has to find ways of talking about hypothetical situations, releasing conversation from the concrete to more abstract situations, inviting speculation about cause and effect, and invoking imaginative experience. Perhaps the most important task in school is to preserve and foster the child's sense of wanting to know.

Behaviour and personality

Some researchers have talked about a special personality of the deaf with its own special psychology. Myklebust (1964) has argued that severely deaf people think and behave differently from hearing people in order to make sense of the world. In his view abstract thought is more difficult for the deaf than concrete thinking. In the following example:

> The dog is asleep.
> He sleeps in a box.
> The box is under the table.

deaf children may comprehend the individual sentences but be unable to make the logical leap to infer that the dog is under the table. It could be argued that the problem is linguistic: lack of familiarity with language usage to know that the subject of the first sentence is implicitly present across the sequence. Myklebust, however, has argued that the problem is symptomatic of a rigid, literal and egocentric learning style which cannot cope with hypothesis or inference.

Severely hearing-impaired children have been variously described as impulsive and socially immature; less able to care for their own needs; lacking self-direction; and more dependent on adults, than normally-hearing peers (Meadow, 1980). They may be viewed as being less well motivated to achieve; unable to see other people's points of view; poor at making friendships; restricted in general knowledge and experience; and requiring greater adult direction and external control (Quigley and Kretschmer, 1982). The stereo-typed picture of the unique deaf personality is one of passive dependency on others; unquestioning styles of learning and un-critical, self-centred and naïve assumptions about the world.

This is, of course, a classic example of the deficit model in action, whereby styles of behaviour and personality are attributed to the child's disability. A much more positive view is that it is not deafness *per se,* but the indirect effects of deafness which influence social adjustment, emotional development and learning strategies. We have pointed out that deafness not only interrupts auditory input but also interferes with early patterns of social and linguistic interaction between children and their caretakers. In turn this may lead to different parenting styles, such as over-protection, less permissiveness, heightened direction and control; more particularly, the nature of the child's linguistic experiences may be unwittingly less nurturing. The point is that characteristic behaviour traits in the hearing-impaired are a product of learning experience and may be specific to those situations in which learning takes place, rather than being part of a 'deaf' personality.

Some of these environmental obstacles may be avoidable. A child with impaired hearing is inevitably cut off from some sources of learning, such as overhearing the interactions and discussions of others. Information may not be absorbed so rapidly because of the stresses of listening. Children dependent on hearing-aids for auditory input will find many school situations unbearably noisy acoustic environments. Language is both process and product of learning and enables us to construct a framework for new concepts, for relating new information to old, and to escape beyond the here and now. We arrive at a considered view of events in experience by discussion, listening to opposing points of view in the 'to and fro' of conversation, and in gauging the reactions of others to what we say. Children learn in a context of linguistic interaction which may be very difficult to achieve with hearing-impaired individuals. Nevertheless, the positive aspect of this view is that the problem is one of finding routes around the obstacles which deafness creates for the child. The deficit model leads to a much more pessimistic outlook of the limitations *inherent* in the child's condition. The alternative view puts the locus of the child's learning difficulties in the teaching environment. It is the teacher's responsibility to adapt strategies to meet the child's needs. As we have seen, teachers and schools do vary in their effectiveness and adults can be helped towards changing the way *they* behave, to good effect.

Language development in deaf children

The vast majority of research efforts with the severely hearing-impaired have been concerned with evaluating the products rather than the processes of learning. The purpose has usually been to establish how far behind normal peers deaf children fall in terms of their achievements. Similarly, researchers have tried to evaluate the effectiveness of one method of communication over another (i.e. speech versus sign) by measuring outcomes. The problem with the latter studies is that it is usually impossible to find children who have been exposed to just one kind of language system. Indeed, deaf children are often exposed simultaneously to gestures, signs and finger spelling as well as speech. So any attempt to focus on the success of one method compared with another will be impossible to achieve. The consensus view, summarized in the very comprehensive survey by Kretschmer and Kretschmer (1978), is that regardless of *how* language is learned, severely hearing-impaired children are likely to be very poor communicators at the time of school entry and beyond, when comparisons are drawn with normally-hearing peers.

Some very early observations of deaf babies, in the first few months of life, suggest that they do babble, coo and cry like hearing infants. In hearing babies the production of speech sounds proper begins at around 9 months, when the child learns the sound contrasts which signify meaning. A few studies suggest that deaf babies produce a reduced range of babble sounds, in less quantity and with a flatter tone; and of course, the speech sounds of babies who have restricted auditory experience are much slower to become language-specific than hearing counterparts. We pointed out earlier that phonological aspects of speech occupy a position left of centre in our language model (Figure 3.1). However, a lot of attention has been given to the characteristics of the speech of hearing-impaired individuals which make it different from normal. Several aspects are usually highlighted: slow, laboured and breathy speech; distortion of vowel sounds; omission of consonants; incorrect speech rhythms. (See summary in Ingram, 1976.)

Speech intelligibility has been used as a measure of educational success. Markides (1970) reported that untrained listeners were able to report correctly on only 19 per cent of deaf children's speech. In Conrad's (1979) survey of deaf school leavers, measures of speech intelligibility showed results of a similar limited nature. However, in the study of the speech of deaf children by Dodd (1976), 11-year-olds were felt to be using more than half of the forty or so distinctive sound units of English; sounds were used systematically, albeit very delayed. Difficulties in mastering the sound system are attributed to the incomplete auditory information received by the child, even when hearing-aids are worn.

The importance of these studies to subsequent reading development, concerns the nature of the language which is internalized by the child. Normally-hearing children are felt to have inner speech-like experiences which correspond to their outer use of speech sounds. In other words, when thinking or reading, most children use a covert speech code intended only for themselves. Access to an inner speech code is felt by some to be the critical factor in the child's potential for reading. The argument proceeds that if deaf children have a distorted or very limited experience of spoken language, they may not even develop an inner speech code. The lack of internalized language has been blamed as the major cause of the deaf child's literacy problems. We shall be examining this line of argument in some detail in the chapters on reading and thinking. Suffice it to say here that this explanation of reading failure in terms of lack of inner speech, presupposes a theory whereby the child decodes text into speech sounds in order to achieve understanding.

Turning to studies of the grammatical development of deaf children (the central area of syntax in our language model), research on very young infants suggests that there are similarities in the early stages between deaf and hearing groups. Hearing-impaired children of deaf parents who sign are likely to make rapid progress in using signs themselves, and the sequence of emergence of signs and combinations is felt to mirror normal development. For example, *over-extension* can be seen in infant signing: one sign such as 'more' being used in two-word combinations to indicate different meanings: 'more play', 'more food', 'more sock' (Collins-Ahlgren, 1975). The appearance of spoken language is also felt to reflect the early stages of normal development, although much delayed. Schlesinger and Meadow's (1972) data for pre-schoolers suggests that the majority of deaf children by the age of about 4 years would be using the language structures of normal 2-year-olds, but some were less advanced. In a more recent study the spontaneous language of 4- to 15-year-old deaf children was analysed (Geers and Moog, 1978). Interestingly, the most rapid language development was observed between the ages of 4 and 9 years. More than half of the group, most of whom had hearing losses in excess of 90 decibels, were using language with a syntactic complexity less than the average 3-year-old hearing child.

The consensus view is that deaf children continue to make slow but consistent progress throughout the school years in their grammatical skills. The most comprehensive studies of the range of syntactic structures which deaf students can use and understand were carried out by Quigley and his associates (1976). It should be noted that this work used a written test format. It examined the abilities of children aged 10 to 19 years in dealing with isolated written sentences of varying complexity. It did not, therefore, include a range of factors involved in the child's understanding of spoken language, such as the social context of conversation. Deaf children were presented with series of sentences with a variety of grammatical structures: negation, conjunction, verb processes, determiners, use of pronouns, question forms, relative clauses. Even when it was known that the children understood the vocabulary and concepts involved in the sentence structures, it was found that particular kinds of sentence pattern caused difficulties in comprehension, while others did not. For example (Quigley and Kretschmer, 1982), when given the two sentences:

The boy kissed the girl.

and

The boy ran away.

most students understood them, but were unable to respond correctly when one sentence was embedded in the other:

The boy who kissed the girl ran away.

Most deaf students, even up to 18 or 19 years, believed it was the girl, rather than the boy, who ran away. However, in relation to almost every aspect of syntax tested, very slow but consistent progress could be measured throughout the age range.

Two aspects of the language competence of deaf children can be found in younger hearing children. Earlier we drew attention to the strategies which children use in order to make sense of language. One such strategy, shared by younger hearing and older deaf students, is to assume that sentences in English follow a Subject-Verb-Object pattern. Children who use this rule will quickly come upon problems of interpretation with sentences which do not follow it, such as passives. We have also highlighted the 'minimum distance principle' as a strategy which hearing children use up to the age of 6 or 7 years in comprehending sentences such as:

Joe fed the dog and went in the garden.

Deaf children may persist up to and beyond school-leaving age in misconstruing such a sentence to mean that the dog, and not Joe, went in the garden. It will be recalled that the principle at work identifies the noun closest to the verb in the surface structure of the sentence as being the subject. It is important to remember that the weight of evidence indicates that deaf children do develop a system of grammatical rules which may be greatly delayed but which nevertheless parallels in many respects the normal developmental process.

We have seen that when attention is drawn to the social context in which language development takes place, deaf children face additional hurdles because adults may, unwittingly, provide a less facilitating interactive environment. In order to discover how aspects of meaning develop in language, the learning context is all-important. For the deaf child we have identified several ways in which the behaviour of parents and teachers appears to change in the direction of greater control and an impulse to work on language rather that natural dialogue. Deaf children appear to be cut off from some of the ordinary learning experiences available to hearing children: they never *overhear* the conversation of others. It is for reasons such as this that we have hypothesized different learning styles, more restricted experience, and perhaps a less flexible grasp of the semantic richness of language use in the deaf.

Some examples from personal experience of working with deaf children illustrate a more limited flexibility of usage, which sometimes causes misunderstandings in the classroom. One child had learnt the literal meaning of the word 'time', in the sense of 'What time is it?', or 'Is it time to go home?'; but was totally confused by expressions such as 'Have a nice time', or 'All in good time'. Similarly, whilst this child could cope with some familiar usages of 'get', such as 'get on the bus' or 'get a book off the shelf'; other phrases were much more elusive, such as 'get on with your friends', or 'get on in life'. A hearing-impaired child might understand prepositions in sequences such as 'on the chair', 'in the car', 'by the river'; but be overwhelmed by the less literal meanings of 'on Sunday', 'in the middle' or 'by Easter'. There may in fact be some thirty or forty senses in which words such as 'see', 'come' and 'do' have varying nuances of meaning. Hearing children will acquire these extensions of usage by hearing the same word used in a multiplicity of different contexts. It is easy to see how many of the metaphoric expressions which enrich the English language, such as 'a biting wind', 'clean as a whistle', 'raining cats and dogs', are potential sources of comprehension breakdown.

Some researchers have gone on to say that deaf children are not simply delayed in their language competence: they are also *deviant*. Deviancy implies that a child is using language in a way which has no parallel, even in the immature patterns of younger hearing children. We shall be examining this concept of language deviancy in some detail in relation to the writing of deaf children, since that is the context in which descriptions of deviancy have usually arisen. Suffice it so say at this point that deviant language is better understood when we look at the specific context in which it arises, the intentions of the child in using language, and the cognitive demands made by the task itself.

Studies of reading

We conclude this chapter with a brief survey of some of the evaluative research carried out with more severely hearing-impaired children in the areas of reading and writing. Severe deafness has been described as a 'promissory for reading failure' (Brooks, 1978). The first studies to appear left no doubts about the massive deficits in reading skills when deaf children were compared with hearing subjects on traditional reading tests. Pintner and Patterson (1916) found that the majority of deaf children aged 14 to 16 years were unlikely to have a measured reading age of more than 7 years. This degree of retardation has been reported consistently by many investigations since (Pugh, 1946; Fusfeld, 1955). Of the more contemporary studies, one widely quoted source has been the North American Survey of Wrightstone *et al.* (1963). A sample of 5000 children aged 10 to 16 years was given the elementary reading test from a battery called the Metropolitan Achievement Test. For the age range 15½ to 16½ years the mean reading grade achieved was 3.5, equivalent to a reading age of about 9½ years. In Di Francesca's (1972) survey of 17,000 deaf children across the entire school age range, a paragraph comprehension test produced a reading grade of just over 3 for 16-year-old deaf readers, equivalent to a reading age of 9 years.

In the United Kingdom surveys of reading in the deaf have been much smaller in scope. However, Redgate (1972) in a study of the effects of using the Initial Teaching Alphabet with deaf children gives data from the Southgate Sentence Completion Test (Southgate, 1962). At age 15 to 16 years the mean reading age on the Southgate test is given as 7 years 8 months. Hamp (1972) surveyed reading levels of deaf children aged 9 to 16 years in eight schools for the hearing-impaired in the United Kingdom, in a study aimed principally at validating his own picture vocabulary test. The comprehension tests he used gave a mean reading age of 8 years 10 months at age 15 years. The most comprehensive and recent figures for almost all of the school-leavers in units and schools for the hearing-impaired in England and Wales has been provided by Conrad (1979). His data suggests that deaf school-leavers achieve a mean reading age of 9 years on the Wide-span Sentence Comprehension Test (Brimer, 1972). There would appear to be a consensus of evidence that at the end of their school careers a large proportion of hearing-impaired adolescents will not have achieved generally-accepted levels of basic literacy.

What is perhaps more disheartening is that several researchers have concluded that severely hearing-impaired children reach a plateau in their reading development (Brooks, 1978; Reich and Reich, 1974). A plateau effect implies both cumulative and progressive deficiencies in reading skill over time: a theoretical ceiling beyond which the child cannot achieve. Typically, the reading plateau is put at a reading age of about 9 years on traditional reading measures. Once again this kind of approach to assessing the skills of the hearing-impaired reflects the deficit model. The child shows the symptoms of disability in terms of poor reading. This has been amply demonstrated in the repeated efforts which have been made to show the extent of the hearing-impaired child's failure in comparison with hearing children.

One alternative possibility which has been rarely entertained is that the methods we have used to assess the deaf child's reading ability, based as they are on hearing norms, are less than sensitive when applied to the deaf. It may be that hearing-impaired children tackle reading differently from hearing children. Consequently, reading tests may *obscure* the particular reading skills which deaf children have. We shall be examining the whole issue of reading assessment in some detail in the following chapter. Indeed, there are some fundamental questions to be raised about the use of traditional reading tests, standardized on hearing children, and then applied to a totally different population. It is also fair to say that evaluative studies can never address the problem of *how* children learn to read. What is required is a much finer-grained analysis of the strategies the child adopts in order to make sense of the linguistic and cognitive puzzles which reading tasks present.

Studies of writing

The written language of severely hearing-impaired children has perhaps received more research attention than any other aspect. That is probably because a piece of writing is static and less open to ambiguity. Almost all of the earlier studies attempted to describe and then quantify elements of sentence structure found in the child's writing. Schulze (1965), for example, simply tallied the growth of various categories of vocabulary over time. Simmons (1962), on the other hand, counted the ways in which verbs and nouns were used. Myklebust (1964) assessed word and sentence output, as well as qualities such as 'abstract–concrete'. He also totalled the number of grammatical errors that children made, in categories such as substitution, omission, addition, and change in word order. Some of the characteristic errors in deaf children's writing are often referred to as *deafisms*. Because many errors and departures from written standard English can sometimes be seen, this has led a few researchers to suggest that the writing of the deaf reflects a state of non-language.

A less extreme view is that one can detect certain recognizable features in the writing of the deaf. Cooper and Rosenstein (1966) suggest that deaf children use shorter and simpler sentences compared with hearing peers. They use more 'content' words, such as nouns, verbs and adjectives. The least frequently used are 'function' words, such as articles, auxiliaries, prepositions and conjunctions. Sentences are said to be more rigid and stereotyped. Numerous errors and non-standard deafisms are noticed.

In Figure 3.3 (overleaf) a 9-year-old profoundly deaf girl of average IQ, is describing her pony. Some of the features found in this girl's writing are thought to be typical of many hearing-impaired children. Shorter, simpler sentences are preferred, with less variety. When the child attempts more complex patterns than

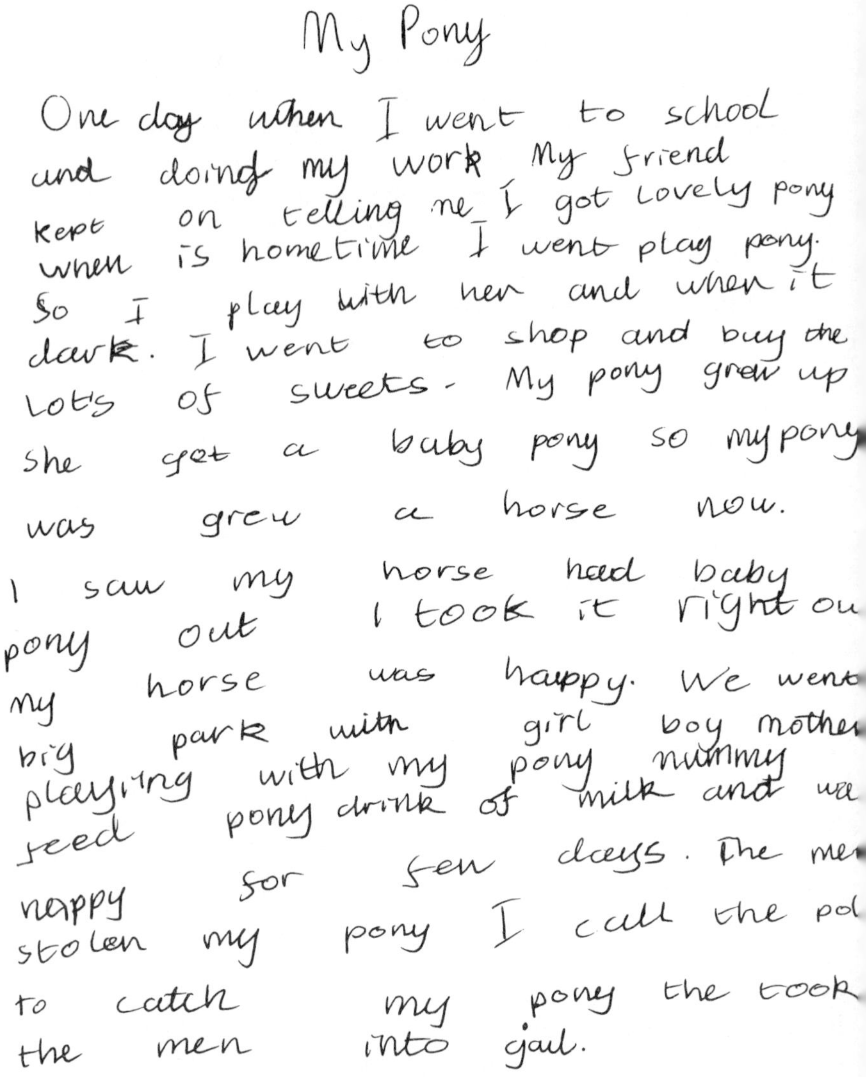

My Pony

One day when I went to school
and doing my work My friend
kept on telling me I got lovely pony
when is hometime I went play pony.
So I play with her and when it
dark. I went to shop and buy the
Lots of sweets. My pony grew up
she get a baby pony so my pony
was grew a horse now.
I saw my horse had baby
pony out I took it right ou
my horse was happy. We went
big park with girl boy mother
playing with my pony nummy
feed pony drink of milk and we
nappy for few days. The me
stolen my pony I call the po
to catch my pony the took
the men into gaul.

Figure 3.3   Piece of writing by a 9-year-old profoundly deaf girl

Subject-Verb-Object, control of grammar is lost. There are a lot
of errors. Determiners are omitted ('I went to shop'), or used
inappropriately ('the lots of sweets'). There are disagreements
between subject and verb forms ('The men stolen'), structures are
omitted ('When is hometime'), and the verb tense changes ('I

went to school and doing my work'). One has the impression that the child has a very poor awareness of the rules which govern how words are used together.

Some writers, such as Wilbur (1977) have pointed out that the hearing-impaired child appears to tackle the writing task 'sentence-by-sentence'. In the sample given here the child is unsure about the connecting devices which can be used to link items in a sentence together. At some points she resorts to juxtaposition ('with girl boy mother playing') and puts her ideas together without formal grammar. Perhaps the most important feature is the difficulty in linking sentences together through co-ordination and subordination of clauses ('and', 'if', 'when'). Similarly, there are few examples of cross-reference or other cohesive devices which help the flow and continuity ('then', 'afterwards', 'however', 'next').

Some authors have reached the conclusion that deaf children use their own grammatical rules in generating writing (Ivimey, 1976). Other researchers have tried to separate out the English grammatical rules which deaf children use, from the idiosyncratic features which seem specific to the writing of the hearing-impaired. Quigley *et al.* (1976) show that 18-year-old deaf students do master aspects such as negation, conjunctions, 'wh' and 'yes–no' questions. However, they continue to have the greatest difficulty in using sentences with embedded or relative clauses, the passive voice, and in all sentences with a structure more complex than SVO. A considered and fairly well-accepted view of the written language of the deaf is that it is both linguistically delayed and different. In Chapter 5 we shall be looking at aspects of both reading and writing in the severely hearing-impaired which appear to have processes in common. We shall also be examining writing from an experimental framework which may account for some of the idiosyncrasies with which the deaf have been attributed.

Chapter summary

1   This chapter introduces several models which may influence our thinking about deafness and child development. The deficit

model has constrained researchers to evaluate levels of achievement, to think of problems lying within the child, and not to
examine how children learn. A model of language study drawn
from linguistics and which describes three areas of phonology,
syntax and semantics, is felt to be a useful reference framework for
organizing research findings.

2   The normal sequence of development in the three areas of
language study is outlined. Acquisition of grammar has a more
central position in this model than the sounds of language.
Particular emphasis is laid upon the social context in which the
meaning of language is negotiated with adult caretakers. The
importance of strategies for interactive learning is highlighted,
such as turn-taking, cohesive devices, word order and the 'minimum distance principle'.

3   The effects of conductive hearing loss on early development
are discussed. Even mild and transitory losses have an effect,
perhaps by confusing the child at a critical period. Research, however, has many design flaws. How far middle-ear problems actually
cause developmental delays is compounded by high associations
with other factors, such as poor health and environment. The
nature of auditory processing problems in children is explored.
The evidence suggests that there is a strong link between early
middle-ear disease and delays in language-based skills, but not
necessarily a specific auditory deficit.

4   Otitis media is discussed in relation to educational achievement. Three groups of children are identified: those with histories
of middle-ear disease but no current loss; those with histories *and*
current hearing loss; and children with poor reading. There is no
clear evidence of specific auditory deficits. Rather, learning difficulties, environmental factors and middle-ear disease are interrelated. The effects of early otitis media are not insurmountable,
although a current loss will create school problems for the child.
A single principle such as poor phonological skills cannot explain
reading failure and the majority of poor readers are reported to
have a broad range of language-dependent weaknesses, as well as
adjustment problems.

5   The effects of severe sensori-neural impairments on development can be devastating, although we should be wary about

making generalizations about 'the deaf', since they are a very varied group. We approach deafness not merely as the deprivation of sound. The important early social context of adult–child inter-action is disrupted. Parents and teachers may unwittingly change their behaviour and try to teach or direct the deaf child. Produc-tive and ineffective teaching strategies are outlined, such as the role of questioning. We ask the question: 'Does deafness con-strain adults to make fewer intellectual and linguistic demands on the child?'

6 Some of the effects of deafness are charted in the child's learning styles and experiences. Evaluations of achievement usually show massive deficits in comparison with hearing chil-dren, whatever teaching method (sign, speech) is used. Speech intelligibility, grammar and strategies for meaning, show delays both in development and deviance. Summaries of research into reading and the reading plateau are presented. These show the extent of the child's deficit but throw little light on the processes of reading. Are traditional reading tests appropriate? Similarly, in studies of writing we can describe characteristic features in samples from deaf children, but do we know why this should be so?

4

UNDERSTANDING AND APPRAISING READING

What is reading? That may seem like a naïve question to ask, but it is not so easy to give the kind of definitive answer which everyone would accept. We could confine our definition of reading to activities involving only books: sometimes described as *authentic* reading tasks. A few teachers might narrow down the sphere of reading proper to include only serious works of 'acceptable' literature. However, there are many literate people for whom books are only a minor part of what they read. As well as books many people read the special offers on cereal packets over breakfast; the part of the gas bill which shows how much is owed (but not the fine print); the headlines in the newspaper, football results, TV guide, adverts and weather forecast; road signs and map directions to get to a place of work; magazines, pamphlets, brochures, tickets, menus, lists, agendas; and a myriad of notices, titles, instructions and labels which enable us to function in our daily lives.

All of these aspects of reading have one factor in common: they communicate information. So, whilst a universally acceptable definition of reading may be impossible, we can at least refer to a range of situations and contexts in which reading takes place. Since we need different kinds of information in different contexts, the reading that one does in order to get on the right train will be different from reading a chemistry textbook in order to do a homework exercise. What the reader does in both situations is to find the information needed. A very important underlying notion of our view of reading is that it is a fairly *active* process. We need to consider how readers make sense of written materials, what questions they ask and how they actively interpret what is in front of them in print. For present purposes then, a working definition of reading must include the strategies the reader brings to text, in its many forms, in order to gain meaningful information.

We need to address the question 'What is reading?' for two important reasons. Firstly, having decided what the skilled reader is able to do, we can then consider what the beginner is attempting to learn. In this chapter we shall be examining several views of the normal reading process in order to help understand what it is that the hearing-impaired child has to do to become a reader. Secondly, there is a great danger that the way we teach reading, and even worse, the way we assess reading, becomes confused with *how* we read. Neither teaching techniques, nor testing methods may bear much relation to what children do when they read. Some experts would say that children learn to read *despite* the way they have been taught or tested. One shortfall of the deficit model discussed in Chapter 3 is the steering of research away from processes of learning towards outcomes. A great deal of research energy has gone into measuring the extent of children's failure (including both deaf and hearing children) whilst ignoring how children learn what they do. We shall discover towards the end of this chapter that traditional techniques of evaluating reading may in fact obscure the very information which would help us to understand how children go about the process of reading.

It would be unfair to claim that there was a consensus view of the reading process or that we had come anywhere near an adequate psychological explanation of reading behaviour. What is true is that reading involves a wide range of complex intellectual activities. Reading has been described as a kind of natural laboratory for studying visual perception, pattern recognition, word identification, short-term memory, comprehension, language, thinking and reasoning. It seems highly unlikely, when attention is turned to children with difficulties in learning to read, that any single, unitary factor will have the power to account for all of the problems which children experience, since there may be a multiplicity of factors involved.

Psychologists do not always agree on what children need to know in order to read. Some would say that for the beginner there are two key insights. First, that we can split our spoken language into separate units such as sounds, words and sentences. Secondly, that these spoken features correspond roughly to units that can be written down and then read. The fluent reader seems to reach the point of not being aware of the clues that are attended to in text in order to read for meaning. In other words the skill has become an automatic one, not consciously controlled. None of us can remember how we learned to read and that is one reason why there are many different views on the matter. A fairly safe bet is that there is more that one successful path to reading, that children's reading strategies change as they become more proficient, and that different reading tasks demand different skills of the child.

Reading strategies are sometimes described as being 'bottom-up', 'top-down', or a mixture of the two. The term 'bottom-up' simply suggests that the reading process begins with the print on the page. Taking clues from written features such as letters, the reader works upwards to the 'higher' levels of words and sentences, until the meaning of the whole is discovered. 'Top-down' processing suggests that reading is guided by decisions made by the brain. The child draws on knowledge of language and experience of the world in order to make predictions about what is likely to be found in print. The one approach emphasizes the printed code, the other stresses aspects brought to reading by the child. As we have suggested, these reading routes are not mutually exclusive and it is likely that children use both sources of information to reach meaning.

'Bottom-up' models of reading

According to one view, reading can be described as a series of stages in a hierarchy. Each stage performs a specific operation on its input, which is then passed on to the next level, where further processing takes place. For example, a reader might approach the following sentence step by step:

I had an apple for lunch.

The first step might involve fixating the eyes on the first word of the sentence starting from left to right. The letter 'I' might be identified by its shape and then recognized as the visual symbol which stands for the personal pronoun: in this instance, the subject of the sentence. The next step might be to fixate the second word in the sentence, a group of three letters: 'had'. The reader might proceed by converting each letter into its component speech sound: 'huh-ah-duh'. In this way the reader works out how the word is pronounced. The written word is thus translated into a series of sounds which is already known in the reader's spoken language. Put another way, the visual code makes contact with the oral symbol and is then understood. This information will need to be held in memory until the rest of the words in the sentence have been analysed in similar fashion and the meaning of the whole sentence discovered.

Psychologists sometimes refer to an inner store where word meanings are kept. This mental lexicon holds information in the way a dictionary does. We can look up an entry to find out how a word may be pronounced, what part of speech it may be, and what range of meanings it may have. In terms of information-processing the most important issue is how the reader uses the information presented on the page in order to locate an entry in the inner lexicon, where the meaning of the word is stored. The reader has to extract information from print, use this to find the appropriate lexical place in the mental dictionary, and then recover the details needed to understand the text.

This view of reading begins at the level where the reader perceives letters and then works up to higher levels of data, such as the word, phrase or sentence. For that reason such models of

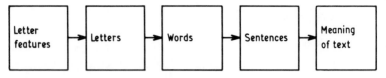

Figure 4.1   A 'bottom-up' model of reading

reading have beeen called 'bottom-up', 'data-driven', or 'text-based' (Stanovich, 1980). Most 'bottom-up' research has been directed at identifying the many subskills implicated in fluent reading ability. As indicated in the example above, the usual place to begin is with the eye movements readers make as they read. What kind of visual information can be picked up in the rapid succession of jerky leaps that we know the eye makes across the printed page? How do we recognize what we see?

Visual features

One potential source of information is the features of letter shapes. A good reader might use this awareness of the invariant features of letter shapes to identify the string of letters which make up an individual word. The reader would then have to use the visual representation of the word in order to recover the word's meaning from the internal dictionary or lexicon. In other words, the reader identifies the letters which make up the word and then recovers details of the word's pronunciation, grammatical class and what it means, from an inner store built up from language and reading experience.

It is possible that poor readers may be less good at directing and controlling their eye movements. Alternatively, they may be less good at extracting visual information from the page. They may be poor at using visual features to recover a word from the inner dictionary; or the lexicon may have a limited quality of information stored, which prevents the reader from recognizing what the word means. Some studies have shown that good readers have greater knowledge of the *orthography*, or letter structure, of words than poor readers (Allington, 1978). This kind of letter-by-letter analysis of reading has a lot of commonsense appeal. It is also true that there are differences in some of these basic subskills, such as the pattern of eye movements, in good and poor readers. It is often felt that children who confuse letters such as 'p', 'b' and 'd', who make inversions or reversals of letter sequences, may thus have problems in reading. The child's errors are thought to arise from a decifit in visual perception. Two things are worth noting: *all* children confuse letter shapes when learning to read; poor readers persist in doing so for longer. Efforts have been made to detect visual perception deficits in poor readers. In Jorm's (1977) experiments, children were given tests in which the mirror image of an abstract design had to be picked out from a choice of four (pool reflections test). According to Jorm, if poor readers had any perceptual problems which led them to confuse similar letter shapes, then they would have run into difficulties on his mirror image test. However, poor readers of all ages did just as well as good readers.

We cannot assume that the process of learning to read begins with the identification of letter shapes. Neither can we assume that deficits in these visual subskills are a *cause* of problems in reading. A strong case can be made that being able to read helps children to organize their perceptual abilities, co-ordinate eye movements, and be more consciously aware of visual features like distinctive letter shapes. One researcher who felt that good readers identified words too quickly for them to be analysing print letter by letter, suggested that reading cannot be understood by studying 'the most primitive aspects of the reader's performance and working up' (Kolers, 1973).

Instead of taking the letter as the basic visual building-block, some researchers have argued that the reader identifies individual word patterns. Information might be got from the spelling regularities, or from the length and distinctive visual character of a word. A number of experiments have been concerned with the question: 'Can subjects recognize whole words more easily than isolated letters?'. Typically, a subject might be given a very brief display of letters to look at, and then asked to report as many letters as possible, or to say whether letters given afterwards, appeared in the original display. A very well-established finding of studies of this kind is referred to as the *word superiority effect*. Subjects are more accurate and can recall more when the letters displayed are real words. Letter recognition improves when the stimulus is a whole word rather than just a string of isolated letters. This suggests that readers do respond to some property possessed by words but not letters, and that the word unit carries more significance than the sum of its parts.

The point needs to be made that subjects' behaviour in experimental situations may bear little relation to what people do when they read for meaning. Reviewers of experimental findings in the visual subprocesses of reading (see Mitchell, 1982) also point out that the strategies which subjects adopt in tackling these processing problems change markedly from task to task, and from one situation to another. Finally, when good and poor readers have been compared in their sensitivity to spelling patterns in words, it is the *poorer* readers who seem to be more sensitive to violations of spelling rules, rather than the good readers (Stanovich and West, 1979). So, despite the experimental effect of word superiority, there is little evidence to suggest that good readers depend entirely on word features in reading, or that poor reading is caused by the child failing to use spelling or word knowledge.

We have suggested that the way we teach reading should not be confused with *how* we actually read. The *whole* or *sight–word* method is a case in point. In the early stages teachers may present the child with individual whole printed words which are learnt by the child as sight vocabulary. Several reading schemes used in schools expect the child to be able to recall twenty or so sight words before the child is allowed to embark on the first reading 'books', where these words will be met. The teacher might be led to believe (particularly by those who sell reading schemes) that reading grows incrementally word by word, and therefore can be taught through repetition of key sight vocabulary and word recognition. The picture is undoubtedly more complicated than this, and that point becomes obvious when we look at children's active efforts to make sense of written materials as they encounter print.

Sound features

Perhaps the most popular line of approach is that the basic building-block of reading is acoustic rather than visual. An important source of information for the reader may be the set of rules for pronouncing letters, blends and sequences, which enable print to be decoded into corresponding speech sounds. It is suggested that a reader converts letters into a series of sounds already known in the reader's spoken language. This acoustic information enables the reader to locate a word in the inner lexicon where the meaning of the word is discovered. This might be described as the phonological route to recognizing words. Teachers often refer to this method as reading by *phonics*. Once again there is much commonsense appeal in this approach. In Chapter 2 we said that there were some forty or so distinctive sound units or phonemes in spoken English. The underlying argument is that we have a set of rules which *efficiently* relates the spelling patterns of English print to the sound patterns of speech.

The fact that good readers are able to pronounce letter strings such as 'dilp', 'thrind', 'ut', 'gorp', and find agreement on how such nonsense words should be pronounced, suggests that readers can use a phonological decoding strategy when words are unfamiliar. Experiments have shown that words which follow regular pronunciation patterns are easier to read. Baron and Strawson (1976) asked subjects to read lists of words aloud as quickly as they could. When words conformed to normal phonic rules, such as 'sweet', they were more rapidly read than irregular words, such as 'sword'. Studies like this suggest that phonological coding does play some part in reading performance. Similarly, experiments have shown that the pronunciation of words helps subjects to decide whether a phrase makes sense. Baron (1973) gave subjects phrases like 'tie the knot' where the words are both sensible and sound right. Some phrases, such as 'tie the not', sounded right but contained spelling errors. Other phrases neither looked, nor sounded, correct. Subjects were much more likely to make errors when the words *sounded* correct. In other words the phonological information confuses the issue and makes it harder for the reader to decide about meaning.

Experiments suggest that pronunciation rules do influence behaviour on these specific reading tasks. What is less clear is whether the phonological features are necessary for recognizing words, or whether effects such as auditory confusion, arise *after*

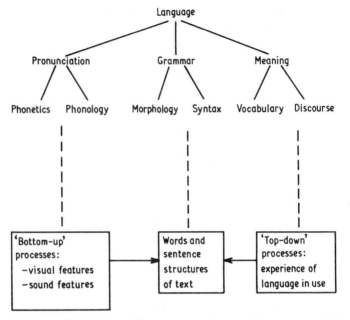

Figure 4.2   Three areas of language study in relation to models of reading

the word has been recognized. More importantly, how do these findings relate to more authentic reading tasks? We have already mentioned that psychologists differ widely in their views about what children need to know about language in order to read. For some researchers it is the insight that speech can be split into sound segments or phonemes which is crucial. According to this view, success in reading then depends on the child associating these speech segments with elements of the printed word (Liberman *et al.*, 1974). In Figure 4.2 we have enlarged on the model of language study presented earlier, to include the different approaches to reading. Phonological aspects of spoken language, together with spelling correspondences, occupy the far left of the diagram and ignore the rest. So, in terms of the three major areas of language study, a phonological theory of reading involves the peripheral aspects of language.

Most of the evidence in support of a phonic approach to reading comes from the differences found between good and poor readers. Another commonsense argument is that good readers develop phonic strategies so that they can tackle new visual patterns which they have never met before (Gibson and Levin, 1975). In one study, thirty-two children who were reading fluently, well *before* they got to school, were given a whole range of tests to see how they differed from normal (Clark, 1976). These children were, in fact, remarkably ordinary on most tests apart from auditory discrimination. On the Wepman test (1958), in which children have to distinguish between the sounds in spoken word pairs, such as 'pork–cork', 'dim–din', 'vow–thou', 'gum–dumb' and 'fie–thigh', these early fluent readers showed excellent auditory awareness.

Similarly, many experiments have been carried out where nonsense words which can be decoded phonetically are given to good and poor readers, who are then asked to pronounce each one as quickly as possible. All of this work suggests that poor readers make more errors on the pronunciation task and are less quick. In one of these studies, Snowling (1980) gave children nonsense words written on a card. The child was shown the word and the examiner pronounced the word out loud, rather than the child. All the child had to do was to indicate on the sheet whether the examiner's pronunciation was correct. For example, the word 'dron' might be given the child whilst the examiner said 'dorn', or the word 'brap' presented whilst the examiner said 'barp'. What this task demands is that the child first decodes the nonsense word *covertly*. The child's own inner version is then compared with the examiner's pronunciation. The poor readers in Snowling's study found this task much more difficult than did good readers.

Snowling also compared children on this task who had been matched for reading age but not chronological age. In other words she was able to find a group of older children whose poor reading achievements could be matched with younger children reading at the expected age level. Children were thus matched on the basis of their scores on a reading test. In this study the less able readers also found the nonsense word task more difficult than their younger counterparts. One important aspect of this study is that children matched for reading age may be very different in their reading behaviour. The older children in Snowling's study may have been able to identify words using a sight recognition strategy rather than a phonological approach. We should be very careful not to assume that children who attain the same reading age score necessarily have the same reading strategies. We have already suggested that children may take more than one route towards reading and the strategies that children adopt change as they become more proficient. These points will have obvious relevance when we come to make comparisons between normally-hearing readers and readers with hearing-impairment, particularly if comparisons are drawn on the basis of scores on a standardized reading test.

One other well-known piece of research which has often been referred to in demonstrating that poor readers have phonological decoding problems is the study by Rozin and others (1971) of black American children. They identified a group of eight children who were progressing very poorly at reading by the second grade. They were unable to pronounce nonsense words such as 'zif', 'wat', 'ren', 'gub', and were not helped to identify words by knowing that a set of words rhymed, like 'cat', 'fat', 'sat', 'mat'. What these researchers did was to teach the children in the study a number of Chinese characters which could be used to read sentences and stories in English. Chinese characters represent *whole* word meanings rather than sounds. Although the children were struggling to read English print and had little phonological awareness, they did manage to read stories made up of Chinese characters in a relatively short period of teaching time. The conclusion was drawn that children with reading difficulties find it much easier to recognize words when they are presented as visual wholes than by phonic analysis, and therefore suffer from a disability in constructing words from sounds.

A great deal of weight has been given to phonological skills in remedial approaches to poor reading. Bradley (1980) on the basis of her early work with good and poor readers, suggests that having an ear for sounds, alliteration and rhymes, are important diagnostic factors, and a remedial programme should be designed around these auditory skills. Gittelman and Feingold (1983) present evidence from a study which compared different treatment strategies for children with reading disorders to show that a remedial programme which emphasizes phonetic skills may be much more effective than any other.

Notwithstanding the claims that have been made on behalf of phonological skills in learning to read, there is still a great deal of dispute about the role which phonological coding plays in skilled reading. If we look back at some of the experimental findings presented we can see where the problem of interpretation lies. Most of the evidence comes from studies where subjects are asked to interpret *nonsense* words. Children are given isolated word-pairs, pronouncing letter patterns or comparing one version of a word with another, in tasks which are totally devoid of any context of meaning. It is a fair comment that what children do in these experimental situations is task-specific and cannot be generalized to normal reading tasks.

A fundamental problem concerns the assumption that phonological skills enable a child to identify real words more efficiently than the straightforward visual route using the features of the whole word unit. It may be true that the evidence for phonological coding is only apparent in tasks where words are presented in isolation or as nonsense strings, and where the whole process of word identification is slowed down and dissected. An equally valid case could be made that being able to identify words through the direct visual route is rapid and efficient. Being able to read in this way helps the reader to locate words in the inner lexicon or dictionary. It is there that the child finds information about pronunciation. So, visual identification of the word may *precede* and foster awareness of phonic components. Put simply, the very fact of being able to read may provide the child with insights about the spelling-to-sound correspondences of written language, rather than the other way round.

In a recent review of the research literature, Briggs (1983) weighs the evidence regarding good and poor readers and whether they use a phonological code in reading. Poor readers are typically said to have weak phonological coding skills where 'decoding' is defined as the ability to recognize nonsense strings. Briggs suggests that in word recognition tasks, both poor and good readers are able to use phonological skills in recognizing words. The difference between the two groups lies in how *automatic* the child's word recognition skills become. Poor readers seem to be unable to master the pronunciation rules. If good readers use phonological information to identify new words, they very quickly come to rely upon direct and immediate visual access to word meanings. Good readers, therefore, do not always need to go through the stage of sounding out letters in order to recognize words, once they are familiar. Poor readers, according to Briggs, never achieve such rapid and direct access to word meanings. What poor readers do instead is to direct their attention to other clues within the reading context. Paradoxically, poor readers have to be much more flexible in their decoding skills, and have to draw on other sources of information during reading. Good readers succeed because their understanding of 'bottom-up' rules is very much more explicit. Their decoding skills are so efficient that they have no need to develop alternative strategies (such as using context clues or information from pictures) in order to derive meaning.

'Top-down' models of reading

We have so far considered models which view reading as a bundle of component subskills. There is an opposing point of view which says that reading does not proceed letter-by-letter, or word-by-word. Instead, the reader approaches the printed text with a specific intention or purpose in mind. The reader expects to find particular things in print. Knowledge of language and knowledge of the world are used to predict what might be found in the text. In other words, the reader looks for meaning rather than letters or words. It is this prior anticipation or expectation of the written word which guides the reader. The reader could be said to bring meaning *to* print, rather than deriving meaning *from* it.

A very well-known proponent of the 'top-down' view is Smith (1978). He vehemently attacks the use of phonics in teaching children to read. He argues that there is in fact very little consistency in the spelling patterns of English which justify the learning

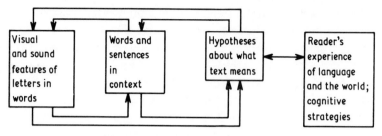

| Visual and sound features of letters in words | Words and sentences in context | Hypotheses about what text means | Reader's experience of language and the world; cognitive strategies |

Figure 4.3   A 'top-down' model of reading for meaning

of a set of rules. He says that the spelling-to-sound correspondences are so confusing and unreliable that children who depend upon them are likely to be *disabled* in their reading. Smith provides a model of reading skill in which the child is a scientist, making hypotheses about the written word, endeavouring to make sense of it. Hypotheses come from the child's understanding of the properties of language. The child tests out predictions by sampling text. The printed word enables the child to confirm or reject the hypotheses which have been made.

Several accounts of the 'top-down' view of reading have been given (Goodman, 1976; Neville and Pugh, 1976–7). All of these see the reader as being receptive to all kinds of clues in text. These would include the printed letters on the page, together with features which might be termed *pragmatic:* information beyond the text itself, such as the child's experience of how the world works. Hypotheses about what the text means could conceivably originate from the letters, words and sentences on the page, as well as in the child's head; and might also be tested out at any of these levels. The major difference between 'bottom-up' and 'top-down' models of reading is that the latter has no sense of a *fixed* progression through different stages of analysis in a hierarchy. The 'top-down' view of reading is a continuous sampling and testing cycle, whereby the child asks questions of print which are checked out and give rise to new questions. Because the child is actively predominant in this view of reading, terms like 'reader-based', 'prediction-based', or 'schema-driven' have been used to describe this class of models (Stanovich, 1980).

In Figure 4.2 we have aligned the different reading models with the separate areas of language study, covered in Chapter 3. 'Top-down' approaches reflect many of the important features which characterize the interactive context of semantic development in spoken language. Both are concerned with the active efforts required to communicate: the processes of negotiation out of which meaning arises. Both share the idea that flexible strategies are required to make sense of a language context. In the diagram, they occupy the right-hand side, whilst the central position is occupied by syntax. Grammar is the study of the organizing principles of language, which in reading determines how the sounds and meanings of the language are related.

The 'top-down' view of reading is a useful reminder that reading is a complex intellectual skill, more than the sum of its parts. Psychologists have tended to dissect reading into component subskills to make it easier to study. 'Top-down' theorists, on the other hand, tend to underplay the contributions which subskills such as letter recognition may make to reading. In its pure form the 'top-down' model has its own drawbacks. One argument against it is that it is not a very efficient way to read. If one had to generate hypotheses about words, sentences and context all the time in order to read, this might be very laborious. Much quicker, one might argue, to recognize words *directly* from print. One series of studies which addressed just this question was carried out by Mitchell and Green (1978). They measured the speeds at which subjects presented printed sentence material to themselves using an on-line visual display.

In one experiment subjects were given passages based on an extract from Tolstoy's *War and Peace*. The material was delivered three words at a time. At different points in the passages phrases were inserted which were much more predictable. It might be presumed that text which is more predictable will require fewer hypotheses and checks on interpretation. Fewer predictions should imply easier processing since the text needs to be sampled less often to confirm each prediction. In fact, contrary to the hypothesis-testing view, processing was no faster in more predictable parts of the text. Instead, reading rate seemed much closer to the speed at which individual words are recognized. In other words, there is evidence which suggests that context clues do not facilitate word recognition to the extent proclaimed by 'top-down' theorists.

Much of the research cited in support of 'top-down' models uses a variation of the *cloze* task. In cloze procedures subjects are given a sentence or paragraph to read and asked to fill in gaps in the text. Subjects do this by using clues in the context to predict what might appear in the gap. In fact this technique has been used in the compilation of silent reading comprehension tests. Later in the chapter we shall be discussing the use of two such cloze tests (Wide-span and Southgate) with hearing-impaired children. The errors which children make in cloze procedures can be very revealing. They may reveal what the child knows about linguistic forms, the structure of sentences, the content of a passage; together with some insights into the strategies the child adopts in order to make sense of the linguistic puzzles the test presents. In a similar vein, 'top-down' theorists such as Goodman (1969) and Clay (1968) have developed methods of examining the oral reading, or cloze errors of children, in the light of what these 'miscues' tell us about the child's approach to the reading task.

According to Goodman, a reader who makes a mistake is not necessarily guessing at random. The reader is essentially a user of language. During reading the language user responds to the graphic display in an effort to reconstruct the message that the writer wanted to communicate. Information may be gleaned from letters and sounds, the grammatical structures of sentences, or from the context of meaning. Not all the available information may be utilized since there is a great deal of redundancy in text. The reader picks out just enough information to make predictions about meaning. There is no precise relationship between the visual features on the page and what is eventually reconstructed as the message. Proficient readers have developed their sampling and prediction strategies to the point where they use the least number of clues necessary. When a child makes a mistake it may be that more attention is being paid to the syntax or meaning context, than to the graphic information. The reading process miscarries because the poor reader is less efficient in the samples taken and the predictions put forward. However, unexpected responses to print are generated by the same 'top-down' processes as expected responses.

Goodman has developed a taxonomy which provides a number of questions which can be asked of reading miscues. At the word level the child may give an observed reponse which is graphically similar to the response expected: 'went–wanted', 'was–saw', 'quickly–quietly', 'batter–butter'. At the clause level the child may insert or omit elements: 'The book which you gave me was exciting – the book was exciting'. At the semantic level the child may make miscues which alter the meaning ('The boy shouted down – The boy fell down'); or simply adjust it ('The lady's wig was . . . – The lady's fake hair was . . .'). Important in Goodman's analysis (and indicative of the strength of the reader) is whether the child's miscue preserves the sense of the sentence, whether errors are self-corrected by re-reading, whether substitutions are of the appropriate grammatical class to fit the syntax of the sentence, and whether the child's overall interpretation is in line with the deeper meaning of the text. Finally, Goodman argues that for the child to be able to develop strategies and profit from miscues, reading can only be learned as the child encounters real language materials, as opposed to 'flash' cards or phonic charts.

Goodman's description of the reading process has been challenged at several points. An important issue is the belief that good readers are more effective in their use of contextual cues. 'Top-down' theorists firmly believe that fluent readers are much more sensitive than poor readers to the information provided by the context, and that this facilitates *ongoing* word recognition. This view has prompted Smith (1973) to say that 'reading is not primarily a visual process'. The meaning that the reader derives stems from behind the eyeball, from the brain. The reader utilizes only as much visual information in the text as is required to check that what is understood matches the author's intentions. Unfortunately, when good and poor readers are compared in their use of contextual cues, it is not the case that fluent readers use contextual cues more effectively. Juel (1980) compared the oral reading errors of good and poor readers on a set of target words which varied in terms of 'text' factors, such as how frequently they occurred, the number of syllables and the degree of difficulty of a word, together with variations in 'contextual' features. Contrary to the 'top-down' belief, it was the poor readers who were more reliant on the context, whilst the good readers made errors which showed that they were responding to features in the text itself.

This brings us to a third and intermediate model of the reading process. To summarize: the 'top-down' view suggests that it is quicker to read by generating hypotheses about what is on the page rather than identifying words directly from their visual patterns. This has been challenged because it may be more efficient to identify words directly from text. Using hypotheses to facilitate word recognition could be inhibiting and use up some of the cognitive resources that the child needs in other high-level processes, such as integrating new information with old, or simply thinking about what is being read. If poor readers can be shown to depend more on the context of a passage, that may be a good indication that their word recognition skills are slow and non-automatic: they need to draw on other sources of information to make sense of the material. A more adequate account of reading really needs to incorporate features of *both* 'bottom-up' *and* 'top-down' processes.

Interactive models of reading

The interactive or compensatory model of skilled reading holds that both 'bottom-up' and 'top-down' processes can occur alongside each other. The reader has several sources of information: letters, sounds, words, clauses, which arise upwards from the page. The reader also makes predictions which act downwards upon the lower levels. Each of these levels operate independently and simultaneously and influence each other. So, information gained from the word being identified will influence expectations about meaning, and vice versa. The interactive view differs from the 'top-down' view in its pure form, in emphasizing that low-level, data-driven strategies are very important for good readers. It has been argued that these direct, efficient low-level strategies for word identification are necessary in order to 'free-up' the child's thinking and comprehension capacity (Stanovich, 1980).

When word recognition is slow, the reader can compensate by drawing on sources of information at other levels, such as context-redundancy or hypothesis-testing. But to do this the reader may sacrifice some processing or cognitive capacity. For the good reader, word recognition may become automatic early in reading development. However, it may be speed of word recognition that is the crucial difference between poor and fluent readers. The good reader may be skilled at a direct, context-free, word recognition level. The poor reader has deficient word-analysis and shows a greater reliance on contextual factors or hypothesis-testing. In so doing the reader may have less *attentional capacity* left over: the hypothetical thinking space in which the child relates new concepts to old.

One paradoxical fact should be noted. Teaching practice has been very heavily influenced by 'top-down' models of reading. Good readers are often taught to rely heavily upon context, whilst poor readers are taught low-level decoding skills, such as phonics. The former emulates the strategies of the less-able reader, the latter denies the child access to supplementary sources of information in text. We shall be returning to some of the implications of this paradox when we consider teaching strategies in Chapter 6.

The assessment of reading

Reading assessment, like any other line of enquiry, needs to have a specific purpose. Testing for its own sake, collecting data at random and with no particular question in mind, is futile. Before using test materials, professionals need to have a clear idea of the questions they want to answer, the scope and limitations of individual test techniques, and the status of the findings revealed by the test in relation to those aspects of the child they are interested in. There are a great number of pitfalls in testing children, and it is well to know where these lie. A useful place to begin is with the range of function and purpose different assessment techniques serve. A survey of national standards of literacy needs to be carried out differently from a head-teacher's screening programme in school. When teachers want to know more about an individual's specific strengths and weaknesses in reading, a different set of factors is highlighted, and other cautions are necessary.

In order to monitor standards of achievement, *normative* test materials are required which give some idea of the levels attained by a wide population. Knowing the average test results on a particular measure of reading achieved by a large group of 11-year-olds, enables comparisons to be made between an individual or class-group of 11-year-olds in one school, and the population mean. Over the last decade or so the trend has been to move away from large-scale evaluative surveys of levels of achievement in reading. Two influential studies: *The Trend of Reading Standards* (Start and Wells, 1972) and *The Bullock Report* (DES, 1975) epitomize the earlier preoccupation with literacy levels and relative standards in a particular geographical area, age group or period of time, in normal school children. The direction in which most research with hearing children has moved appears to be towards identifying *intra-group* factors associated with reading achievement. Despite what we have said about the lack of a definitive model of normal reading skill, there have been persistent attempts to find factors associated with reading readiness, failure or success, to identify the strengths of good readers and the weaknesses of the reading disabled. There is some agreement (Clark, 1980) that the direction in which reading research needs to go, if we are to understand the reading process, is towards fine-grain analyses and detailed observations of individual children as they learn to read.

In contrast, almost all the reading research with hearing-impaired children to date has been descriptive or evaluative. With both mild hearing losses of a conductive nature and more severe sensori-neural impairments, research effort has gone into highlighting *inter-group* comparisons. A great deal of energy has been expended in measuring the limited achievements associated with varying degrees of hearing loss, in charting the extent of the deaf child's failure when comparisons are drawn with normally-hearing counterparts. It is particularly true of more severely hearing-impaired youngsters that the predominant question which has been posed is 'What proportion achieve literacy?'. This emphasis on evaluating outcomes we have attributed in part to the thinking which underlies the deficit model approach. So, the nature and purpose of the majority of studies of reading in hearing-impaired children has not moved on from the monitoring stage. As we have suggested, evaluative research is unlikely to contribute towards an understanding of the processes involved. Researchers working with both deaf and hearing children will need to pay much closer attention to the 'fine-grain' of emergent reading behaviour in individual children over periods of time.

The next point which needs to be made about reading assessment concerns the wide descrepancy between the techniques we use and the complex processes we are attempting to measure. What we have described as a natural laboratory for studying intricate cognitive behaviour involving perception, language and thinking, is diminished by the terms we use to describe it: the reading age or quotient. Every reading test samples only a limited area of a child's reading ability. What is more important is that test materials may sample aspects of a child's behaviour which may bear little relation to what the child does when tackling authentic reading tasks. There is the danger, too, that how we set about testing reading, influences what children think they ought to be doing as they read. Testing children's phonic skills may leave them with the idea that phonic decoding is what they should be attempting to do with printed words. Suffice it to say that the kind of assessments of reading teachers choose to make will often reflect their own view of the reading process, rather than reflecting how children actually read.

Testing individual readers

Those who devise reading tests usually adhere to a particular model of the reading process, and this provides the rationale for appraising reading skills in a particular way. The majority of this chapter has been devoted to different models of reading and we can use this framework to determine what skills test authors hope their materials will reveal. It should also be possible to relate tests of individual reading skill to the areas of language study outlined in Table 4.2, in terms of the different levels which tests endeavour to tap. Many tests are designed to assess individual strengths and weaknesses in reading. Assumptions are made about the skills which the child needs to have mastered in order to be able to read. Any gaps which are revealed by a test can then be used to plan a teaching programme.

Several points need to be made about this apparently straight-forward recipe of pinpointing difficulties and then teaching to make good the gaps. Firstly, since we are still very far from knowing what skills the child does need in order to read, most test materials are contructed *intuitively* rather than upon a firm theoretical foundation. It should not be taken at face value that the content of reading test materials gives useful or relevant guidelines for teaching. Secondly, the question of *validity* arises: how far does a test measure what it is supposed to? There can sometimes be a wide gulf between what researchers think tests measure and what they actually reveal about a child's behaviour. Finally, a point made by Raban (1983) in her introductory survey of reading tests is important in the present context. Teachers are well advised to utilize *informal* aspects of testing procedures. Normally, a pupil's correct responses are observed and counted to form the raw score on a particular test. It is more valuable, in order to find out something of the pupil's test strategies, Raban suggests, to look at the mistakes that are made. Incorrect responses on a test may reveal a great deal about a child's underlying approach to the reading task.

'Bottom-up' measures of reading

Some test materials sample 'bottom-up' aspects in line with a view of reading as being a bundle of component skills. Tests such as the Infant Reading Tests (Brimer and Raban, 1979) or the Macmillan Diagnostic Reading Pack (Ames, 1980) include a range of procedures designed to tap subskills felt to be important to reading. The Infant Reading Tests include items where children have to match a spoken word with a printed visual symbol; items which involve recognizing speech sounds at the beginning, in the middle, or at the end of words; and items where the child has to match squares containing sets of shapes, letters and words.

In the Macmillan Diagnostic Reading Pack the early stages of beginning reading are approached by tasks which include the matching of letters in a series or in a nonsense word, with its partner in a number of alternatives, e.g.:

swzc szwc czsw swzc scwz czws

Children are also asked to match upper- and lower-case letters; to write letters and letter groupings from memory; and to write down the first letter of a word which is spoken. There is also an item which presents pairs of words to the child and then requires a same/different discrimination to be made on the basis of sound, e.g.:

short–thought, could–good, shop–shot

Children are also asked to blend letter sounds together to make words; to recall a sequence of numbers in a test of short-term auditory memory; and to identify nonsense words spoken by the teacher in a printed list of alternatives.

There is a danger that teachers may view these subskills as being prerequisite to reading and that measures such as the above give an indication of *reading readiness*. Tests of orthographic knowledge, or the ability to make auditory and visual discriminations, may simply reflect a child's experience of print. They do not necessarily have any predictive value. The same criticism could be levelled at tests such as the Early Detection of Reading Difficulties (Clay, 1979), which check *concepts* about books which are felt to be prerequisite, such as knowing where the book begins, that print and not the picture tells the story, that the reader attacks print from left to right and from top to bottom of the page, and that spaces between words have a function. In other words, the child's insights about units of language and their correspondences in text are being ascertained. But do these insights develop independently of reading and can they be taught? It may be that such tests are simply monitoring what the child is learning in his encounters with books.

Not surprisingly, since phonic subskills have often been accorded a great deal of importance in beginning reading, and particularly in remedial practice, a number of materials are available which assess phonic awareness. The Phonic Skills Test (Jackson, 1971) includes a range of letter combinations which the child has to read aloud correctly: final consonant blends, such as 'damp' or 'gasp'; vowel digraphs, such as 'loud' or 'boy'; together with multi-syllabic words, such as 'partridge'. The Domain Phonic Test (McLeod and Atkinson, 1972) also taps the child's ability to decode phonically regular consonant and vowel blends in various positions in words, by asking the child to read isolated words aloud, such as 'sip', 'plod', or 'swipe'. Whilst in the Swansea Test of Phonic Skills (Williams *et al.*, 1971) the teacher pronounces a stimulus word and the child identifies the word which matches the sound from a group of five. Sixty-five nonsense words are given, each of which is placed in a set of four decoys, and each is said to provide information about the child's phonic knowledge which can then be used as the basis for a remedial programme (e.g. 'yug', 'pulf', 'woft').

In our discussion of phonological coding, we suggested that, notwithstanding the claims made on behalf of auditory clues in learning to read, an important possibility is that being able to read provides the child with insights about grapheme–phoneme correspondences. So, tests of phonic skills, like tests of orthographic knowledge, suffer from the same shortfall: they may simply reflect, rather than predict, developing reading competence in the child.

At the whole-word level there are a number of tests in popular classroom use which tap sight-word recognition skills. The Burt (1921), Vernon (1938) and Schonell (1942) graded vocabulary tests, despite the length of time which has elapsed since these materials were originally devised and standardized, are still used as measures of the child's sight vocabulary for whole words. More often than not these quick and simple-to-administer tests are also used to provide an index of a child's wider and general reading competence. Strictly speaking, such tests are measures of word identification: the ability to produce the spoken component of an isolated written word. It is not necessary for the child to recognize this vocabulary in the sense of *knowing* what each word means. In any case, word reading tests are generally devoid of any meaningful context.

Some reading tests, such as the first stages of the 'Primary Reading Test' (France, 1979), ask the child to select one word from several given, to match a picture stimulus. For example, a picture of a cake is accompanied by several distractors including 'cat', 'make' and 'cape', together with the target word 'cake'. The distractors are selected, presumably, because they are auditorily or visually similar to the target word ('cake–cape'). There is the possibility that test items like this present *hidden* clues to the child which enable responses to be made. The picture stimulus must be unambiguous and will inevitably represent an object. How then to represent a word like 'make', which could be dismissed as an incorrect choice because it would be difficult to represent in picture form?

'Top-down' measures of reading

Techniques of assessment have been described so far in which the reader is viewed simply as progressing through a hierarchy of basic subskills, mastering letter, sound or word features. However, many diverse efforts have been made to assess reading where the reader is acknowledged as an active language user. The least successful of these simply provide an isolated sentence for the child to read, wrested out of any meaningful context. So, for example, the Salford Sentence Reading Test (Bookbinder, 1976) presents the child with a series of unrelated sentences, such as:

Look at the book.
The sun is red.

Essentially, this is a test of word recognition in which the reader can derive some information from the sentence frame (the grammatical constraints) in order to unlock possible word entries in each sentence. But like many word recognition tests this taps largely passive, mechanical reading skill.

Some attempts have been made to assess children's awareness of language, and the concepts about the functions and features of print which are brought to reading. The principle underlying these techniques is that factors such as visual perception or letter-name knowledge are far less important to beginning readers or struggling readers, than the child's grasp of the purpose of reading. The Linguistic Awareness in Reading Readiness Test or

LARR for short (Downing *et al.*, 1983), could be described as a 'top-down' approach to the conceptual prerequisites for reading success. It aims to probe into the child's awareness of the different kinds of information communicated by print. The foundations of flexible reading strategies are said to depend on such insights. In one section of the LARR test children are asked to select which picture in a series shows a person finding out what time a bus goes, when the circus is coming, or how to cook a stew. Children have to use the material to sort out who is sending a message, leaving a note, telling a story, giving directions. This, then, is a test of the child's inferential reasoning: the inferences he draws from the graphic information given about the varying *functions* of reading. One possible source of difficulty in giving this test is that it assumes a sophisticated level of comprehension of language in order for the child to be able to follow the instructions and explanations which accompany it. Children may, therefore, fail to do well on this test because they do not understand the nature of the task as it is presented. For this reason claims for good predictive validity of the LARR test (the extent to which it predicts children's later achievements in reading) may not be entirely due to conceptual readiness factors.

There is a range of test materials which have been designed to investigate emerging reading *comprehension* in children. Many people have argued that tests which enable the child to draw on semantic and syntactic features of language in text are much closer to the real business of reading itself. The Holborn Reading Scale (Watts, 1980) is a series of thirty-three sentences of graded difficulty, which are unrelated and which principally test word recognition in a sentence frame. However, an attempt is made to move away from a purely mechanical reading test by asking the child a question about each sentence. In this way a limited insight is gained into whether the child has also read with understanding. For example:

Quench your thirst by drinking a glass
of our sparkling ginger ale.
It says that ginger ale will stop you
from being . . .*what?*

This kind of test has been criticized because the demands which are made on the child are minimal. In fact, little more than recall is required. The child does not have to make judgements about, or draw inferences from, the text. There is little need for the child to seek out new information, ask questions of the material, or evaluate it. Nevertheless, this approach does move a step closer to authentic reading tasks since the child has to recall the main idea of what is read. What it does not do is reveal the kind of active strategies children use to interrogate text as they read for meaning.

Similarly, the Neale Analysis of Reading Ability (Neale, 1958) sets out to assess accuracy of word recognition by giving a series of self-contained little story passages to the child. The story material may not appeal to the children of today in the same way that it did to children of the 1950s. However, it is possible, using the Neale Analysis, to assess comprehension of main ideas in the stories. There is also a very simple framework for analysing any reading errors that the child makes in terms of addition, substitution or omission of words. The supplementary test material is specifically designed to test letter, sound and phonic-blend knowledge. So, whilst the test does present a narrative reading task format to the child, the language and content is dated and the teacher is encouraged to identify gaps in the child's low-level decoding skills. The Neale will not elicit whether comprehension fails because the child has a limited grasp of word meanings, or is simply overwhelmed by some of the complex and unfamiliar syntactic structures:

On to the stage was raised the shy but happy Swiss puppet.

There are several available test materials designed to assess reading comprehension through *silent* narrative reading tasks. Some of these are based directly on the theoretical work of researchers such as Goodman who have argued that the reader searches for meaning, makes hypotheses about print, then checks out the predictions. The cloze technique invites the child to guess what should appear in sentences which have words deliberately deleted. What the child inserts into such gaps may reveal the strategies the child adopts, the clues paid attention to in the material, and what the child knows of the structure of language. The Cloze Reading Tests (Young, 1982) for example, present the child with a series of short graded passages, from which words have been deleted:

Snow is bad for traffic . . . all times.

It is suggested that the reader scans ahead selectively for clues, creatively combining what is being read with anticipation of what is still to come. Good readers rectify the deliberate omissions in the text by using their grasp of the meaning of the whole. The claim is made that the cloze method provides a means of assessing those reading skills which make use of, but also transcend, the recognition of print and individual words.

Later in this chapter we shall be looking at some recent research where cloze-type tests have been used with severely hearing-impaired children. It appears to be true that the child's responses in completing the cloze task provide some insight into the strategies which readers use, particularly in relation to available linguistic cues in the material. However, it is clear from research that children are inconsistent in the way they tackle reading tests, and what the deaf child does may be very different from the hearing child. There are some important implications of this for interpreting the results of reading tests and comparing one group of children with another.

There is one very thorough battery of reading comprehension tasks which deserves mention: the Edinburgh Reading Tests. These are a series of separate subtests designed to sample a very wide range of reading skills in children from 7 years to 16 years. There are four stages appropriate to different age bands with some overlap. The first stage material covers the following areas: vocabulary, syntax, sequences and comprehension. In the *vocabulary* subtest the child has to select words which fit a picture; *syntax* tests sentence completion by choosing a word to make good the whole, and also by deleting words which have been misplaced in sentences; *sequences* assesses ability to put words into logical order, and by answering questions to show awareness of the sequence of events in a connected passage; *comprehension* gives prose material and asks the child to make inferences, draw conclusions and comment on people's feelings from what they say. The importance of the Edinburgh Tests lies in the efforts which have been made to assess *reflective* reading (the child asking questions of print, seeking out information and making comments about it), in a wide range of 'natural' reading situations. In later stages of the tests, youngsters are given newspaper advertisements, recipes, letters, football reports, posters, and a variety of comprehension exercises drawn from different content areas in school. Teachers using these tests have found them very revealing of the active strategies children bring to reading, and as such they have high relevance to the hearing-impaired. The only drawbacks are the length and complexity of the material in the later stages, together with the important criticism that teachers need not turn to published test materials to find out about a child's learning skills in different areas of the curriculum, when information could be gathered informally just as well.

Informal reading inventories

There may be many sources of dissatisfaction in using formal yardsticks of reading. Some teachers feel strongly that when they wish to appraise children's reading they are not concerned to see whether children pass or fail a test, but to observe *how* the task is approached. An 'outcome' approach, knowing how well a child's test score compares with another's, is scant basis on which to plan a future teaching programme. Much more important is to decide upon those skills which are significant in reading and make observations of the child which will reveal what skills have been mastered and what the child needs to do better. Skill-based methods of observation are sometimes called *criterion-referenced* and are discussed in an article by Pikulski (1978). This kind of assessment provides a framework for studying the behaviour of the reader. It relates to the child's own reading books or other text material, and should be part of the teacher's continuous and ongoing awareness of the child's strengths and weaknesses. This kind of assessment procedure cannot be bought as a standardized test package; however, we shall be setting out a reading-skills profile for hearing-impaired children in the final chapter.

One kind of informal reading analysis has already been touched upon: the study of miscues. Researchers such as Goodman have used miscue analysis to support the view that children's reading mistakes are not random, but display a knowledge of language in use. To look at miscues the teacher first selects a passage from the child's everyday reading matter. A copy of the passage should be made if the teacher wishes to mark the actual text as the child reads. It is also helpful, particularly if the child's speech clarity makes intelligibility a problem, to tape-record the child's reading and analyse it later. It should be noted that with this method the teacher is assessing the child's oral reading accuracy. This is one aspect of reading, not the most central in terms of reading for meaning, but one which adults often request. It is what the child does in order to make sense of text which is most important, not oral accuracy. However, the method is justified as a starting point because it does give insights into the child's learning strategies. Several accounts of miscue analysis in the classroom have been given; for example, Arnold (1982) describes a coding system which teachers can use to analyse oral miscues. Examples of the common miscues made by children during reading aloud and what they might reveal about the child are given in Table 4.1.

If oral communication with a child presents speech intelligibility problems, then asking a child to read aloud may be inappropriate. The child's speech accuracy will be prominent, and what needs to be determined is how the child reads for meaning. Teachers can devise their own informal checklists of reading skills and strategies, which are more finely tuned to a severely hearing-impaired child. The teacher has to decide, first and foremost, which areas of skill the child needs to achieve. These could include aspects such as attitudes to reading, motivation and persistence in face of problems, together with the child's independence in tackling new materials, or need for adult help. An informal profile might include 'bottom-up' factors in reading, such as the child's awareness of letter shapes, sight vocabulary, or phonic correspondences. In this book we have tried to put these subskills and 'word-attack' principles in a larger perspective of the reading

Table 4.1 Types of miscues and what they reveal

Miscue type	Reasons for miscue
Omission (word left out)	Word not in child's vocabulary Uncertainty about pronunciation Keywording (child identifies a few keywords in a sentence)
Substitution (wrong word read but meaning preserved)	Prediction from sentence frame, story context, or language experience Child replaces an unfamiliar word with a known word Reads for meaning not accuracy
Substitution (wrong word read and meaning changed)	Haphazard guesswork; imperfect sampling of letter shapes or sounds Incomplete understanding of sentence, story or picture context Child overwhelmed by vocabulary or syntactic structures
Insertion (reads a word not in text)	Anticipates the sentence material wrongly Guesses words which are often associated together Errors made earlier require additional words to preserve meaning or grammar
Repetition (re-reads words or sentence)	Returns to beginning of word or sentence to confirm or check meaning Unfamiliar vocabulary, grammar or concepts causes child to re-read for further clues Aware that something is wrong child makes several attempts to correct the miscue

process. Nevertheless, if the teacher feels there is merit and relevance in observing 'bottom-up' strategies in the hearing-impaired child, then that is a matter of individual choice. The point of an informal reading profile is that it records observations of the reading process, including mechanical and word-building skills, together with understanding and use of a broader range of language variables in reading, in line with the individual teacher's own philosophy.

Having worked out the skills which are felt to be important to reading, the teacher then needs to think out the likely sequence of skill acquisition: what steps follow each other in the order of teaching and learning. It is not easy to identify objectives and to write them down in such a way that they are not open to mis-interpretation. In other words, the skills identified should be as precisely stated as possible so that an independent judge could check whether or not the child had reached the objectives set. The importance of this kind of assessment procedure is that it analyses the child's strengths and weaknesses without a test having to be passed or failed. A profile of objectives structures a teacher's observations and helps to identify areas where the child needs more attention. Such a profile also serves as a record against which progress can be measured over time. Some examples of teaching objectives from the 'Profiles of the hearing-impaired' prepared by Webster and Ellwood (1985) are given in Table 4.2. Further discussion of the principles behind an objectives' approach or curriculum-based assessment are given in the last reference, together with Ainscow and Tweddle (1979). A detailed profile of literacy skills is given in the final chapter, specifically written for hearing-impaired children.

The assessment of reading in deaf children

Almost all the studies of reading in deaf children share some common factors. They are descriptive or evaluative: designed to establish how far behind their hearing peers, deaf children's achievements fall. As we have said, this 'deficit' approach is unlikely to reveal very much about the process of reading, since it is only concerned with the *outcome* of teaching. Nevertheless, there is close agreement in the literature that deaf children read

Table 4.2 Examples of teaching objectives taken from the 'Profiles of the Hearing-impaired Child' (Webster and Ellwood, 1985)

Hearing and speech
Sits in good listening positions in class without reminder
If using a radio aid, checks proper functioning with teacher
Alerts teacher to difficult listening conditions, such as noise
  interference
Responds to key words
Has control of simple grammatical sentences in speech
Understands and uses a wide range of complex sentence structures
Listens to and demonstrates comprehension of oral instructions in
  large teaching groups
Has a wide vocabulary of everyday objects and activities
Can enter the 'to and fro' of conversation in group situations
Child understands language in the abstract and how to refer out of
  context or beyond the 'here and now'

Social interaction
Shows some confidence and independence in basic self-help, such as
  asking for things at lunch table
In the playground is included in games by hearing children
Regularly has social contacts with hearing peers, such as in after-
  school clubs or at home
Aware of socially acceptable behaviour according to the situation –
  doesn't just follow others' leads
Sees other people's points of view, not just his/her own
Confident and independent in organizing day-to-day needs such as
  bus pass, timetable, books and materials, homework
Addresses others appropriately, enters conversation at proper point,
  holds a sustained dialogue
Other hearing children find him/her an interesting and attractive
  companion
Mature in sexual knowledge and attitudes
Not afraid of informal gatherings with hearing children, such as
  playground, disco, snack bar

Educational achievements
Needs small, well-defined tasks, frequent activity changes,
  reinforcement and checking
Can work independently and with concentration levels expected of
  peer group

Table 4.2—continued

Educational achievements—continued

Reads for information using reference books, graphs, tables, maps, newspapers

Competent in the four arithmetic processes up to 30

Handles money and correct change

Uses concepts such as: 'more'; 'same', 'longest', 'equal', 'below', 'highest', 'shorter'

Able to use contents, index, headings and summaries to gain information

Can read a passage to locate a point of information or main idea

Can digest a paragraph of text and answer questions or make notes on content

Can read a story or text and relate the sequence of ideas or events

---

very poorly. In Chapter 3 we suggested that a consistently depressing picture of the reading achievements of the hearing-impaired had been painted (Di Francesca, 1972; Jensema, 1975; Nordén, 1975). The most recent figures for almost all of the school leavers in units and special schools in England and Wales have been provided by Conrad (1979). His reading data indicate that deaf 16-year-olds achieve a mean reading age of about 9 years, which is below generally accepted levels of functional literacy. Not only does there appear to be a consensus of opinion about poor attainments in reading, but this has also been taken as a reflection of underlying limitations in other language skills: a kind of plateau to linguistic achievement, beyond which the deaf child cannot progress.

One other factor shared by studies of deaf children's reading achievement is that researchers have demonstrated the plateau effect by using reading test materials devised for hearing children. There are no materials devised specifically to assess reading in the deaf, and so researchers have used traditional yardsticks standardized on hearing children, or with special adaptations in format for the deaf. Invariably, the measured reading attainments of deaf children are expressed in terms of reading age norms derived for the normally-hearing. We may be led to believe, for example, that if a hearing-impaired school leaver achieves a reading age of 9 years on a formal hearing-referenced test, then the skills and strategies which are brought to the reading task are similar to a hearing 9-year-old. Reported in this way such findings invite us to make a comparison between the deaf adolescent's performance and the competence of a hearing 9-year-old, not just in reading but in the child's underlying knowledge of language.

Some of the assumptions which underpin the use of hearing-referenced test materials with deaf populations can be challenged. Since there is no reason to suspect that the distribution of intelligence is abnormal in a sample of deaf children (Kyle, 1980a) it seems likely that the deaf adolescent will be much more sophisticated, emotionally, physically and conceptually, than the 8- or 9-year-old hearing child with whom a comparison is invited on the basis of reading-test norms. A basic question of *validity* arises. Do test materials sample identical test behaviour in deaf and hearing children? Can we assume that the same reading-age score in a deaf and hearing child is achieved in the same way? There is, in fact, a strong possibility that commonly used 'silent' comprehension or cloze tests, may be tapping quite different processes in deaf and hearing groups. How far the deaf child's performance on a reading test reflects nothing other than linguistic deficiencies is also open to question. There is the possibility that deaf children may adopt non-verbal strategies in attempting to make sense of the test puzzles with which they are faced.

It may well be true that researchers up to now have asked the wrong question. Not 'Why can't the deaf child read?', but 'Does the deaf child read by a different process?'. Some recent investigations have tried to unravel the problems associated with traditional yardsticks of reading, by focusing on the respective test responses of deaf and hearing children as they tackle reading tests. If there may sometimes be a gulf between what reading tests purport to measure and what they actually reveal, this is even wider for hearing-impaired children. Ironically, observation of children's error behaviour on reading tests, focusing on inappropriate and ineffective behaviour in terms of the test proper, has given considerable insight into the strategies deaf children may adopt as they read.

The Wide-span study

In a recent study (Webster *et al.*, 1981) we replicated Conrad's (1979) measures of reading achievement in deaf school-leavers. Conrad used the Wide-span test (Brimer, 1972) and we also gave this to sixty hearing-impaired adolescents matched for reading age on the test with younger hearing children. To be included in the study each deaf child had to have a hearing loss of more than 70 decibels averaged over five frequencies in the better ear, have no other significant handicap, be prelingually deaf as far as could be ascertained, and be aged between 15 and 16½ years. Three groups of children were got together with reading ages of 7, 8 or 9 years on the Wide-span. Equal numbers of boys and girls were represented. The hearing children who acted as controls had reading ages similar to their chronological ages and were matched for IQ. The main interest lay in whether the deaf and younger hearing children attempted the test materials in the same way. The validity of the test and the conclusions drawn from it depend on the materials measuring the same processes in the population to which it is applied, as in the population on which it was standardized.

The performance of deaf and hearing children was analysed using a system based on miscue research (Goodman, 1969). The test procedure is fairly straightforward. The child reads a cue sentence on the left-hand side of the test booklet and chooses one word from this sentence to fill in the gap in a second, unrelated sentence on the right:

Our dog always lifts his head up when he howls	All tall blocks of flats have _____

The nature of this reading task is fairly complicated. The manual suggests that the test items are constructed to permit hypotheses about the omitted word to be tested 'by abstracting possible words from the semantic and syntactical context' (Brimer, p. 7). Clearly, the task demands an awareness of the grammatical constraints in the sentence, and some idea of the meaning of the sentence will be useful. The task might be described by a linguist as a *metalinguistic* process because the child has to be sophisticated enough in the control of language to be able to think about it in the abstract. In other words, it requires what we have described as reflective or explicit awareness, a kind of disembedded thinking. This task can be tackled at various levels: for example, in the following item a child displays awareness of some of the linguistic constraints, although he gets the item wrong:

The salt of the earth are the
hewers of wood
and the drawers of water.

Alongside the wardrobe
stood a tall chest of *wood*.

The observed response 'wood' suggests that the child was able to work out the meaning of the test sentence and insert a word which is both semantically and grammatically appropriate. In fact we were able to identify several classes of response, all of which highlight some kind of linguistic goodness of fit. In another kind of error, the child selected a word which fitted the syntactic constraints of the sentence (it was judged to be a word of the right 'class') but the resulting sentence did not make sense:

Slowly he lifted the glass not wishing to *pick* a drop.
(correct word: *spill*)

A third type of linguistic error which suggested that the child was deriving some meaning from the text, was one in which the selected word was associated with an adjacent word in the sentence frame:

An *foolish* child is one who has no brothers or sisters.
(correct word: *only*)

We have described as *non-linguistic* errors those responses where no obvious connection could be found between the meaning or structure of the sentence and the word inserted into it. On some items, for example, a child inserted into the gap a word from the cue sentence which occupied the same *spatial* position (the fifth word in the sentence, say). Using these categories it proved possible for an independent panel of judges to reach high agreement on how different errors could be analysed and what level of linguistic organization they revealed in the child.

For normal children with both chronological ages and reading ages of 9 years, 81 per cent of errors could be classified in terms of

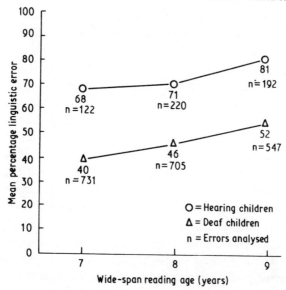

Figure 4.4   Errors made by deaf and hearing children on the Wide-span test

some kind of linguistic strategy. Hearing-impaired adolescents with reading ages of 9 years made twice as many errors and only 52 per cent of them showed some kind of linguistic strategy. The main results of this study are shown in Figure 4.4.

The children achieving the highest reading ages in both deaf and hearing groups also made a relatively higher proportion of linguistic errors than those who achieved the lowest reading ages. To some extent then, success on this test is related to the child's growing linguistic abilities. However, there were some major differences in the way the two groups tackled the test materials. Hearing children always stopped when they felt they had reached their 'ceilings': when they knew they had begun to make a lot of errors. Deaf children, on the other hand, always carried on to attempt every item on the test. Why did the deaf children continue to provide answers, whilst the hearing children stopped at their 'ceilings'? The simple interpretation is that deaf children do not inhibit their responses even when the task is far beyond the limits of their comprehension. The deaf child tries to answer questions to the very end of the test, at which point the reading task must be meaningless to the child.

Clay (1977) in a study of emergent reading skills in normal children sees recognition of errors, self-monitoring, and formation of self-correction strategies, as crucial developmental steps. Her 'high progress' children were able to spot dissonance in the syntax and meaning of sentences. These children always tended to hazard linguistically appropriate guesses and to search for the best-fit solutions in reading. It is clear from the deaf children's performance on the Wide-span test that, whatever else they might be doing, *effective* search and check procedures are not being used. This kind of perseverative behaviour could be interpreted as a legacy of teaching practice: passive, unquestioning styles of learning. We have highlighted the possibility that there may be some pervasive secondary consequences of deafness, which lead to greater dependency on adults, less self-direction and a more accepting, uncritical style of learning. We have preferred to attribute such behaviour and learning strategies to early learning experiences, rather than deafness *per se,* when the child seems to be exposed to heightened direction and control from parents and teachers.

It is also possible that the nature of the Wide-span reading task, uncompromising as it is to the linguistic limitations of the deaf, forces such children into adopting strategies which simply enable them to provide answers. One other major difference between deaf and hearing groups in this study concerns the number and type of errors made. All of the deaf children in the three reading groups and across all of the test-items, including above and below 'ceilings', showed a similar error pattern. Simply put, many more errors were made in comparison with hearing controls and a significantly higher proportion were non-linguistic. Brimer (1972) suggests that for hearing children, success on the Wide-span depends on an awareness of the structure of the language system, ability to comprehend and perceive syntactic and semantic relationships, and skill in reflecting upon and manipulating the sentence elements presented. The deaf child has overwhelming problems in analysing the structures of text, in reflecting upon the answers, in self-monitoring and self-correction. Performance on this kind of linguistic puzzle is different *in kind* from that of the matched, hearing counterparts. The use of a spatial non-verbal strategy shows that the deaf child tries to surmount the linguistic obstacles faced by utilizing other possible cues in the test items. In fact, a purely spatial strategy, which may not entail any reading, has a payoff: many of the items on the Wide-span can be tackled correctly simply by lifting the word from the cue sentence which occupies the same position as the gap:

In the still air of the noon heat the flag hung
limp over the border post.
After the storm the damaged ships had to
. . . back to port.

To summarize, the results of this study show that the strategies which deaf children may adopt in tackling the Wide-span are very different from hearing children. This is true across all the items and not just beyond the child's 'ceiling'. Deaf school-leavers are not only retarded in their reading ability, they obtain their test scores in different ways from hearing children. Deaf children persevere at responses well beyond their level of understanding; they do not self-monitor or self-correct. The many more errors that are made at all levels of the test reveal that deaf children adopt strategies for solution which are often non-linguistic in character. The implications are far-reaching. This specific test does not measure *delayed* processes in the deaf similar to those found in younger hearing children. This raises serious questions about the value of reading estimates of the deaf child, using norms standardized on the hearing. Data provided by researchers such as Conrad (1979) on the deaf child's reading achievements are likely to be misleading since they are tapping different processes in deaf and hearing children. A deaf child's score may resemble that of a younger hearing child but the performance and processes that lead to that score are likely to be different in a number of important respects. Thus, test scores serve as a poor guide for any attempt to estimate the type of material the child could read in books, to locate a child in a language programme or on a reading scheme.

The Southgate study

The reading test performances of deaf and hearing groups were explored in another, quite different test situation (Wood *et al.*, 1981). Analysing test behaviour on only one reading battery might invite the criticism that the results are test-specific and not generalizable to other test materials. So the Southgate (1962) test was given to groups of deaf and hearing children to see whether similar differences could be observed in the strategies adopted. One hundred and twenty children took part in this study: sixty deaf and sixty hearing. The average age of the deaf children was 11 years, and the hearing 9 years. Hearing losses in the deaf sample ranged from 57 to 113 decibels, with an average loss of 87 decibels in the better ear. The average reading age of the deaf children was 7 years 9 months, and 8 years 6 months for the hearing group on the Southgate test. On this test the child is required to complete a sentence by choosing one word from a given selection of five, for example:

She stirred the *soup pages cloth kitchen jumper.*

The test is designed as a measure of word recognition in which the child can test out the correct completion of each sentence by using the grammatical and semantic constraints.

Again it was found that deaf children tackled more of the test items, persevered in their attempts far beyond the level of their understanding, and made many more errors than hearing children of the same reading age. The deaf group attempted over 90 per cent of the questions, the hearing group 85 per cent. The average number of errors made by the hearing-impaired group was 47 per cent, the hearing 18 per cent. We have the same finding as we had in the Wide-span study: that deaf children fail to check or monitor their own performances, and continue to supply answers to questions they do not understand, in many cases right to the end of the test. One possibility is that the deaf children were simply answering questions at random. To explore this a detailed analysis of children's answers to every question was undertaken, particularly where errors were made.

Obviously, many of the 'distractor' words in each test item are included because they either look, or sound like, the correct answer:

Use a knife and *frog fork from fall flake.*

However, the item analysis of the patterns of choices made by deaf children showed that they were not distracted by similar looking or sounding alternatives. Neither did their responses appear to be random. Curiously, there was a great deal of agreement amongst the deaf children upon the words which were chosen, even though the answers they selected were wrong. This pattern of popular choices was also quite different to that of hearing children. If the deaf were not acting at random in answering test items, what were the features of questions that they exploited to reach agreement? Furthermore, what does their pattern of choice tell us about the deaf child's reading strategies?

Examples of those test items on which there was a high consensus of choice amongst the deaf children, are given below:

Birds are covered with *trees skirts sky* **nests** *feathers.*
Ducks can **pond** *swim water farm sing.*
Mice like *chins choose* **cats** *cheese she.*

These examples indicate that selections were made on the basis of word association: a sense of which words tend to appear together in everyday usage and experience. In fact, the deaf reader may be doing nothing other than keywording what is thought to be the main subject matter. However, word association does not explain all the errors that are made: the important paradox is that deaf children are able to get right answers to some difficult questions on the Southgate, using just this strategy. In the following examples, the most (or only) highly associated word in each list of alternatives also happens to be the correct response:

I drink *cake hens* **milk** *picture man.*
There was a bridge over the *rain running* **river** *rest ruler.*

Once again these results indicate that the reading ages given by the Southgate test for hearing-impaired children are not simply reflecting delayed reading attainment. The Southgate study lends further strength to the argument that when deaf children are confronted with test materials of overwhelming linguistic complexity, the responses which they make in order to proceed with the test are not random. Capital is made of specific features of the test materials which enables the child to develop a consistent strategy. Not all the features of test questions have been identified, but word association is one of them. This finding further underlines the weakness of tests based on hearing norms as instruments for assessing the reading competence of the deaf child. The same test score by hearing and hearing-impaired children is likely to have been achieved in quite different ways, and mean different things.

Finally, we have said that all that needs to be attributed to the deaf reader in completing the Southgate Test is a sight vocabulary for keywords and a sense of likely associations. In Chapter 5 where we consider the particular strengths and weaknesses of hearing-impaired readers, we shall be arguing that deaf children have no problems in recognizing individual sight words. Reading difficulties arise when the child is asked to comprehend more complex text. It is precisely the point at which reading test materials demand comprehension of more complex syntactic structures that the deaf child's reading skills have been said to plateau. We shall be pursuing this line of argument further, since it is a possibility that the 'plateau effect' is an artefact of test construction. In other words, many reading measures up to a reading age of about 9 years may be sampling word recognition, whilst beyond that, more sophisticated linguistic skills are required. The rapid increase in linguistic complexity in test materials at that point simply obscures emerging skills in the deaf child.

The Hamp study

Following on the Wide-span and Southgate studies other researchers have also investigated the hypothesis that test scores reflect different processes in hearing and deaf children, using other materials. Beggs and Breslaw (1982) gave the Picture Aided Reading Test (Hamp, 1975) to forty hearing-impaired children. This is a word recognition test with fifty-five stimulus words each supported by four pictures. The child has to pick an appropriate picture from the selection of four to match the stimulus word. On this test the child's reading age is calculated from a 'total score' over all the items. In comparison with hearing children matched for reading age on this test, deaf children are said to achieve their 'total scores' by identifying correctly, quite different subsets of words. For example, deaf children were able to identify some of the later items on the test (such as prehistoric, pyramid, muscular) which the younger hearing controls found too difficult. Conversely, deaf children failed a greater proportion of the easier items on the test than did hearing controls.

Once again the deaf children agreed amongst themselves upon the most appropriate responses to many of the items, even though they were incorrect. The authors identify the deaf children's strategy as being one of selection according to picture *saliency*. In other words, a picture is selected simply because it has the most visual appeal. There was a remarkable similarity between the pattern of responses made by deaf children supposedly reading the stimulus words, and the responses of a group of hearing children who were given *only* the pictures to see, and then asked to choose one. Beggs and Breslaw describe the deaf children's non-verbal efforts to solve the Hamp Test as being indicative of 'fundamental differences between the reading skills of deaf and hearing children'. Whether or not this is true the study substantiates the argument that hearing-referenced tests give unreliable data about the reading skills of deaf children. The Hamp test cannot be relied upon to give any clear indication of emerging reading skills, since there is evidence that the deaf may solve this reading puzzle *without* reading.

In the brief survey which we made earlier in this chapter of different reading assessment techniques, attention was drawn to some of the pitfalls involved in testing children. Principally these concern the scope and function of assessment and the status of any findings. Since most test materials are put together intuitively rather than on any firm theoretical basis, what the author believes a test is measuring and what is actually revealed, may be some distance apart. Reading tests sample only a small part of a child's reading behaviour. How the child behaves on a specific test may bear little relation to the child's reading of authentic materials. One other pitfall is that how we set out to test reading may influence what children think they ought to be doing when they read. For example, almost all reading tests present words or sentences to the child wrested out of any meaningful context, thereby encouraging mechanical word recognition skills, rather than attention to wider discourse features available in continuous text. It is with these questions in mind, drawn from the assessment of reading in general, that we have approached the testing of reading in the hearing-impaired.

All of this recent research suggests that many reading test materials overwhelm the deaf child linguistically. However, what the deaf child does when confronted with a reading test is not random or senseless. Deaf children do adopt consistent strategies which enable them to tackle the puzzles the tests present. That may lead to poor scores relative to hearing norms but it does reveal intelligent efforts to capitalize on some of the cues available in the material, and these may be non-verbal cues. Reading tests tap different processes in deaf and hearing groups. Therefore, any attempt to compare deaf and hearing children in terms of reading age will be misleading. Estimates of reading age do not indicate delayed processes in the deaf, similar to younger hearing children. Neither do such test results give any clear indication of reading development in the deaf, or of how one child's reading progress compares with another, since the deaf child may tackle reading tests *without* reading. Perhaps most importantly of all, these studies cast doubt on the notion of a reading plateau for deaf children if only because of their lack of sensitivity to the actual reading abilities of the deaf. It is also worth pointing out that many of the outcome studies which have tried to evaluate the benefits of one kind of educational treatment compared with another (e.g. oralism versus manualism), have used measures such as reading ages. We now know that reading measures cannot be taken at face value as reliable indicators of children's reading or linguistic progress.

From the deficit model of descriptive research, which is content to document the extent of the child's failure, we have seen how important it is to examine what hearing-impaired children actually do when they read. The fact that formal reading measures tell us little about the individual skills of deaf readers, what strategies are more important for success than others, and which children are better readers than others, leaves us with another set of problems. How best to reveal the skills which the deaf child brings to the reading task? Actually, apart from the fact that formal reading tests reveal marked differences in reading processes between deaf and hearing children, they also hint at what might be important factors for reading success. That would seem to lie in the ability of the child to transcend the linguistic obstacles by being more actively aware of other sources of information in written material. In the following chapter we shall be looking at more *informal* assessments of reading behaviour. The only way to reveal the skills which the deaf child brings to reading is to make much finer detailed observations of deaf children's reading behaviour itself.

Chapter summary

1   We began this chapter by asking the question: 'What is reading?' There is no consensus view of the reading process, and how we assess or teach reading may bear little relation to what children do when they read. Reading involves a range of complex intellectual activities such as perception, memory, language and thinking. A unitary-factor explanation of reading or reading disability is inadequate. For present purposes we define reading in terms of the active strategies the reader uses to gain meaningful information from print.

2   'Bottom-up' models of reading are discussed. These pay attention to *text* factors as basic building-blocks of reading, such as letter shapes, word patterns or letter-sound correspondences. The experimental evidence which highlights separate subskills is reviewed. Letter shapes may provide some information, but all children confuse letters when they learn to read and poor readers may not have perceptual deficits. Whole words may be recognized more easily than letters, but reading is more complex than a

word-by-word process. Decoding print into sound usually differentiates good from poor readers. However, being able to read may provide the child with 'phonic' awareness rather than phonic skills being prerequisite. In terms of our language model, 'bottom-up' features involve peripheral aspects of language.

3   'Top-down' models are discussed which view the reader as a language user who makes hypotheses about text. Reading is seen as a sampling and checking cycle, whereby the child tests out predictions about the meaning of print. The 'top-down' view puts greater emphasis on what the child brings to reading in terms of intellect and experience, rather than what text reveals. This is a view which supports the social context view of language learning (the right-hand side of the language model) rather than a subskills approach. Children learn to read by reading, in the same way and for the same purpose, that they learn to speak.

4   The interactive view of reading integrates automatic processes, such as direct word recognition from print, with 'top-down' processes such as hypothesis-testing. The reader may use several sources of information, including letters, sounds, sentences, context, as well as predictions. Good readers may be quicker at analysing text features which leaves capacity for 'thinking space'. Poor readers may have to utilize other sources of information in text because their 'bottom-up' skills are less efficient.

5   The assessment of reading in children has many pitfalls. Tests usually sample a small area and cannot reflect the complexity of the reading process. What children do on a specific test may bear little relation to how they behave on authentic reading tasks. Tests are usually devised intuitively, and what they set out to measure may be different from what they *actually* reveal. Testing and teaching often reflect the teacher's view of reading and may influence how children think they should read. Together with the scope and status of reading measures, it is also important to know what level of the reading process is being assessed. A survey of 'bottom-up' tests is given, such as orthographic knowledge, phonic skills and word recognition. 'Top-down' tests of sentence, story and text comprehension are discussed, together with cloze material. Informal reading assessments are recommended.

6   The testing of reading in deaf children has usually had a

monitoring or evaluative purpose, in line with the deficit model. Traditional yardsticks, standardized on hearing children, paint a depressing picture of reading achievement with a plateau at around a reading age of 9 years. Recent research on the Widespan, Southgate and Hamp tests has important implications. Deaf children are overwhelmed by the linguistic demands made by tests but their behaviour is not random or senseless. They adopt consistent strategies which sometimes capitalize on non-verbal cues. Reading tests tap different processes in deaf and hearing children: the deaf are not simply *delayed* readers. Comparisons between deaf and hearing in terms of reading are misleading, as is the notion of a plateau. More finely detailed observations of deaf children as they read are likely to lead to greater understanding of the reading process and to teaching strategies.

5

READING, WRITING AND THINKING

Normally, every child has already taken many momentous developmental steps, well before school age. In language we can assume that the hearing 4-year-old will already have an extensive and rapidly growing fund of vocabulary. We can take for granted a sophisticated mastery of the basic patterns of syntax and the ability to generate long and complex sentence sequences. In fact, by the age of 3 years most children have acquired all the main elements of sentence structure and can use simple clauses, questions and commands. All of these linguistic developments depend on the richness of the child's early language interchanges with adult caretakers. We cannot study how the child's understanding of language emerges without paying attention to the social context of language use. We need to look at how children become engaged in communication games, how adults collaborate with the child in negotiating meaning, and how strategies are learned which enable both child and adult to make sense of their linguistic encounters.

We are often guilty of underestimating what the young infant is capable of. In Donaldson's (1978) book, for example, some earlier notions about the pre-school child's inability to use formal and abstract reasoning, are scrutinized. Donaldson challenges many of the interpretations made by Piaget of experiments where the child of 6 or 7 years, seems unable to 'decentre'. In other words, no other point of view is taken into account apart from the child's own. The classic demonstration of this is the three mountains experiment. In this, a three-dimensional model is shown to the child. One of the mountains has a house on top, the second is covered in snow, the third has a red cross at the summit. A little doll is produced and positioned to one side of the model. The problem for the child is to decide what the doll sees. When children below the age of 6 years are shown pictures of the model from different angles, they almost inevitably choose the picture which represents their own point of view: what they themselves can see. Piaget interprets this as evidence of 'egocentrism': an inability to stand back from a situation and infer a different point of view.

Donaldson has several things to say about this. Firstly, that the child may fail to understand the adult's instructions, rather than the nature of the exercise. Secondly, that such experimental tasks fail to make *human sense* to the child. When similar tasks were given to children involving a doll hiding from a toy policeman, young children were able to 'decentre'. This task also involves judgements of what can be seen from different points of view. However, it has an essential new ingredient of presenting a dramatically important, meaningful context to the child. Even 3-year-olds quickly grasped the motives and intentions of the dolls in this task and were able to make the kind of objective judgements which Piaget felt young children to be incapable of.

Donaldson goes on to suggest that it is the infant's ability to interpret and make sense of situations which is fundamental. It is bound up with all other kinds of learning the child is involved in. It enables the child, through processes of hypothesis-testing and inference, to develop a knowledge of the language system. These arguments can also be applied to reading development, in a number of ways. Both language and reading must be seen to have some relevant and meaningful purpose to the child. Both processes involve active thinking and reasoning. Both involve the child's ability to 'decentre'. Both are closely enmeshed with the child's general potential to work out how the world is put together.

Spoken language, for the majority of children, is the principal symbolic system: the vehicle of thinking activity. Initially, children may use spoken language with little awareness of how the system is put together. Language is embedded in the events to which it refers. In time, children do become aware of language as something separate from events in the world. By the time many children get to school they are capable of analysing and reflecting on the language they use as a system of symbols, free of any context. Written language extends this development still further. By its very nature, written language enables the child to think about events which have no context, apart from what the page provides. It could be said that children need to have discovered quite a lot about language as a code, in its own right, before they come to reading.

These aspects of language development in childhood have two major implications. Firstly, it is now well accepted that children use their experiences of learning, in speaking and listening, in order to make sense of reading. In other words, both language and reading have the same purpose and function: achieving understanding, actively creating and searching out the significance of things. So what children learn as they attempt to make sense of the world through linguistic interactions will subsequently be applied to reading. Secondly, if a hearing-impairment disrupts the contexts in which language growth takes place, it follows that the child with a hearing loss will be less well prepared, in a host of ways, for learning to read.

In this chapter we shall be looking in some detail at what the deaf child brings to reading. Indeed, almost all of the factors associated with a hearing-impairment which we have considered so far put the child in a different position as reading is approached. That fact is very simply illustrated by a glance at any of the early books in a typical infant reading scheme. The beginning reader is immediately exposed to complex sentence structures not within the control of many older hearing-impaired children. For the hearing child there is usually no problem. The average 5-year-old has much more sophisticated language under control than the language of early texts. The sentence patterns attempted in first books should be familiar. For the hearing child, reading is a matter of discovering the written characteristics of a language already known. Furthermore, we have said that by school entry many children have an explicit awareness of language as a code that can be manipulated free from the context it represents.

What of the hearing-impaired child? We have discussed the possibility that there may not be the same breadth or depth of verbal concepts. There may be parts of speech that the child does not recognize very easily. The child may never have been able to enter the 'to and fro' of conversation which leads to a rich experience and understanding of how words are used together and how they modify each other. Children who have acquired a sign language as a means of communication may be at no advantage when it comes to reading. One reason for that is the fact that natural sign systems are organized upon grammatical principles which do not reflect spoken or written English. Similarly, children taught signs alongside spoken English as part of a total communication programme, cannot be *guaranteed* to have any better grasp of English syntax. Inevitably, the more limited the child's experience and use of language, the more immature the child's thinking about language will be. The child may be less well aware of language as an abstract system.

Deaf children may have to devise unique strategies for making sense of the world, strategies which enable them to transcend the linguistic obstacles in their midst. They may become used to utilizing other information sources. One commonly held belief is that the more severely hearing-impaired the child, the more that vision will be relied upon as the primary communication channel. This is hard to prove, simply because we do not know which features of a communication situation deaf children are sensitive to. It is likely, however, that children are able to utilize other sources of information together with sound. Reading may thus become a qualitatively different process for the deaf child.

So, the hearing-impaired child may approach the reading task with a set of challenges. First, the printed symbols of the written code have never been met before. Secondly, the child may not be familiar with the words, sentence patterns and discourse features which the code represents. Thirdly, the kind of explicit awareness of language as a code, required by reading, may be less well-developed. For the hearing-impaired child the process of learning to read becomes a *language-learning* process at one and the same time. As Streng (1965) puts it:

> Every language lesson is a reading lesson and every reading lesson is a language lesson.   (p. 31)

The more subtle problems for the deaf child approaching reading are related to the secondary effects of deafness upon the child's learning experiences. We might include here a possible diminishing of the child's active impulse to make sense of language at the hands of unwitting adults and teachers. We have described this in terms of passive, unquestioning styles of learning. Perhaps the first step for these children in approaching the language puzzles of reading, is to learn how to learn?

In this chapter we shall be addressing the questions: What do hearing-impaired children bring to the reading task in terms of their skills and experience? What does the reading task demand? What strategies does the child develop? Where do any difficulties begin to arise? To the last question we could not expect, for reasons expressed earlier, that any single factor would have the power to account for every child's difficulties. However, if we are trying to find the major source of reading problems associated with varying degrees of hearing loss, this is likely to be at an interface: where the child's language and cognitive system meet with text. This line of approach takes us very quickly to the heart of the matter: the relationship between language, thinking and reading. Several recent experimental studies, involving both reading and writing, suggest that one powerful and potentially limiting factor, which must be taken into account, is the child's auditory memory, in turn dependent on the amount of 'inner' language the child can call upon.

Mild hearing losses and reading

Many researchers have been attracted to the idea that in order to be able to read, children must be capable of processing the sound features of language. Two quite separate kinds of evidence have been linked together. On the one hand, studies of normal reading development have sometimes accorded great significance to the ability to relate the spelling patterns of English to the sound patterns of speech. Studies of early fluent readers, such as by Clark (1976), together with assessments of the strengths and weaknesses of good and poor readers, have led people to conclude that auditory discrimination is crucial to reading. The evidence in support of phonological skills being the basic building-block of reading was discussed in Chapter 4. It was concluded that psychologists do not always agree on what insights children need about their language system in order to be able to read. In terms of the language model presented, 'bottom-up' skills such as phonic awareness are aspects which occupy the periphery.

Notwithstanding the doubts which have been raised about the central importance of auditory factors in reading, such evidence has been linked with the learning difficulties experienced by children suffering from conductive hearing losses. On the other hand, then, the suggestion has been made that early middle-ear hearing losses lead to a long-term disability in handling and processing the sounds of language. Downs (1977) has called this an 'irreversible auditory learning disaster'. This body of evidence was reviewed in Chapter 3. Quite apart from the problems of research design in studying this group of children, all of the tests designed to measure auditory discrimination, blending and sequencing of sounds, and the like, generally depend on the child's knowledge of words. The commonsense view of this research evidence is that delayed language is *associated* with early middle-ear disease. There is, in fact, a nexus of associations between poor health, poor environment, poor family circumstances and poor developmental achievements. So the evidence for a *specific* underlying auditory reading deficit in children with early middle-ear disease is not at all clear.

What does the child bring to the task?

It is easy, of course, to see how researchers have skated over some of these complexities in an effort to produce elegantly simple explanations of reading and reading failure. Unfortunately, this is one area of learning and development where simple solutions are both elusive and inadequate. This is not to dispute the research evidence, merely to put another interpretation upon it. To the first of our questions ('What does the mildly hearing-impaired child bring to reading?'), we can suggest the following response. A group of children suffering mild hearing losses from an early age is likely to show marked delays in mastery of speech sounds, with confusions in the perception of speech and in production of sound contrasts. Some particular units of speech are more susceptible to the effects of a slight hearing loss, than others. However, the fricative 'f' or 'v' sounds, nasal sounds like 'm' or 'n', plural endings, and the sounds of speech which are unstressed or of weaker intensity, may be missed.

These children may have problems in discriminating between sounds, in blending sounds together, and in listening out for sounds in noisy conditions. They may have poor auditory memories. Problems in sequencing, distinguishing, manipulating and remembering sounds, generally depend on the child's knowledge of words. Here too, children with mild hearing losses will have poorer vocabularies and a more limited range and flexibility of usage of words than normal. They may have a restricted understanding of what words mean. Their experience of the different forms words take in use may also be impoverished. There may be problems in remembering words and explaining words, and this may be particularly acute in relation to what the child is learning, or failing to learn, in school.

To cope with school, the child needs a good grasp of the structure of language. However, as a group, children with mild hearing losses may also be markedly delayed in their understanding and use of grammar. They may be unable to understand what is said to them, interpret questions wrongly, and be unable to put their thoughts adequately into sentence forms, to formulate a reply. Furthermore, they may be unable to think about the complexities of their language systems. So that, as well as being poor at using grammatical structures such as plurals, different tenses, and rules which govern phrase or clause patterns in English, these children may also have more limited insights into how the language is put together. This is what has been called 'reflective' or 'explicit' awareness: the ability to stand back and think about language independently of its context. Linguists sometimes call this *metalinguistic awareness*. It is a skill which is often demanded in school, for example, in tackling reading comprehension tests, but it is a product of a deep and rich experience of spoken language.

It is worth remembering that by the age of 5 years, most normally-hearing children have reached the stage of language growth where they can generate long and extended sentence sequences. This mastery of the recursive features of syntax enables the child to connect sentences together, embed one within another, and create new and complex expressive patterns. Although at school entry most hearing children have control of the most important elements of syntax, this degree of sophistication continues to be refined during the school years. Karmiloff-Smith (1978) has said children begin to treat language as a 'problem-space' in its own right. In other words, they continue to experiment with, hypothesize about, and reflect upon, the complexity of linguistic form for its own sake. Children who have suffered mild hearing losses over this early pre-school period of rapid language growth may be far less sophisticated in their use of syntax and in their thinking about language.

The areas of linguistic delay which mildly hearing-impaired children bring to the reading task are broad-based and affect the whole spectrum of language-related skills, including auditory processing, knowledge of words, together with grammar: the organizing principles of language. Inevitably, since these children are less well-prepared in terms of a framework of language, full participation in the language-learning experiences of school is also affected. This is particularly true in situations where listening is more difficult, such as a busy classroom. So it is not surprising to find, as one thing leads to another, that mildly hearing-impaired children develop less effective strategies for learning. These might include short attention span, poor concentration, distractibility, high adult-dependency, poor motivation, and less creative or inquisitive learning styles.

The compounding factors associated with middle-ear disease in childhood, highlighted in the research literature, serve to exacerbate children's learning difficulties in schools. If middle-ear hearing losses tend to occur more frequently in environmental and family circumstances which are themselves less conducive to academic achievement, then these factors, over and above hearing loss, must be taken into account. In Chapter 3 some of the factors were identified which contribute to wider developmental problems and which also predispose children to middle-ear disease: prematurity, low birth weight, general ill health, poor nutrition, poverty, poor housing, family difficulties and quality of parenting. All of these aspects, in themselves, account for some children's poor early development and progress in school. There is a strong nexus of associations within which mild hearing losses are implicated. A model of development has been presented in which the child's discovery of language is deeply embedded in the social context in which the child hears language being used. It should be apparent that a hearing loss, of even a very small degree, has both direct and indirect ramifications for language and reading.

What does the task demand?

'What does the reading task demand?' To the second of our questions we respond by regarding the process of learning to read as a language-acquisition process itself, which reflects the child's developmental progress generally. The reading research reviewed in Chapter 4 depicts a diversity, rather than a consensus, of opinion. The reason for that, quite simply, is the state of the art: we do not know how children learn to read, and in order to try and understand what happens, we have tended to dissect the complex psychological processsses involved into small, manageable pieces. The problem in doing this is that we tend to lose sight of the whole. It follows that an acceptable model of the reading process must be multi-factorial.

One such model has been described as *interactive* or *compensatory*. This outlines some of the basic sources of information which the text presents to the reader and which are available to be used, if required. Letter shapes and the distinctive letter configurations in words may help a child to identify a word. Experimentally, whole words are easier to recognize than individual letters, but it may be that words are remembered on the basis of some of the letter characteristics. This has been called the visual route to word meaning. Another possible route to word recognition, might involve some of the sound features of letters which enable the word to be pronounced. These are text-driven, 'bottom-up' sources of information which arise upwards from the page.

Good readers tend to become very efficient at these low-level strategies and develop automatic, direct word recognition from print. We saw in Chapter 4 that there is some disagreement about which of these decoding skills is *prerequisite* to reading. An equally plausible explanation could be given that these insights into letters, sounds and words, emerge as a *consequence of* reading, rather than being *necessary for* reading. Whichever way we look at this evidence makes little difference to the conclusions we draw about hearing-impaired children. Mildly hearing-impaired children will have confusions in their perception of speech sounds as well as depletions in their knowledge of vocabulary. They may have problems in remembering, sequencing and discriminating sound features. All of these features are as peripheral to language as their written correspondences are peripheral to reading. However, even in low-order, 'bottom-up' strategies, the mildly hearing-impaired child is disadvantaged.

The interactive model of reading also presupposes that larger units of language will provide useful sources of information to the reader. Most written material, even infant reading schemes, present phrase and clause pattterns to the child. One of the expectations of children reading is that they will utilize their sophisticated grasp of the structure of spoken language in tackling the written conventions. The child who makes a successful attempt at understanding:

The dog was bitten by the snake.

must be aware that the use of the auxiliary verb 'was', the modification to 'bite', together with the insertion of the preposition 'by', signify a reversal of the usual SVO pattern to mean:

snake bites dog

The correct interpretation of the sentence in its passive form must depend on prior developments in spoken language. Where a mildly hearing-impaired child is unfamiliar with more complex sentence patterns, has a limited experience of language in use, and is generally linguistically immature, then some of the larger units of written text will not map onto the child's existing understanding of language forms.

The interactive reading model also outlines some of the higher level sources of information which act downwards upon the printed page. According to 'top-down' theory, children's experience of language in use and their knowledge of the world enable predictions to be made about what text means. The reader samples and checks hypotheses about what the author intends to communicate in print, and actively reconstructs the message. There is disagreement here too, about the relative efficiency of having to make predictions all the time when reading, compared with direct word recognition. Nevertheless, 'top-down' strategies are yet another route towards reading for meaning. In this respect also, mildly hearing-impaired children are disadvantaged. One asks the question:'Where do children derive hypotheses about what an author intends to communicate in print?' The answer, of course, is that these insights develop hand-in-hand with the child's growing experience of the world, particularly as a language-user. The successful child will draw on a rich fund of early language encounters, including spoken interchanges with others, but also experience of listening to stories, of being read to, and of discovering with adults a world in books.

To summarize, the reading process is disrupted in children with relatively mild hearing losses, not simply because of specific auditory problems, but because of a much more diffuse discrepancy between the child and the task. Much greater emphasis has been placed upon those features of deafness, language and reading, which are deeply embedded in the social context. The child's social experience and mastery of language, style of learning, more general cognitive development and control of reflective thinking, are all implicated. Reading both requires and encourages an awareness of language as a system which enables the child to think about events not immediately present. If anything, general linguistic and intellectual immaturity are responsible for reading difficulties in children with early middle-ear disease, and those factors may have socio-cultural determinants.

Interestingly, some 'dyslexia' theorists have begun to take a much broader view of the possible origins of reading difficulties in the wider population. It is now well-accepted that there are no single characteristics of 'dyslexia' other than a difficulty in reading. Any group of children collected together as 'dyslexic' will have different skills and difficulties. This has to make sense if we accept the complex nature of the reading process. However, researchers such as Vellutino (1979), have begun to set 'dyslexia' within a language-learning model. Rather than postulating deficiencies in aspects such as visual perception, Vellutino suggests that 'dyslexia' is a problem of language experience. The child fails to get 'printborne' because of mismatches arising at any of the points along a language-learning dimension.

We have not been able to answer all the questions posed about reading in relation to mildly hearing-impaired children. There is little evidence, for example, relating to the kind of reading strategies which this group of children adopt as they tackle reading materials. The reason for that is the largely evaluative nature of the research literature. The other major problem in researching this group of children is that they are often identified in retrospect as being children who have had histories of middle-ear disease. The most revealing study would need to chart a child's acquisition of reading skill over time, together with monitoring middle-ear function. But of course, the child found to have middle-ear pathology would have to be left untreated: an unethical proposition.

Reading and the severely hearing-impaired

In responding to the questions, 'What does the severely hearing-impaired child bring to the reading task?', and 'What does the task itself demand?', useful reference points are provided by the model of language depicted in Figure 4.2 as it relates to a framework for reading. Let us begin with the left-hand side of this model: the lower level skills involved in recognizing letter shapes and associating these with speech sounds. This is the obvious starting point in view of the deaf child's difficulties in mastering the sound system of the language because of the gaps in auditory experience. What implications might this have in an alphabetic system where some of the sound features of speech are represented in the written units of print?

In fact, some researchers have looked at the low-level, 'bottom-up' reading skills of hearing-impaired children. In Kyle's (1980b) studies he looked at the development of basic perceptual processes such as letter identification, discriminating and matching letter shapes, and the ability to associate words and pictures together. Over a 3-year period these skills showed no developmental differences in deaf and hearing children between about 7 and 11 years. In other words, if one simply examines 'bottom-up' processes such as the ability to learn sight vocabulary, there may be little difference between young deaf and hearing children. The hearing-impaired child's reading problems begin as soon as an attempt is made to understand more complex text. This is precisely the point at which some researchers have said the reading skills of the deaf begin to plateau. Our contention is that tests of reading up to that point tend to tap low-level skills such as word recognition, and beyond a standardized reading age level of about 8½ to 9 years many tests tap more complex language skills. The plateau effect may well be an artefact of test construction whereby the deaf child's slowly emerging grasp of language is obscured by the sudden, overwhelming exposure to linguistic complexities in test materials. Traditional tests are insensitive to what the deaf child is trying to do with the reading task.

It should be clear by this point that the importance of 'bottom-up' skills such as grapheme–phoneme awareness in reading is debatable. If one is interested in reading for meaning then the ability to decode and pronounce a printed word correctly may be irrelevant. Certainly, for the deaf child the focus of interest must shift to the wider linguistic difficulties experienced by the child.

The sensible view of this area of reading research, which was summarized in Chapter 4, is that young hearing children may rely to some extent on phonic information as they begin to read, particularly if taught to do so. However, good readers probably come to rely upon more direct ways of identifying word meanings. The very fact of being more proficient at reading may itself lead to greater insights about features such as letter shapes and letter sound correspondences. This might also apply to deaf readers: those who have gained in proficiency may also have gained a better awareness of the phonemic features of words.

One interesting piece of research by Dodd and Hermelin (1977) suggests that even profoundly deaf children can use phonological information through lip-reading. In several experiments on spelling, which we shall discuss later in this chapter, deaf children demonstrated an awareness of the sound features of words which they may have inferred through seeing the accompanying lip patterns. This points up the danger of assuming that we know which aspects of the communication context are either accessible or unavailable to a hearing-impaired child. Nevertheless, some researchers feel that they have located the source of the deaf child's reading difficulties in the child's loss of access to speech sounds.

Inner speech

In Conrad's (1979) work the issues of the deaf child's 'inner speech', phonetic skills in letter sound decoding, and poor reading, are closely linked together. What do people mean when they refer to inner or internal speech? Loosely, this is usually taken to mean the speech-like experiences people use covertly, only for themselves. It is the inner experience, corresponding to the outer use of speech sounds, which people reserve for themselves, when thinking or reading. Many people may be aware of this internal, unvocalized speech, when they read. Some support for this comes from studies using electro-myographic techniques whereby electrical impulses are recorded from the speech muscles (Sokolov, 1972). This kind of electrical activity can be shown to accompany reading, especially when the text is difficult. It has also been observed that when text gets hard people read aloud, where they would normally read covertly. This might suggest that hearing what text says is an aid to comprehension, whether this is done externally or internally. This is not far from what some reading theorists have said about needing to hear the sounds in words, in order to discover the meaning. All children begin by reading aloud to their teachers and parents, and only later read covertly for themselves. So, inner speech may be something that children are able to use as they get older or as they become more proficient at reading.

It is worth looking more closely at how Conrad (1979) set about measuring inner speech in deaf children. If a list of words is given to a hearing person to read and recall, one factor which affects how well people do on this task is the phonemic similarity of the words in the list. To put this another way: words which sound alike, such as 'zoo', 'blue', 'screw', will be more difficult to recall than words which sound different, such as 'door', 'home', 'lane'. The similarity of the sounds in the words confuses people and interferes with their recall performance. Conrad used this effect as a measure of inner speech in deaf children. He gave children word lists to remember, using homophonous and then non-homophonous words (i.e. the words either sounded alike, or were phonemically different). Many deaf children in Conrad's study found the homophonous list no more difficult than the non-homophonous. There was no phonemic *interference* on recall. The few deaf children who did show phonemic confusions during recall could be said to be using an inner speech code. They have to be mentally 'hearing' the words when they read, for this effect to take place. On the other hand, children showing no interference may be said to have no inner speech and to be using some other kind of coding strategy. That is, they may be relying on the visual features of words, rather than the sound features.

Conrad puts such a lot of weight on inner speech because the better readers in his survey of deaf children almost invariably showed phonemic interference. Conrad interprets this to mean that inner speech coding is the defining variable for the deaf child's success. Children displaying more inner speech were more likely to lip-read well, to speak more intelligibly and to read better, and to be thought by their teachers to be more generally competent in language. In reading, Conrad says that inner speech enables the child to 'escape into full phonetic coding' (1979, p. 163). Conrad backs up his argument with reference to the more profoundly hearing-impaired, less-able readers in his study, most of whom read very poorly and showed no evidence of inner speech. Finally, Conrad proposes that many deaf children reach a ceiling in their achievements, a reading plateau beyond which they cannot progress, because the lack of inner speech imposes a limit on how much written language can be acquired.

There are several things wrong with this line of reasoning. We can start with the loose definition of inner speech. Presumably, the concept of internal speech is broad enough to include speech articulation without sound, together with auditory speech imagery which is purely inferred without articulation or inner sound experience. There is no doubt at all that deaf children use some kind of inner code. This might include aspects of gesture, sign language, finger-spelling, as well as inner speech sounds. Where children are taught a sign-language system they can be observed reading into sign, in the sense that signing accompanies 'reading aloud'. We must assume that signing, for this child, can be implicated in the child's inner language code in some way. So, there is uncertainty about whether inner *speech* coding is a prerequisite for reading development.

More importantly, Conrad's test for internal speech is a highly specific short-term memory task. It is a pure assumption that because children elect to use a phonological coding strategy in this short-term memory task, they will always prefer to use the same code in other, more authentic reading tasks. Children do change strategies from task to task and the fallacies of such an assumption have been pointed out with regard to the testing of reading generally. We have already seen that when deaf children are faced with reading tests, such as the Wide-span or Southgate, they may attempt to capitalize on whatever features or cues are available to them and this might involve aspects of speech coding as part of a *mixture* of strategies.

Finally, it has to be said that Conrad's explanation of the link between internal speech and reading is a weak one. The relationships between speech sounds and reading are far more complex than he suggests. If deaf children without internal speech are trapped at a pre-phonetic stage of reading from which they are unable to escape, then we have to dismiss the importance of other linguistic factors to reading: the central aspects of grammar and the important area of semantics. Internal speech within Conrad's explanation of the reading process has a fairly limited, low-order role. This is too simplistic an underlying mechanism which ignores most of the recent ideas about the importance of 'top-down', higher-order, organizational factors for reading. This is not to query the experimental evidence that deaf children are unlikely to use inner speech. But there may be another interpret-ation which accounts for some of the deaf child's problems in reading and writing, which we shall discuss later in this chapter in relation to working memory.

The deaf child's grammar

One of the interesting findings which emerged out of the recent research into reading assessment of the deaf (see Chapter 4) is that children may elect to solve the linguistic puzzles of reading tests by non-verbal strategies. This happens when children are over-whelmed by the complexity of the written material facing them and try to make sense of what they are asked to do by using other available cues in the text. Since deaf children may use non-linguistic or non-syntactically based strategies on reading tests, the question could be asked: 'Do deaf children develop any grammatical com-petence at all?'

We have described syntax as the organizing principles of language which relate sounds to meaning; accordingly, syntax occupies the central position in our model of language study in Figure 4.2. In syntactic skills we can perhaps see the greatest dis-parities between deaf and hearing children in terms of what the child brings to reading, and what reading demands of the child. The research literature reviewed in Chapter 3 indicates that severely hearing-impaired children may be very delayed in their acquisition of the grammar of English language, and this is true of children brought up in an 'oral' or a 'signing' teaching environ-ment. Deaf children are likely to acquire vocabulary more slowly, the different stages of grammatical development appear later, and control of more complex syntax may be much more difficult to achieve, in comparison with hearing children. The consensus view, however, is that deaf children continue to make slow but consistent progress throughout their school years in their grammatical skills.

Undoubtedly, the best approach to assessing the functional linguistic skills of the hearing-impaired is to make detailed observations of deaf children themselves. It will be recalled that traditional evaluations of deaf children, for example, using reading yardsticks designed for hearing groups, are insensitive to emerging reading skills in the deaf child. The work by Quigley and his associates (1976) is the only comprehensive attempt to date, to find out what deaf children do when they read, and which gives reliable insights into the underlying syntactic competence of the deaf. There are some constraints on this work in that it presented children with isolated sentence material and not an authentic reading context. Nevertheless, since the research was more finely tuned to what the deaf children could actually do (rather than what they *failed* to do), it demonstrated very clearly that developmental progress is made over time, albeit slowly, and this runs counter to the idea of a plateau of language achievement.

To summarize, Quigley demonstrates that deaf children up to and beyond school-leaving age continue to have problems in interpreting particular kinds of sentence structures, such as embedded clause sequences. In contrast, a simple, active, declarative sentence such as

Richard eats an apple.

may be understood very readily. Deaf children master sentences with the Subject-Verb-Object pattern and may tend to apply such a rule to all sentence constructions. Since the SVO pattern does occur very frequently in English, the child following this rule will interpret many sentences correctly. The child assumes that the surface structure of the sentence reflects the deeper meaning, and this is often confirmed in practice. In other words, the first noun encountered is the actor, followed by the action and the acted upon. Unfortunately, English frequently departs from this simple relationship between surface word order and deeper meaning. In passive constructions, for example:

Richard was bitten by the cat.

the deep subject of the sentence is not Richard, whilst the cat is the actor, not the acted upon. Most hearing children by the time they reach school age, will have a sophisticated enough grasp of syntax to know that this is a sentence in the passive voice and should be interpreted accordingly.

Another principle which deaf (and younger hearing children) adhere to in interpreting sentence structures is the 'Minimum Distance Principle'. Using this strategy the child may identify the noun closest to the verb in the sentence as the subject. In the sentence:

Richard stroked the cat and went to bed.

the subject of the second clause is deleted and has to be inferred. Younger hearing and older deaf children may interpret this to mean that the cat, and not Richard, goes to bed.

We could put forward the suggestion that the imposition by children of rules, such as SVO or MDP, occur because they do not understand what else to do. The strategy simply tells us that children will make an active effort to make sense of language structures which are beyond their control.

Several questions arise from these findings. Why is it that deaf children adhere to these rules for much longer than hearing children? Is it because deaf children never move beyond simple sentence structures in their control of oral, spoken language? If so, why not? Could that be a product of learning experiences at home and at school: less rich, less nurturing language interchanges? At least some of the answers to these questions are partly resolved when we consider the role of auditory memory, discussed later in this chapter. However, one argument which has appeal to a lot of researchers is that the reading problem experienced by the deaf child is caused by a straightforward mismatch between the child's control of syntax and the more complicated syntax of written materials. If that is correct, the logical step to take would be to reduce the linguistic mismatch in both written and spoken language input to the child, such as by modifying the text in books. In the following study an attempt was made to address that particular question of whether the reading difficulty of hearing-impaired children is caused by a discrepancy between existing syntactic skills and the language met by the child in books.

A diagnostic reading battery

Most of the earlier evaluations of deaf children's reading have given scant information about how children read, which children are progressing better than others, and what skills and strategies are important to foster. To try and observe the 'fine grain' behaviour of deaf children reading we devised a new informal reading comprehension test (Webster, 1983). We were interested in what readers try to do with the task and how they go about solving the linguistic puzzles presented. The framework of investigation advocated by Clark (1980) in mainstream reading research seems most likely to yield relevant information here: the study of what the skilled reader can do and what the beginner is attempting to do. There is interest, too, in the emergence of skills in deaf readers over time: how different age groups move on in their reading. Close observation of deaf children as they interact with reading material is likely to reveal the strengths and weaknesses of deaf readers. Hopefully, this kind of study will reveal more about the strategies deaf children adopt as they encounter reading materials and how they attempt a synthesis of the written message, given the linguistic abilities they bring to the reading task. In the end, the utility of this research can be assessed in terms of how it translates into teaching practice: what can we teach the child to do better?

Eighty children took part in the study. Each child had an average hearing loss of more than 70 decibels in the better ear, with no other handicap, and with a pre-lingual hearing-impairment as far as could be ascertained. The sample had an equal number of boys and girls in four age groups of 8, 9, 10 and 11 years, with twenty children in each. A battery of graded reading materials was devised to look more systematically at the points at which reading difficulties arose when the child reads for meaning. One possible source of reading failure is the syntactic complexity of the sentence material. So we controlled the complexity of the grammar used according to the LARSP framework devised by Crystal, Fletcher and Garman (1976). Essentially, LARSP provides a profile of the grammatical patterns which appear in children's language as they progress from the most primitive stages, through to the stages at which most of the grammatical features of the adult language are mastered. Using LARSP as a reference, it is possible to devise written materials which only contain syntactic structures occurring at one particular stage in the sequence of normal language development. LARSP enabled us to 'hold' the syntactic complexity of the sentences used in the reading battery at the stage where complex, co-ordinated and embedded sentences being to appear. This is the point at which deaf children have problems, but of course, these features are normally mastered by hearing pre-schoolers and are commonplace in text.

One other source of reading failure is the amount of information contained within written material. Even though two sentences may have similar grammatical complexity, one sentence may have many more elements of meaning than the other: there may be more information presented to the reader. This aspect too, can be controlled. Yet another source of reading failure for the deaf child is lack of familiarity with vocabulary. Here too, it is possible to control the difficulty level of the words used in text. In order to make the present material as accessible as possible to hearing-impaired children, vocabulary was drawn from the spoken vocabulary lists prepared by Bench and Bamford (1979). In this instance the vocabulary for our reading test was that known to be familiar to children aged 8–10 years, across the normal ability range, and with hearing losses in excess of 80 decibels. In summary, the interest lay in how children read for meaning, in sentences with graded amounts of information, using familiar vocabulary, but in grammatical patterns of a consistently challenging complexity.

The reading battery consisted of a series of pictures and accompanying sentences. The child is asked to look at each picture and select one of three or four alternative sentences which goes with the picture. For each sentence presented to the child there is a vocabulary check: if the child fails to understand the meaning of an item in sentence form, the sentence is presented again with the important vocabulary highlighted. So, for example, in the first section of the battery a picture of an object, such as a bus, is presented and the child is asked to pick the correct sentence from amongst:

A. What you are looking at is very much like a car.
B. It is something like a train that you can see.
C. Perhaps it is a bus which is in the picture.

All of the sentences have a grammatical structure with 'recursive' features which allow clauses to be embedded one within another, and the co-ordination and subordination of one clause with another.

If the child fails to select the sentence which is associated with the picture of a bus, the child is then asked to read the important vocabulary:

A. car
B. train
C. bus

In the second section of the battery a typical picture shows apples on a table. The child has to pick the appropriate sentence from these four:

A. Those are apples which are on the tree.
B. Those are bananas which are on the table.
C. Those are bananas which are on the tree.
D. Those are apples which are on the table.

If the child fails, the sentences are presented again as follows:

A. apples   tree
B. bananas   table
C. bananas   tree
D. apples   table

An item drawn from the third section of the battery shows a spoon behind a cup. The child has to find the target sentence from amongst:

    A. The cake has been put behind where the plate is.
    B. The spoon has been put in front of where the cup is.
    C. The cake has been put in front of where the plate is.
    D. The spoon has been put behind where the cup is.

The target sentence in this case would be presented in degraded form as:

    D. spoon   behind   cup

In the fourth section of the battery the child is given a picture such as a cow trampling upon flowers on a hillside. There are four sentences in the item, which remain at complex-clause level (stage 5). However, each sentence now has four elements of meaning:

    A. The cow is breaking the flowers which are on the hill.
    B. The cat is jumping the fence which is in the field.
    C. The cow is breaking the fence which is on the hill.
    D. The cat is breaking the flowers which are in the field.

The degraded target sentence appears as:

    A. cow   breaking   flowers   hill

For every child tackling the reading battery we have two scores: firstly, the number of items passed where the child was able to read for meaning in grammatically complex sentence structures; secondly, those items where the child needed to be shown the important vocabulary in order to make the right choice. If children failed on the first presentation of the sentences, but succeeded when given the vocabulary in isolation, we assumed that they had been confused by the syntax. Some children failed at both levels. The major findings of this study are that hearing loss itself, bearing in mind that all the children were severely hearing-impaired, was not a major factor in determining success on the reading task. Overall scores on the test showed that the older the child, the better the scores became. So, reading comprehension on this test continues to improve across all the age ranges: it does not plateau. The different age groups tended to produce different patterns of errors.

The youngest children made many more errors involving grammar; they were more easily confused by sentence syntax, but could usually succeed when given the vocabulary. Older children made fewer errors over grammar or vocabulary and approached 100 per cent success. Perhaps the most surprising of the findings was that many of the children found the sentences with the most information content more easy to get right than the sentences with only limited elements of meaning. In other words, many of the groups of children found the four-element sentences just as easy, or indeed, easier to get right, than the three-, two- and one-element sentences. The scores often improved in the later, and what might be felt to be the most difficult, sections of the reading battery.

How can this be explained? It will be helpful at this point to consider one aspect in which spoken language differs from written language. In written language there are no situational or social clues to meaning. In spoken language the social, non-linguistic context provides the child with clues to interpret what is being said. The younger the child, the greater the reliance upon evidence provided by the context of conversation. Print, on the other hand, is *decontextualized* in the sense that the child's understanding must come from the printed page. Nevertheless, there are many ways in which written materials do provide clues to meaning, quite apart from syntax and vocabulary. One of the findings from the studies of assessment of deaf children's reading, reported in Chapter 4, is that deaf children often adopt consistent strategies which capitalize on the less obvious sources of information in test materials. We could anticipate that this might also occur with the reading battery which we devised.

An examination of the reading strategies adopted by the children tackling the test battery is very revealing. Analysing the items which many children made errors upon, shows yet again, that the deaf children often agreed on what should be the preferred sentence choice, even though this was the incorrect response. So deaf children did tackle the material systematically and were exploiting some particular features of the test items in order to make their decisions. What might these features be? In the following item there was agreement amongst the deaf children, beyond chance, upon the sentence which is in italics (the correct response is marked with an asterisk):

> There is a cat and it is sitting on a roof.
> * There is a fence which has a boy sitting on it.
> *There is a boy who is falling off a roof.*
> There falling off a fence is a cat.

Here a specific rule akin to the minimum distance principle, mentioned earlier, would appear to be operating. There are three competing nouns in subject position. The child who is uncertain of the syntax structures seems to select out of the sentence frames the nearest available sentence subject, in the sense of first to emerge going from left to right. Since the picture illustrates a boy sitting on a fence, we have to accept that what the child does is to disregard some of the meaning content of the sentences. Some elements do not enter into the decision-making process. So the child simplifies the nature of the task that is faced, since some of the grammatical and meaning features are outside the child's awareness. In essence, it is the child's over-simplification of the reading task which creates problems of understanding. The child disregards some of the important modifications to meaning which are embedded in the sentence syntax.

In this particular test the pictures and sentences are presented together so that the child can seek out the critical sentence features which the picture primes. At this point, we can suggest, the child uses a broader knowledge of language use, beyond syntax and literal meaning. In terms of our language model the child draws on experience of the semantic aspects of language in use. These would include the child's anticipation of how reading tests are usually devised, the kind of responses expected from previous experience, the likely intentions of the test author, together with all those potential cue sources not contained within the sentence itself. Semantic features enable the child to negotiate between the picture and the sentences provided in order to make a response to the question: 'What does this picture represent in relation to the sentence elements I can identify?'. Certainly, it is these factors which the child utilizes rather than syntactic information.

The sentences in the reading battery which carried the most information (or number of elements of meaning) were more likely to be answered correctly than the sentences which presented less information content to the child. One very important point then, is that children may be helped in their search for meaning, if there is *more* rather than *less* information, upon which to base a choice. To put this another way, the child is helped in his search for the critical features in sentence material if there are more rather than fewer, to differentiate. This point we shall be pursuing further in the following chapter when we consider the modification of reading materials for deaf children.

To summarize, we do not have a published reading test in the United Kingdom based on close observations of what deaf children try to do when they read. There is a need for such an instrument to assess vocabulary knowledge, growth of grammatical skills together with the child's ability to use information outside the sentence context. Detailed observations based on the deaf themselves do show improvements in all these skills over time. The concept of a plateau of achievement seems likely to be a product of insensitive test procedures which obscure the slower developments in deaf children's language skills. It is clear that children with more limited vocabulary and syntax resources will try to make sense of written material in different ways: by simplifying the questions asked of text, and utilizing other cue sources. In order to do that the child depends on the richness of information in text, and that has important implications for the kind of materials we give to the child, as well as for the reading strategies that we endeavour to teach. We may find that it is more effective to modify the way in which the child seeks out meaning in text, rather than modifying the materials themselves.

How do these findings relate to the framework of description introduced in Chapter 4: the different approaches which have been made to the reading strategies of ordinary readers in mainstream research? 'Bottom-up' factors in terms of identifying keywords may be involved. However, when the deaf children were asked to read the sentence material they did not rely very much on 'bottom-up', text-based strategies such as decoding symbols into sounds or signs. From the behaviour observed it is unlikely that this group of children saw the reading task as one of decoding word-by-word into speech or sign, because that is not what they tried to do. Instead, they were much more likely to use alternative cue sources and strategies, those indirect 'top-down' routes to meaning.

In the reading battery, deaf children did attempt to resolve their uncertainties by making predictions about what the picture represented, which features in the sentences were critical, and which aspects to disregard. They sometimes imposed over-simple hypotheses when they sampled too narrowly and made errors. Nevertheless, these were skills which improved with age and which enabled the older children to achieve a high degree of success. In more authentic text-reading situations there are many more 'pragmatic' clues based on everyday experience which the reader can utilize. It is precisely because the activity of reading embodies such higher level expectations of meaning in text that we can conceive of reading with very little attention to individual words. Inevitably, descriptions of 'top-down' processes in reading, where the reader *interacts* with text in solving the linguistic puzzles therein, are fairly complex. What it is that good readers exploit in text and which aspects of text attention is paid to are difficult to disentangle.

As we hinted in Chapter 4, there is still a lot of debate about the relative contributions of 'bottom-up' and 'top-down' skills in reading. Some researchers have opted for the compromise view, which integrates aspects of both approaches (Stanovich, 1980). Stanovich's view of reading and its difficulties gives a useful perspective on the problems faced by deaf readers. He argues that good and poor readers rely on different kinds of information whilst reading. The more skilled readers have efficient and automatic 'bottom-up' processes, such as decoding graphemes into phonemes. They arrive at a stage of direct access to meaning through word identification. Poor readers, however, gain less information from the lower 'bottom-up' levels and never arrive at the direct-access stage. Instead, they achieve comprehension of text by making greater use of higher order clues to meaning. They attempt to problem-solve using grammatical, semantic and pragmatic features to generate and test out hypotheses about text. This, of course, requires much more thinking and effort than the automatic processes used by good readers. That explains why poor readers read more slowly, make more errors and have to work harder at getting the meaning. Stanovich uses the term 'attentional capacity' to describe the thinking space required during reading, for example, in order to integrate new information with old. 'Top-down' routes to meaning may be more hazardous than reading at a direct, context-free, sight-word level, because they are inefficient and use up more of the available attentional capacity, or thinking space. So, the poor reader may have problems in relating what is read to what is already known (which is how comprehension might be defined) because of the effort that has to be put into reading in the first place.

In the studies of deaf readers as they tackle reading tests, as well as in the reading battery, the children relied on special strategies which use cues over and above low-level decoding cues and even, in some instances, utilizing non-linguistic information. We may have to accept that deaf children may never achieve the kind of underlying linguistic mastery and sophistication enjoyed by their hearing peers. It seems unlikely then that the deaf child will ever perceive reading as a process of transducing print into spoken language, where print is derived from spoken language structures in the first place. We may need to accept that the deaf child will depend more heavily upon indirect routes to meaning, using a wide range of potential sources of information. When we come to consider teaching intervention it may be sensible to work from the child's strengths and help the child to be a more effective 'top-downer'.

In this respect, some of the ideas which have sprung from 'top-down' models may be relevant, such as the emphasis on making better predictions of meaning. Low-order skills, such as decoding into sound, may be less relevant; although paradoxically, remedial teachers have often taught these low-level skills to poor readers, whilst asking good readers to rely more on context.

Reading and the thinking code

The problem-solving strategies of deaf children when they tackle reading materials do seem to be different in kind from those of hearing peers. In Chapter 4 attention was drawn to some of the passive, uncritical styles of learning which deaf children present, such as a reluctance to self-monitor or check responses in a reading test. It is also apparent that deaf children may well be looking to non-verbal cues in written materials, beyond the boundaries of the sentence. Some researchers, such as Quigley *et al.* (1976) believe that it is the *mismatch* between the linguistic complexity of written materials, which is the source of reading problems. It is certainly evident that major difficulties arise when deaf children face complex syntactic structures in text. But the nature of the reading problem is not so straightforward as mismatching. At this point we turn to the heart of the issue: the relationship between how the child thinks about and *codes* experience, and what is found in print.

It has been said that inner language, the internal speech of the normally-hearing child, provides both the major tool for thinking and the foundation stone for reading and writing (Quigley and Kretschmer, 1982). As a corollary, lack of inner speech has been taken to be the primary cause of the deaf child's deficiencies in reading and writing. Conrad (1979), for example, using a test for internal speech, has claimed that this is the critical variable (rather than hearing loss or intelligence) for success in reading.

The assumption which is made is that the child's inner coding system is implicated in some intervening way during reading. The typical reader is felt not to go directly from the written word to meaning, but must first decode print into its spoken form, to allow the reader to discover its meaning. We have discussed the relative status of these auditory factors in relation to reading and language generally. There is a lot of disagreement about whether inner speech is necessary for reading and whether good readers depend upon it. What can be said, without a doubt, is that at some point in the reading process, the written message must make contact with the child's own inner language system: the child's inner code for thinking. For the hearing child this does not pose much of a problem since we can take for granted that an inner code must relate in one way or another to a grasp of the spoken language. For the deaf child, on the other hand, there is the crucial problem of determining what kind of inner coding is used. If severely deaf children do not use inner speech, then what do they use?

Almost all of the existing research into cognitive mechanisms and the deaf has been concerned with the coding systems which individuals adopt when given a specific task (usually a memory task) to do. In one experiment (Chen, 1976) hearing, moderately hearing-impaired and deaf students, were given a passage to read and told to mark out all the 'e' letters as they read. The researcher thought that if subjects were decoding the material using a speech form, then the silent 'e's, such as the final 'e' in 'bite', would be overlooked because there is no sound component when this silent 'e' is pronounced. On the other hand, 'e's *with* an acoustic image, such as the 'e' in 'bed', should not be missed if a speech code is being used. As predicted, the hearing students and those with only moderate hearing losses, were much more likely to miss silent 'e's than the deafest group with hearing losses greater than 80 decibels. The conclusion was drawn that the greater the hearing loss, the more likely that a visual recoding system is used.

Other workers have looked at the influence of finger spelling on the recall errors of deaf children learning pairs of letters. Locke and Locke (1971) showed that children who had been taught to use finger spelling were more likely to rely on visual finger shapes as they memorized letters. Letters which looked the same on the fingers were more likely to be confused. Just as finger spelling can be a viable memory code, so sign language can serve as a memory code for those children who have been taught to sign. Many studies show that when children are familiar with signs they may remember words according to sign features. The sign for 'vote' has the same handshape as the sign for 'tea', and deaf children asked to remember the word 'vote' often recalled it as 'tea'. This research, and a body of studies on the symbolic mediation used by deaf children, addressing the question 'What kind of inner code?', is reviewed by Hirsh-Pasek and Treiman (1982).

The research evidence on the thinking codes available to deaf children seems very diverse in its findings and there is a good reason for this. The deaf child's coding system must be based on features which have significance for the individual. Some aspects of the speech signal will still be accessible, even to profoundly deaf children, such as rhythm, intonation, or residual sound signals. In natural communication situations non-verbal cues may mark linguistic forms, such as facial expression, lip movements, or gestures. In reading, there will be fewer context clues, but it is not impossible for deaf children to infer aspects such as lip patterns which accompany the sound features of written language. The fact is we do not know which aspects of communication situations, spoken language or print, can be utilized by the child as a tool for thinking. When children read for meaning they may elect to use one of a number of options. Their inner representations of the written language may have a mixture of features, including auditory clues as well as information beyond the sound signal. Unfortunately, non-speech codes may be at a disadvantage when used to transduce printed words, since these derive from spoken forms in the first place. The implication of this will become clear when we come to consider the child's working memory and how this depends on the kind of inner coding the child is able to use.

We have argued that the deaf child's inner language may be a much more idiosyncratic system than the hearing child's. The deaf child may 'think': in terms of visual patterns seen on the lips, or in sign; in terms of sound features; by utilizing some elements of vocabulary and syntax; together with any other sources of information. These are all potential facets of an inner thinking code. The question is: Does this choice of inner code place any limits on the child's thinking capacity for spoken or written English language forms?.

Working memory

Recent work on the processes of short-term memory in hearing children has important implications for the hearing-impaired. It has been argued that one facility which everybody needs in order to understand and use language is a means of storing verbal material. If we did not have such a storage system it would be hard to deal with spoken sentences, because information at the beginning of a sentence has to be retained long enough to work out how this relates to information at the end of a sentence. This would be especially true of more complex sentences where the relationship between the words and the meaning is not straightforward. We have seen that in passive sentence structures the surface order of the words in the sentence may not reflect the deeper meaning. In order to be able to infer meaning we have to be able to hold on to the word sequence in our heads, until we have worked out the sense of what is being said.

Baddeley (1976) has tried to explain how we might process verbal material in terms of a theory of working memory. He proposes a dual memory system. One part of the system is used for the temporary storing of speech-like material. Baddeley describes an 'articulatory loop', which is a kind of slave system where sound sequences are stored and rehearsed. This articulatory loop retains verbal information just long enough for a decision to be made about what it means. The verbal loop depends upon the child having inner speech. The second component of working memory is the 'central executive'. This is the part of the system responsible for processing and decision-making. The verbal loop maintains material until it can be organized centrally by the executive.

One of the characteristics of the ear as a sensory organ is that it processes information along a time dimension. Unlike the eye, which can take in a lot of visual input simultaneously, or at the same point in time, the ear processes input as a succession of events over time. We need some kind of rehearsal system to hold these events in store in order to make sense of a whole sequence of speech input where meaning is inferred from the relationships between individual words. Inner speech and the rehearsal loop are specially designed to cope with speech-like information. If a child does not have inner speech, but some other kind of code, such as a visually-based system, there may be consequences for the verbal loop system. In other words, severely hearing-impaired children may be disadvantaged in their *processing* of language because they lack inner speech and access to working memory systems.

Baddeley has suggested a number of areas in which the temporary storage system of working memory plays a part. One important area is in reading (Baddeley, 1979). The articulatory loop is said to have a useful role for normal children learning to read. It enables the child to rehearse the word order of print, to retain the surface structure of text until meaning is derived. Experimental studies have shown that poor readers are less able to rehearse and retain serial information. Work with deaf children (Lake, 1978) suggests that the ability to recall sequential information on a short-term memory task is closely related to the child's skills in using syntactic structures in writing. So, in understanding language and in language-related activities such as reading and writing, some kind of temporary store is required. Information about the grammatical structure of a sentence, together with information about individual words, must be retained long enough to discern the semantic relationships between words in a sentence. The more complex, embedded or co-ordinated the relationships between phrases and clause structures, the greater the demands upon such storage facilities. But it is difficult to see how speech and language comprehension could proceed without some kind of short-term store.

This throws a different light on the function of inner speech. We have so far discussed inner speech in relation to reading. Conrad (1979), for example, gives internal speech a limited, low-order role. He links inner speech to the phonological abilities of the reader. In his view, internal speech helps the child to become phonetic: to decode print into speech sounds. This is an overly simplistic view of the factors important to reading, and to language generally. Viewed simply in relation to phonological skills, the significance of inner speech must be very limited. This is particularly true of hearing-impaired children, who may rely less on these low-order skills in reading than on 'top-down' strategies.

However, if internal speech is looked at from the point of view of working memory, it assumes a much greater significance. It is not so much decoding which is the problem, as a more central limitation on the child's cognitive processing capacity. An attempt was made in the following studies, reported in this chapter, to investigate the role of feedback mechanisms and re-hearsal systems in reading and writing. We begin with a study which tested out the importance of short-term memory in the reading comprehension of deaf children.

Critical features, short-term memory and the articulatory loop

In the diagnostic reading battery described earlier the child was given several series of sentences, carefully graded according to grammar and meaning, and asked to select a target sentence to go with a picture. The test was given in such a way that the child was able to see both the sentences and picture together. Since the sentences and picture could be seen at the same time the child was allowed cross-reference between the two. Many of the children, particularly the older deaf children, did very well on this test and approached 100 per cent success. An account was made of how the child tackles this material by locating the salient features of the written sentences, primed by the picture stimulus. The success of the deaf child in this task appears to be greatly aided if there is more information presented. Sentences with fewer semantic features were more difficult. Data from the item analysis suggests that children do identify what seem to be the critical features of each sentence relative to the picture. In order to succeed with more complex test items the child has to hold one critical feature in memory and then search for other features which will enable the child to make the right sentence choice. Sentences with four critical features of meaning posed little problem. We have identified some of the cue sources which enable the child to do this, including syntax, as well as pragmatic information beyond the sentence, such as what experience tells the child will be the likely answer. When children agreed on an incorrect choice this was often because they oversimplified the critical features required. The children always made partial solutions: they got some features right, but disregarded others.

In a follow-up study (Webster, 1983), a variation was intro-duced on the original task which tested out the processing capacity of the deaf child. We wanted to know how far this specific reading task depended on good short-term memory. The task as it stood did not require much short-term storage capacity, because the pictures and sentences were presented together for the child to see. With slight changes, the reading battery could be made to depend more heavily on short-term recall. This would give important evidence in relation to the question of whether internal speech was involved in phonological coding, or more centrally in processing capacity, when the child reads.

Twenty hearing-impaired children took part in the study. To be included, each child had to have an average hearing loss of more than 70 decibels in the better ear, have no other significant handicap and be pre-lingually deaf as far as could be established. The sample had an equal number of boys and girls aged 11 years. A control group of twenty hearing children was selected with equal numbers of boys and girls between the ages of 8 and 9 years. These children were matched with the deaf subjects on the basis of IQ and reading age. We also included a group of normally-hearing 11-year-olds in the study who were matched according to chronological age, but who were much better readers than any of the other groups.

What we did was to give a section of the reading battery to all of the children. For example, in the following item the material consists of a picture of a man giving a doll to a boy and the correct sentence has to be located from amongst:

A. Mummy gave the ball to the girl who was there.
B. Daddy took the ball from the girl who was there.
C. Mummy took the doll from the boy who was there.
D. Daddy gave the doll to the boy who was there.

All the children were given the sentence and picture material to inspect together with cross-reference allowed, as in the original procedure. Shortly afterwards, the same sentences were given to every child without the picture present. The sentence and picture material could not be looked at together or cross-references made between the two. After a delay of 10 seconds the picture was introduced, whilst the sentences were removed, and the child asked to recall, by marking a selection from A to D, which sentence fitted the picture.

Under the original conditions of the reading battery the deaf children achieved over 90 per cent success, a similar finding to the earlier study. However, under the revised procedure correct responses dropped to about 45 per cent. The younger hearing children under the original conditions made 70 per cent correct choices, but this dropped to 52 per cent under the revised procedure. Scores for the older hearing children were not really disrupted by the change in procedure and they were still able to achieve more than 80 per cent. What these results indicate is that the 'top-down' reading strategies of deaf children, as they search out the critical features for meaning, are easily disrupted. Once the children were asked to hold the information in a short-term store, even though they had just tackled the same material successfully, correct responses fell drastically. Young hearing children were also affected in the same way, although older hearing children were not affected. This would suggest that short-term memory, and perhaps access to the inner rehearsal facilities of working memory, improves alongside growing expertise in reading itself.

In this chapter we have characterized deaf children as readers in terms of the 'top-down' strategies they endeavour to use. Arguably, the most efficient approach to reading is to access meaning directly from print. The interactive model of reading suggests that good readers are so efficient in their ability to maintain the flow of information upwards from the page, that these 'bottom-up' skills become automatic. Good readers then have the capacity to think about what they are reading, and to engage in other cognitive processes, such as relating new information to old. The deaf child on the other hand, may make efforts to derive meaning from text by utilizing cues from a multiplicity of levels. Our knowledge of normal reading development suggests that reading strategies which involve searching around for clues amongst the visual, phonemic, syntactic, semantic or pragmatic features of text, will make heavy demands on the child's thinking and processing capacity. In this respect the deaf child might be compared with the poor hearing reader, who also depends more on prediction-based and hypothesis-testing strategies. This less efficient approach to reading presumes that there is a flow of information outwards from higher intellectual levels to the page; the brain directs the eye to the sort of information the reader expects to find in print. The question is – at what cost to the child's thinking capacity?

One thing which emerges clearly from the experiments reported here is that the deaf child's strategies can be disrupted very easily by putting extra demands on short-term memory. The importance of inner speech in short-term memory, particularly when the child is dealing with verbal information, is critical. Those who have written widely about the deaf (such as Conrad) have never really discerned the central role which internal speech plays in language-related activities. The important implication of the present studies is the role of internal speech, not to phonological coding, but in providing access to the articulatory rehearsal system of working memory. In hearing children, facility in using internal speech may develop alongside emerging reading skills. For the deaf the limitations of access to working memory because of the lack of inner speech may explain why these children continue to have difficulties in language-related activities, since the basic cognitive framework for handling extended verbal sequences is undeveloped. The deaf child is forced into adopting processing strategies which are to some extent incompatible with the patterns of spoken language reflected in print. In the following section the important role of feedback and short-term storage mechanisms is explored in relation to another aspect of language activity: writing.

Writing and deafness

Writing is not a simple process of transcribing speech into printed symbols; nor can it be considered as the equal, but opposite process to reading: encoding information in words, as opposed to decoding. When professional writers have asked themselves what seems to be involved in the act of writing, most describe three distinct stages. (Beard, 1984; Smith, 1982). In the first stage, writers compose: they decide what they are going to say. This is really a *pre-writing* phase when writers 'listen' to their own ideas before setting them down on paper. The activity in the second stage involves translating ideas into the formal structures of written language. A network of skills is demanded. Handwriting and spelling affect the ease with which a reader may respond to a person's writing. However, the more central aspects which affect the meaning of what is written involve the vocabulary chosen, how sentences are constructed, and how sentences are linked together to make a cohesive text. The third stage is one of subsequent review or inspection of what has been written. Without the reappraisal stage it is difficult to imagine how writers could develop the cohesion of their texts: the interweaving of sentences by devices such as pronouns, conjunctions, and various forms of cross-reference (Halliday and Hasan, 1976).

In the present book much more space has been devoted to reading than writing, and this reflects the relative priority which is usually assigned to the two activities. Despite a predominant view that reading is more important than writing, in fact, the written language of the deaf has been studied more extensively than any other aspects. Writing is easier to study, in the sense that it can be inspected visually and the marks on the page stay still. Almost all of the earlier research on the writing of deaf children is descriptive: quantifying the number of nouns, verbs, adjectives and kinds of error made. In this section, a rather different approach to writing is attempted, focusing on the cognitive aspects of writing. We shall be discussing the broader linguistic skills involved in writing. But we shall also be discussing the notions of short-term storage and articulatory feedback loops in relation to the writing act, particularly as they affect stages of pre-writing and inspection.

The background research on deaf children's writing was discussed in Chapter 3, and much of this is summarized in the study by Cooper and Rosenstein (1966). They suggest that deaf children use shorter and simpler sentences, with less-flexible word order. There are more 'content' words, such as nouns, verbs or adjectives, and fewer 'function' words, such as prepositions, articles and conjunctions. Deaf children tend to keep to one particular sentence pattern, such as Subject-Verb-Object, and there are many errors and non-standard usages, or 'deafisms'.

The major limitation of descriptive studies is that they tend to point only towards a lack of organization in the deaf child's language. This factor we have highlighted in reading assessment too, as part of a deficit model approach. It is only recently that writers such as Quigley *et al.* (1976), have looked at the systematic nature of the deaf child's written language. Quigley's work suggests that deaf children have the greatest difficulties in writing sentences with embedded relationships, relative structures and passive voice. In fact, any sentence patterns beyond SVO may be difficult. However, deaf children do improve their writing skills over time. One question which has often arisen in relation to the writing of the deaf is whether it reflects a delay or a deviance in language development.

Ivimey (1976) addresses this question of deviance in his study. Deviance in language refers to characteristics which are never seen in normal children's usage; that is, they are part of a unique system used by deaf children only. Ivimey feels there is evidence of both deviance and delay. Some of the features of deaf children's writing can be seen in much younger hearing children's written efforts. Older deaf children, despite the fact that they may have a much poorer grasp of the language system, will be attempting to express more sophisticated ideas and concepts than hearing infants. It could be said that the unusual features of the written language of the deaf result from a breakdown of the child's language system, inadequate to the pressure of the older deaf child's communication needs.

Many normally-hearing children and children with only moderate hearing losses may have difficulties in writing. The piece of writing in Figure 5.1 is taken from a 10-year old girl with a moderate sensori-neural hearing loss, of above-average intelligence. There are several positive aspects one can draw attention to in this piece of work, as well as some weak aspects. The child has learnt a good deal about story structure. She begins the piece in traditional style: 'One day . . . ', and ends it with an appropriate summary of the events in her story: 'So that is our favourite summer holiday.' Hearing-impaired children may find the use of a complex function word, such as 'that', very difficult. A word like 'that' has an abstract meaning: it refers back to the child's story.

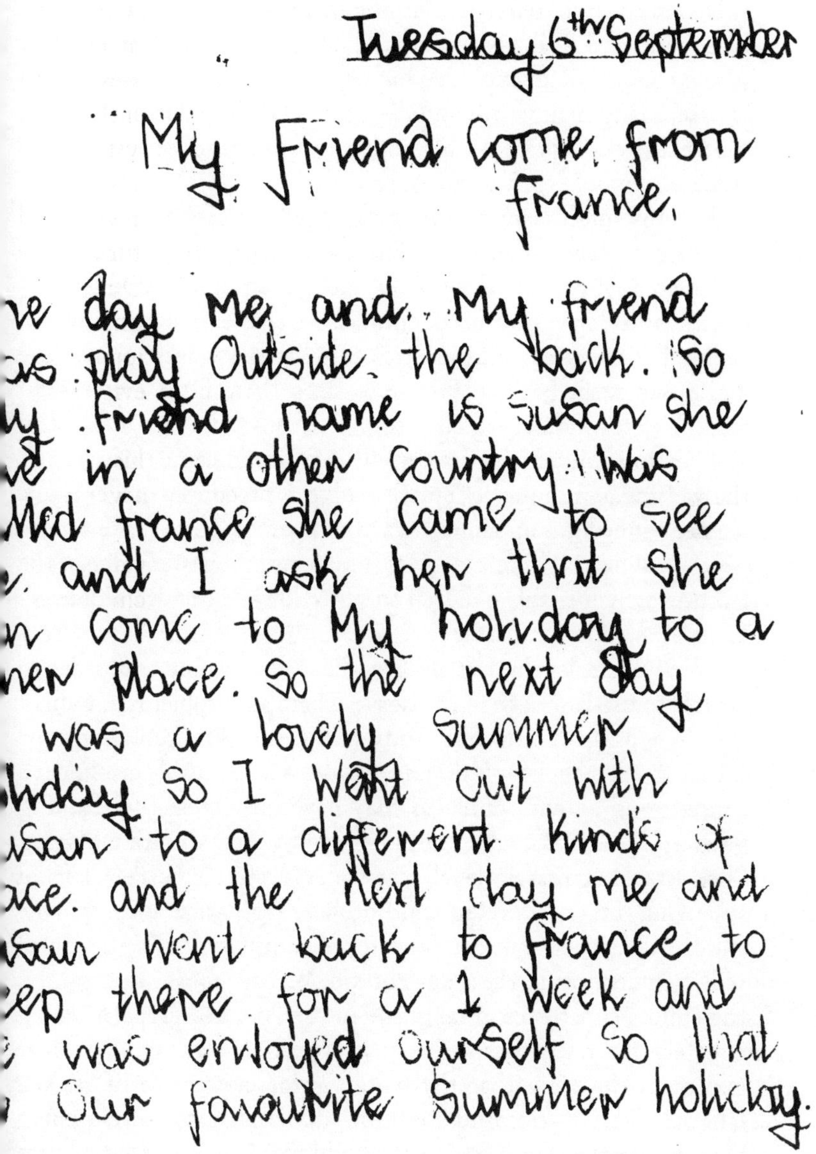

Tuesday 6th September

My Friend Come from france.

ne day Me and My friend
as play Outside the back. So
y friend name is Susan she
e in a other Country was
lled france she Came to see
. and I ask her that she
n come to My holiday to a
ner place. So the next day
was a lovely Summer
liday So I Went out with
san to a different kinds of
ace. and the next day me and
san went back to france to
ep there for a 1 week and
was enloyed ourself so that
Our favourite Summer holiday.

Figure 5.1 Written work by a 10-year-old girl with a moderate sensori-neural hearing loss

It has no concrete referent; it is not an object or an action that can be experienced. It is a grammatical device which has meaning only in the context of an extended sequence of language. There are, of course, many such words and the child's facility in using complex sentences will depend on his mastery of function words, such as 'where', 'who', 'but', and 'which'.

Throughout the piece this girl is generating some long and complex sentence sequences. The use of connecting devices like 'the next day' give some sense of time sequence. Many of her sentences have fairly advanced phrase and clause structures which enable her to extend and interrelate what she wants to say: 'me and Susan went back to France to sleep there for a 1 week and we . . . '. Pronouns, again a source of difficulty for many deaf and hearing children, are used well: 'My friend name is Susan . . . she'. Using a pronoun to replace a subject introduced earlier is one way of connecting up sentences across a paragraph to make a more cohesive whole. This child, then, has begun to master some of the features which enable children to write long, extended sequences to make a coherent passage.

What obstacles do deaf children have to surmount in order to be able to use language in this way? There are problems in each of the three areas of language study outlined in Figure 4.2. At the sound level, the key function words which enable a child to connect and extend sentences may have only weak and fleeting stress in speech: they may not be heard by a child with a hearing loss. At the syntactic level, these devices are relatively late in appearing in the development of language structures, so the child's inexperience in handling more complex syntax structures will include most of these devices too. Perhaps most importantly, the child's experience of language in use does not prepare her adequately for the structures which appear in writing. We have expressed the view that the child's prior experience of spoken language, its function and intention, underpins later development in using written language. If the child has only limited exposure to function words, embedded sentences, and complex syntax in spoken discourse, then she will be less well prepared to recognize and use these features in written language. So, it is not simply a problem of mapping the rules for spoken sentences onto written sentence structures. Rather, the problems of sustaining dialogue and enjoying complex linguistic interactions with deaf children in conversation constrains the range of usage to which the deaf child puts written language.

The child's writing in Figure 5.1 shows, through its awkward lack of fluency, that there is still a lot to learn. A feature which characterizes the passage is that she consistently keeps to one sentence pattern beginning with: 'So . . . '. The use of 'So' invites us to expect that the ideas expressed in each sentence follow on as a result of what went before. Since this is not usually true of this child's piece it could be said that the child has learnt the device mechanically, and does not always use it with the appropriate intention. It is one means by which the girl links up her material. She may not have mastered the broader range of devices available to help connect her ideas together. In several places where there is uncertainty as to how to relate one element to another, she simply disregards the formal grammatical means: 'She live in a other country was called France she came to see me'. An embedded sentence using 'who' or 'which' is well beyond her control. The end product is that ideas come flooding out of the sentence without the organization of formal syntax. This is what is meant when it is said that the pressure of the child's communication needs bursts out of the limited language structures at her disposal.

This difficulty in writing extended sentence sequences and in connecting sentences together in discourse, has been highlighted by many researchers working with the deaf, and is also shown by less able and younger hearing children (Kretschmer, 1978). We have said that such skills are acquired later on in the development of spoken language, and one important factor is the child's prior experience of discourse and complex language forms in communication generally. Children with good writing skills are reflecting their knowledge of vocabulary, sentence syntax, together with insights about the way in which meaning emerges in context, gained from a wider experience of language as communication. In the final chapter, the possibilities of actively teaching discourse features to children for use in creating written language are discussed.

This child's writing shows some features held to be character-istic of the hearing-impaired, although it is likely that these aspects characterize the written work of many hearing children who have more limited language experience and control. There is immaturity in the girl's awareness of the critical features of words which govern their use with other words, such as 'a other', 'a different kinds of', 'for a 1 week'. There are particular problems in using correct verb forms and auxiliaries ('was play', 'we was enjoyed'); in using plurals, and possessives ('My friend name', ' a different kinds of place'). Nevertheless, there is an effort to express some fairly complex ideas: 'she came to see me and I ask her that she can come', even though the piece is lacking colour, description and variety. Notice that there are few spelling mistakes, a point we shall take up in the next section.

In Figure 5.2 an 11-year-old, severely hearing-impaired girl is writing about a picture of a busy kitchen scene. This child is much less confident in her use of long, extended sentence sequences and is happy to use a succession of simple sentence structures of three elements, such as Subject-Verb-Object: 'the little girl wanted some strawberries cake'. However, this child makes better use of the noun phrase, such as Determiner-Adjective-Noun: 'The little boy', 'the black boot'. Similarly, she has mastered Preposition-Determiner-Noun: 'under the table', 'behind the step'. In terms of the stage analysis of spoken language which we discussed in Chapter 3 (Crystal *et al.*, 1976) this child is using many structures which appear in the spoken language of most hearing children, at around stage 3, or about 2 to 2½ years of age. These include past tense ('the little girl wanted'); plurals ('vegetables'); and the 'ing' inflection ('drinking'). This child is reaching out to more complex structures, such as connecting sentence elements together with 'and', 'but' or 'then'. An attempt is made to use 'Because', but not very successfully: 'Because he make the aeroplane'. It is clear then, where the child's syntactic control begins to get shaky.

Overall, this piece of written work is very much writing sentence-by-sentence. Wilbur (1977) argues that this is simply to reflect the limited exposure which deaf children have to the discourse features of spoken language: how sentences in a context cross-refer, interrelate and sustain meaning. We have said that

e cat Sitting on the floor. and
-inking the milk. the little girl
-anted Some Strawberries cake.
-e little boy Sitting down under
-e table. Because He make the
-eroplane. the vegetables on the
-uble for dinner. the milk-
-an Came Knock the door. then
-e Lady came open the door.
-e gave a Seven milk to the
-dy. She pay £1.70p to his
-r. him the Black Boot behind
-e Step. the plant blind was
-pen. the rain Coat and rain hat
-ang them. the toys was all.
-ver the mess. the draw was
-pen. the brown Clock. what is
    time? it is 5 past 12.
-nummy Said it is dinner time
-ow.

Figure 5.2 Description of a kitchen scene by an 11-year-old, severely
hearing-impaired girl

one aspect of communication is always difficult for deaf people:
participating in the to and fro of conversation. The suggestion is
that such experience is necessary for writing. To write properly
children require a sophisticated awareness of communicating with
the audience, the reader. It is obvious that this child's concern is in
controlling simple sentence structures, selecting the right verb
and auxiliary: 'the cat sitting on'; putting words in the right
sequence: 'What it is time?'; as well as trying out some personal
ideas about grammar: 'man came knock', 'lady came open'.

The small extract in Figure 5.3 is the writing effort of a profoundly deaf, 9-year-old boy. This is a child whose general communication skills are very limited and his mastery of speech,

The lady is walking at ~~the~~ giving. big
The man is standing at the care big
The children are at the car looking.
The man is car. at the looking big.
The playing at the man. looking boy.
The lady and eating at the looking the

Figure 5.3 Writing by a profoundly deaf, 9-year-old boy with poor communication skills

gesture or sign is such that it is difficult to sustain conversation. His writing reflects to some extent his inexperience of language generally, a severely delayed grasp of grammar, together with some unusual features which may be unique to the child's inner language system. What is clear is that the organizing principles of language which young hearing children grasp at around stage 2, or approximately 1½ to 2 years, are only just appearing correctly in this child's written work, with some features at stage 3 or 4, but little beyond. For example, Determiner-Noun is used correctly together with auxiliary verbs and the correct inflections: 'The lady is walking . . . '. All of the sentences follow a rigid pattern beginning with a subject, verb and then a phrase structure, which is difficult to interpret. The child is unable to extend what he wants to say by grammatical means and simply inserts words. 'Big' appears several times at the end of a sentence perhaps in accordance with some unique grammatical rule operated by the child. There are obvious problems in ordering the sequence of language correctly. None of the features which allow children to connect one sentence with another appear, such as 'and' or 'but', because these are much later developments. So too, the devices which allow cross-reference between sentences, such as pronouns, are well out of the child's range. This is a good example of a child who finds the formal structures and sequences of English language overwhelming. His effective range of vocabulary and syntax is very narrow indeed.

The invisible ink experiment

It is likely that the child's ability to write is closely dependent on other linguistic skills, such as reading and speaking. The work by Griffiths (1983) shows that if you measure the deaf child's language abilities, the child scoring well on a reading test is also likely to make longer and more accurate utterances in conversation, and to produce grammatically correct writing. Such measures are all good predictors of each other. The implication is that if you examine a variety of situations in which language is used by deaf children, behaviour shows a clear and consistent relationship with an underlying language facility. According to Griffiths, this is quite independent of the severity of hearing loss or intelligence.

At various points in this book we have said that there is no straightforward explanation of why deaf children may, or may not, become proficient users of English language. A simplistic view is that loss of access to speech sounds for some children means there is little or no perception of particular elements of the speech message. Put another way, there is no spoken, auditory experience on which to map the features of print. However, the child's difficulties in mastering English syntax must also be taken into account. In order to understand that, reference has to be made to the social context in which children are actively engaged in constructing for themselves the nature of the language system. It is here that we see secondary influences at work, not dependent on deafness *per se,* but which foster different styles of learning in the deaf.

In the following study we examined the possibility that there were other, more subtle influences at work in the task of writing (Webster, 1983). Authors who have thought about what they do when they write usually lay great stress on the stages of pre-writing and review. These are the stages of thinking about what should be said, and subsequently inspecting or reviewing ideas as they are put onto paper. For most hearing people, both these stages depend on some kind of inner language experience. Most people *rehearse* before and after writing. Rehearsal of material in one's head and then on paper would be impossible without some inner language code. Earlier in this chapter the role of inner speech coding was considered in relation to working memory and reading. One possibility is that information in complex sentence sequences must be held in store long enough for the reader to work out the relationships between the different elements in a sentence which contribute to meaning. Inner speech gives the child access to the rehearsal systems of working memory and helps the child to deal with the amount of information revealed in reading text. We have argued that this may be one reason why deaf children tend to attack verbal sequences in different ways from hearing children. But can these limits to 'handling capacity' have an effect on writing as well?

The important stages of rehearsal in writing must be difficult for deaf children if they are unable to use inner speech. The child who has poor access to the articulatory feedback loops described by Baddeley (1979), will be limited in the inner evaluation of language. Without processes of rehearsal and inspection of what has been written, writing cohesive text must be difficult: the interweaving of clauses and sentences by devices such as pronouns, conjunctions and linking markers such as 'because' or 'but'. If this is correct, we have an additional reason for thinking that the deaf approach writing 'sentence-by-sentence'. In order to examine this hypothesis experimentally, a writing task was designed to explore the analogous situation to reading without auditory feedback, of writing without visual feedback.

Twenty severely hearing-impaired children took part in the study with average hearing losses greater than 70 decibels. An equal number of boys were included, aged between 11 and 12 years. A control group of twenty normally-hearing children was selected, also between the ages of 11 and 12 years, matched for intelligence. The experiment involved the children writing about a picture stimulus in two conditions. In the first condition the children were given a picture, a sheet of A4 paper, and asked to write for 30 minutes about what they could see. In the second condition each child was given two sheets of lined A4 paper with carbon paper sandwiched between. Each child was given an expired ball point pen to write with: this functioned as a stylus, leaving no visual trace on the top copy, but a permanent record on the bottom copy. Children were not able to see what they had written since the copies were stapled together. In effect, the 'invisible ink' condition makes it difficult for the child to inspect and rehearse what has been written, because there is no visual trace. Samples of writing were obtained from each child in both conditions. These were analysed and compared to see what differences, if any, there were between the two.

The system of analysis used on the children's scripts was based on the LARSP procedure (Crystal *et al.*, 1976). The LARSP profile classifies the different structures and features of language which arise in the course of language development. At each stage of development the LARSP highlights the new linguistic structures which occur: patterns of clause structure, phrase structure and word structure, together with patterns of sentence connection. Using a LARSP analysis an assessment of the maturity of a child's written language can be made. We can also assess weak and strong features, the number and kinds of errors made, as well as less specific aspects such as the number of words and length of sentences used. For those familiar with LARSP, accounts of its usefulness with hearing-impaired children are given in Crystal (1979).

What then, did this profile approach reveal about the respective writing skills of hearing and hearing-impaired children matched for age and ability? One way in which the data collected in this study can be used is as a straightforward contrast between deaf and hearing children in the normal writing condition. The present study confirms some of the descriptive factors which are prominent in the background literature. Hearing children use fewer sentences, more words and make fewer errors than deaf children. Deaf children prefer to use simple sentence structures with fewer words, many more examples of ungrammatical or non-standard usages, and a higher proportion of 'content' words, such as nouns and verbs, rather than 'function' words, such as prepositions or conjunctions. One important finding is that the vast majority of the deaf children's writing could be accounted for in terms of the LARSP developmental profile. In other words, the deaf child's language follows the normal pattern of acquisition, although it is very delayed. For example, the deaf group tended to use only those grammatical features which they were confident in getting right: they made few attempts at more complex structures which they were likely to get wrong.

The LARSP analysis pinpoints the stage at which a child shows the greatest control of language. For the deaf child this was usually at three elements of clause structure, such as Subject-Verb-Object. The language profiles are far less advanced for the deaf group in terms of clause, phrase and word structure, than the hearing children. Features such as pronouns, adjectives, use of negatives and the 'copula' (or verb to 'be'), appear very rarely in the deaf children's writing. At the word level, many of the more mature word endings were not present in the profiles for the deaf group, although they appeared in the hearing, such as comparatives ('bigger', 'biggest'), and possessives ('the man's hat'). At the clause level, of particular importance in the deaf sample is the absence of recursion at stage 5. Recursive structures are the means by which a child begins to generate extended sentence patterns. Co-ordination and subordination of clauses using 'and' or 'if', occurred rarely. Instances of connecting devices such as 'however' or 'then', use of cross-reference and other discourse features were also very rare, giving the impression once more, of sentence-by-sentence writing. These results confirm and expand the findings reported many times in the literature.

What happened in the 'invisible ink' condition of writing? For the deaf children, the experimental manoeuvre made little or no difference. Writing without visual feedback had no effect on the number of errors made, the length of sentences, or the structure of sentences used. It should be recalled that the 'invisible ink' condition disrupts the normal processes of rehearsal and inspection as the child sets down ideas in print. For the deaf children, internal speech and access to the feedback systems of working memory may already be disrupted. This case was argued for reading. It follows for writing, that removal of the visual trace to *prevent* rehearsal, will have a negligible effect, since there is limited rehearsal in the first place.

Hearing children, on the other hand, fared badly in the 'invisible ink' experiment. In the latter, children's errors more than doubled, while the mean number of words and sentence length is depressed. Children began to be much more conservative in their choice of sentence patterns and were reluctant to use more complex sequences. Most noticeable is the dramatic fall off in hearing children's use of connectivity, recursion, and the sentence linking features of discourse, in the 'no feedback' condition. Hearing children began to make some of the mistakes which are often called 'deafisms', such as inappropriate word endings, omitting determiners and auxiliary verbs. In Figure 5.4, extracts are given from the work of a normally-hearing child aged 11½ years, of average IQ, in the two conditions of the writing task.

The fluency of the picnic description (a) is achieved by appropriate use of pronouns, cross-reference: 'When they got there', and clause links such as 'when', 'later', 'then', 'while' and 'but'. The child has good control of advanced noun-phrase construction, subordination, co-ordination, complementation and the grammatical devices which allow sentences to be interrelated into cohesive text. Sentences are long and a wide variety of clause patterns is used. There are few errors. Writing without visual feedback (b) produces some remarkable changes. The child begins to make fundamental errors in the use of prepositions and determiners ('set out table'), auxiliary verbs ('the calendar saying'), and in simple clause construction. Verbs are omitted or used in the wrong form, word endings disagree. The child resorts to rigid sentence patterns, often beginning clauses with 'which'. Most strikingly of all, the child uses juxtaposition in order to extend his sentence material: 'The wooden chair, the milkman . . . '. The clause patterns which the child adopts are those which reflect the surface structure organization of the sentence material. Control over co-ordination and subordination is lost. There is little cross-reference or recursion, and the writer has been unable to sequence and interweave his sentences to produce a fluent, cohesive text. The overwhelming impression is one of writing sentence-by-sentence.

It was well beyond the scope of this study to judge whether those features which are said to characterize deaf children's written language are part of a unique language system, or simply a result of writing without rehearsal and feedback. 'Pseudodeafisms' can be produced experimentally in a normally-hearing child. One important conclusion that we might reach is that some

(a)

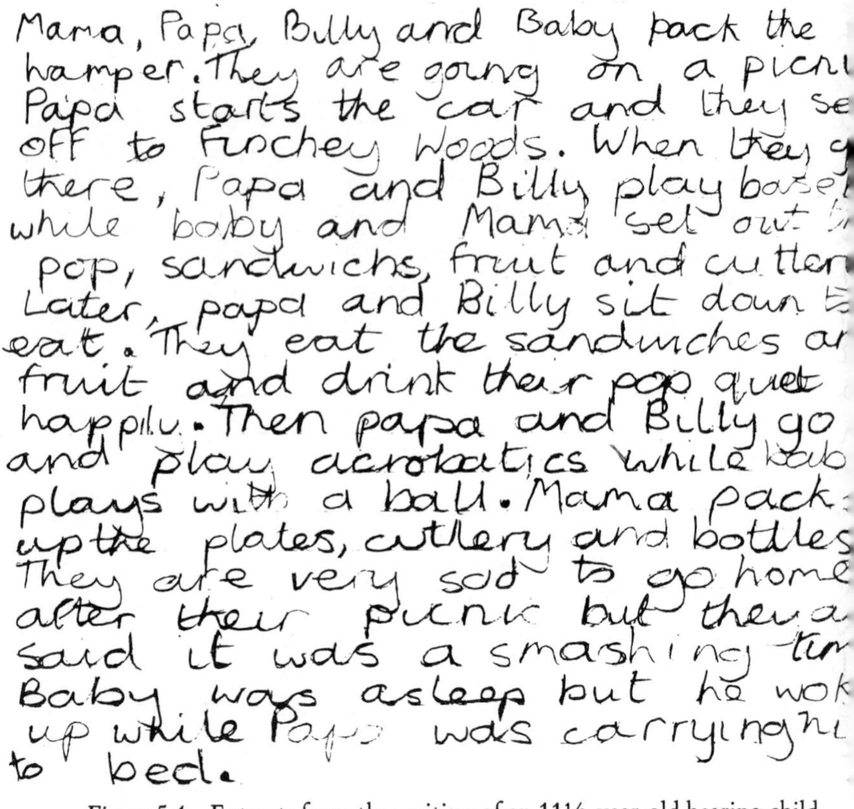

Mama, Papa, Billy and Baby pack the
hamper. They are going on a picni
Papa starts the car and they se
off to Finchey Woods. When they g
there, Papa and Billy play base
while baby and Mama set out
pop, sandwichs, fruit and cutler
Later, papa and Billy sit down t
eat. They eat the sandwiches an
fruit and drink their pop quiet
happily. Then papa and Billy go
and play acrobatics while bab
plays with a ball. Mama pack
up the plates, cutlery and bottles
They are very sad to go home
after their picnic but they a
said it was a smashing tin
Baby was asleep but he wok
up while Papa was carrying hi
to bed.

Figure 5.4 Extracts from the writing of an 11½-year-old hearing child
in two writing conditions: in normal writing conditions (a), and
without visual feedback (b).

of the deaf child's writing difficulties are not necessarily to do
with auditory perception *per se*, since they can also be produced in
hearing children. What can be said is that the written language of
the deaf takes the form it does because it is early patterns of normal
language made to operate under additional constraints. It breaks
down because a developmentally primitive language system is
inadequate to the pressure of what the child needs to say. To these
additional constraints we can add the problems of creating,
writing and rehearsing sentence sequences, when the child has

(b)

e old kitchen with the grinder
et out table. The cooker and mi
ixer, the wooden chair, the multma,
t the doorstep with the woman pay-
ng here feet The calender saying
at it is the 3rd of a month."
The sink with the taps dull and
rey The clock which says in its
wn language says 5 minutes
ast twelve. The cat lapping up
ulk with a dool beside it. The
inese mobile opposite the blind,
hich covers the window which
pposite that a child reaches for
. jelly. The messy books which
e children under the table are
laying with. The dinner getting
ld while the woman wanting to
at but keeping a smile.

poor access to working memory. Feedback and rehearsal appear to facilitate both reading and writing, particularly in dealing with complex discourse features of text. The effectiveness of the deaf child's strategies in both reading and writing must be affected by the child's inner capacity for processing verbal material.

Spelling and hearing-impairment

Spelling and reading may well be independent processes, and achievements in one may not imply corresponding achievements in the other. Each area merits study in its own right (Bradley and

Bryant, 1979). The present book has its major focus on reading, and secondarily, writing. So it is not intended to cover spelling with the thoroughness it deserves. Interested readers are referred for a comprehensive survey of the literature on spelling in mainstream literacy research to Frith (1980). However, the primary justification for not devoting much more space to spelling is that this appears to pose very few problems to hearing-impaired children. At first sight this may seem paradoxical. Surely, of all the processes we have studied in relation to deafness, spelling is the one area most dependent on auditory awareness; in other words, most parasitic on the child's ability to segment speech into sound?

This view stems from a misunderstanding of what children do when they learn to spell, to encode words in print. The misapprehension is that there is one single route to storing and retrieving the spelling patterns of words. In just the same way as there are many possible sources of information in reading text, many routes to reconstruct the meaning, so there are many cue sources in relation to how words are spelt. Both reading and spelling depend on the redundancy of information in print: more cues available than are strictly necessary. In reading, and perhaps in spelling also, we have seen that hearing-impaired children may pay attention to different cue sources in text and therefore may tackle literacy tasks in qualitatively different ways from hearing children. What possible sources of information might there be in learning the distinctive spelling features of words?

In attempting to write a word such as 'apple', the child may decide to segment the spoken sounds of the word into its component syllables and find the letter groupings which sometimes represent those sounds: 'apul'. Spelling errors such as this reveal that the child is trying to use knowledge of phoneme–grapheme correspondences, but the vast majority of words in English do not yield entirely to such a phonetic transcription. Another strategy might be to find the whole visual pattern of the word in one's inner store or lexicon. Some idea of the context in which the word is to be used must be known, otherwise it would be impossible to decide which of two words that sound alike, such as 'pair' or 'pear', is the right choice. Some words, of course, might be remembered on a purely visual basis without any interference from the sound of the letter components, such as 'yacht', 'egg', or 'school'. It is more than likely that children may attempt to copy, learn and write spelling patterns by utilizing a variety of letter, sound and visual-whole features.

One interesting experience which most people have when faced with a word they are unsure about spelling is the wish to write down a version of the word, to see if it 'looks right'. That is probably a fair indication that words are more easily recalled as visual patterns. In a discussion of the development of spelling in children, Marsh and his colleagues (1980) describe a shift in strategies as children get older. When children are just beginning to learn to read and spell they may attempt to use letter–sound correspondences, even though such correspondences are less predictable in spelling than in reading. For example, the rules for pronouncing the printed letter 'k' are fairly predictable, except before 'n' where it is silent. However, the spelling of the sound 'k' is very variable, and the only way to know that a 'k' begins the word 'kitten', but not 'cat', is to remember it visually. Similarly, the correct spelling of words with an initial silent 'k' before 'n', as in 'kneed', but not 'need', depends on visual memory. By the age of about 10 years, most hearing children can use an 'analogy' strategy. When faced with an unfamiliar word, they may try to recall a related word as a basis for spelling the new word. (e.g. critical–criticize). Very proficient spellers appear to make greater use of visual patterns, in the same way that good readers have direct visual access to meaning in reading. This shift in spelling strategies obviously relates to the child's growing experience in reading and spelling, through which an inner visual store is built up.

In the 'invisible ink' experiments described earlier, both hearing and hearing-impaired children produced a number of spelling errors. Although this was not strictly part of the experimental procedure, inspection of the children's scripts reveals a number of important facts. Hearing children writing in the normal condition displayed a high proportion of spelling errors where the child is attempting to use phoneme–grapheme correspondences. Out of fifty-one recorded spelling errors in this group, some 60 per cent were of this kind; for example: 'cud/could', 'anuther/another', 'choclat/chocolate'. Hearing children in the 'no feedback' writing condition, where they were unable to see their spelling attempts, made many more errors, and these were more likely to show visual confusions. Of ninety-nine recorded errors, 64 per cent were of this kind: 'fisrt/first', 'talde/table', 'kictken/ kitchen'. So, in the writing condition deliberately designed to disrupt inner rehearsal, hearing children were thrown back upon a visually based strategy. In contrast, hearing-impaired children made a very small percentage of sound-based spelling errors in both writing conditions. They appeared not to be unduly affected by the change in condition and around 90 per cent of all errors were in visual recall of the letter patterns: 'balk/black', 'clindren/children', 'aporn/apron', 'sicossors/scissors'.

There is one set of studies addressed specifically to the spelling abilities of profoundly hearing-impaired children which confirms most of what has been said here. This work by Dodd (1980) was concerned with the type of information deaf children use to spell words in different experimental conditions. In one experiment ten children, with a mean age of 14½ years and average hearing losses of over 99 decibels, were asked to write down words presented orally in a sentence. Hearing children, used as controls, generated spelling patterns based on direct phoneme–grapheme correspondences. Deaf children, however, performed equally well with phonically regular or irregular words, and we can assume that is because they were using different spelling cues, based on visual features. The same deaf children in a second experiment were forced into using phonological recoding strategies in order to remember a list of nonsense words which were phonically regular. Dodd concludes that deaf children are just as good at using this 'bottom-up' information relating spelling-to-sound, although they usually prefer not to do so. In a third task, Dodd demonstrates that deaf children may be able to extract phonological information from lip-patterns as words are spoken. When presented with spoken nonsense words such as 'thrib', 'multh', or 'trog', deaf children were able to spell these patterns correctly, even when they could not pronounce the words accurately. Dodd concludes that her deaf subjects sompensate for their hearing-impairment, by using information from lip-reading in order to spell.

If we accept these findings it is easy to understand why deaf children may be just as good at spelling as their hearing peers. They seem to be able to use sound as well as visual information. The fact that they tend to rely on visual cues to recall spelling patterns aligns them with good spellers generally, since that seems to be the most successful route to good spelling.

Chapter summary

1   Most hearing children bring to reading a sophisticated mastery of spoken language acquired in a social context. We usually underestimate the infant's ability to grasp the meaning of things and to 'decentre'. Children who have taken active part in learning to speak use the same strategies to make sense of reading. If the social context in which deaf children learn language is disrupted, they will be less well prepared to read. They may have a narrow range of vocabulary and concepts, a poor understanding of English grammar, and a limited ability to think about the language system. They may be less active users of language and turn to other information sources, such as visual. When they face reading, deaf children may not only have to learn the code of print, but also the words and sentences which the code represents. Learning to read therefore becomes a language-learning process at one and the same time.

2   The question is asked: 'What does the hearing-impaired child bring to reading and how does the child respond to the demands of the task?'. Children with conductive hearing loss are considered first. A link between poor auditory processing and an awareness of sounds in print is often made. This is felt to be over-simplistic. Children with early, persistent otitis media show delays in a broad spectrum of language skills. These include auditory perception, word knowledge, syntax and meta-linguistic skills. They may have poor listening ability, short attention span and poor motivation. Environmental factors such as nutrition,

family circumstances, and poverty are associated with middle-ear disease as well as school achievement. If conductive deafness occurs more often in disadvantaged homes, this in itself may contribute to poor progress.

3   Reading demands a range of skills from the child. 'Bottom-up' skills such as discrimination of speech sounds are affected by mild hearing loss. The more central aspects of syntactic structure are also likely to be delayed in this group. 'Top-down' skills such as prediction may be affected because of the child's general immaturity as a language user. A diffuse, as opposed to specific, relationship between otitis media and poor reading is suggested. The socio-cultural determinants cannot be ignored. Some theorists have suggested that a broader view of language disability is relevant to 'dyslexia'. Studies of otitis media children are fraught with research problems, such as the need to look back to periods in the child's development when the child might have been suffering from otitis media.

4   Children with severe hearing losses are considered in relation to the three areas of language study. In this group, 'bottom-up' skills, such as the visual perception of letters or sight-word recognition, show few developmental differences. Even phonic clues could be available through lip-reading. The concept of inner speech is examined. Conrad (1979) argues that inner speech is important for phonetic recoding in reading. Visual coding is less effective and imposes a ceiling or plateau upon achievement. This low-order view of inner speech is challenged. In our view, reading problems begin to arise in the comprehension of complex text, not in decoding print to sound. More important, then, to consider syntactic skills, such as the deaf child's strategies in using principles like subject-verb-object, or minimum distance. Is the deaf child's reading problem a case of mismatch between reader and text?

5   A reading test was devised to answer this question, controlling vocabulary, syntax and amount of information. The most difficult parts of the test were those with restricted information content: from this we conclude that deaf children utilize alternative information sources in text, beyond the sentence boundaries, to decide upon meaning. It is not so simple as a mismatch between

reader and text. The deaf choose a different route in reading. For them reading is a *search for meaning* process, largely 'top-down', with a heavy pragmatic basis. This study also shows that more-sensitive reading tests do register growing skills in the deaf and the older children continued to improve their performance. The 'plateau effect' may be a product of traditional test construction, which produces difficulties which suddenly overwhelm the child at around a reading age of 9 years.

6   A different view of inner speech coding is presented. Its importance lies in providing access to the systems of working memory. Rehearsal of speech-like material during reading holds information in store just long enough for us to make sense of it. Long, complex, embedded sentence sequences depend on the reader's processing capacity. This gives inner speech a higher-level, cognitive role. Deaf children do have inner coding systems, but they may be based on signs, finger-spelling, visual features, or a mixture, including sounds. Unfortunately, non-speech codes may be less effective in dealing with print, which is derived from speech in the first place. The question is; 'How far does the deaf child's inner code limit the child's thinking capacity for spoken or written language forms?'.

7   The importance of short-term memory in the reading comprehension of deaf children was tested out. The 'top-down' strategies of readers were easily disrupted by putting additional strains on their short-term recall of sentences. Inner speech is important to the child when reading because it allows the child to process verbal sequences; could the same logic be applied to writing?

8   The 'invisible ink' study was designed to study the role of feedback and rehearsal in writing. We began by examining several samples of deaf children's written work. Features highlighted in the literature are short, simple sentences, rigid sentence patterns, more 'content' words, fewer 'function' words, many errors and non-standard usages, and disagreements between word forms. There are particular problems in extending sentences, connecting ideas together and using discourse features, such as cross-reference and pronouns, in order to interweave text into a cohesive whole. The end product is that the pressure of what children have to say,

bursts out of the simple grammar at their disposal. Insufficient prior experience of spoken language accounts for some of the problems. The lack of inner speech in rehearsing and inspecting written work may account for the sentence-by-sentence approach. The 'invisible ink' writing condition which disrupts rehearsal, made little difference to deaf children. However, hearing children in this condition began to use less complex sentence sequences, more errors, and far less recursion or connectivity. The deaf child's processing capacity for verbal material is critical.

9 Finally, spelling is considered briefly. There are many routes to spell a word: using letter sounds, visual wholes or analogous patterns. Good spellers shift their strategies eventually from phonic-based to a direct visual recall of word patterns. Deaf children can be forced into using phonic cues in spelling, perhaps extracted from lip reading. They prefer to use the visual-whole method, which is why spelling is not often a problem for deaf children. In this respect they behave like hearing children who are good spellers.

6

TEACHING STRATEGIES

In this final chapter we shall be considering the different approaches which could be made towards helping hearing-impaired children develop literacy. It is not the intention to be didactic. Teachers suffer too much from over-zealous advice of the 'You must do this . . .' variety. Rather, the hope is that teachers will have an informed perspective, a wider knowledge of the various kinds of teaching interventions which could be made. This book will have succeeded in its major aim if it makes teachers aware of the impact they are likely to have, and which aspects of the child's abilities and skills are involved, when a teaching programme is devised.

There are, thankfully, few teachers who follow a particular method or approach blindly, without thinking out their objectives, or the end products of the learning experience for the child. There are also very few professionals who believe they know all there is to know about the hearing-impaired. With this group more than any other, teachers must be prepared to think hard about why they use particular methods and what they want the child to learn. We began this book by saying our knowledge is still only in its infancy. Since we are still in the starting blocks we have to be flexible, try out new and different techniques, and evaluate carefully what has been achieved at the end of the day.

Can reading teach language?

We have seen that reading demands a complex range of perceptual and cognitive skills from the child. Reading cannot be considered as an isolated learning activity, separate from the child's efforts to make sense of the environment. Reading is also, essentially, a language activity, although people disagree over which aspects of language are necessary for reading. One view is that a child must be able to relate the visual features of print to the sound features of spoken language. 'Bottom-up' skills, such as phonic strategies, may enable the child to attack new words never met before, and to build words up in writing. However, we have preferred to put these sound strategies at the periphery of a model of language.

Much more important, we have suggested, is the child's grasp of syntax: the organizing principles of language which relate sounds to meaning. How words are interrelated, how meaning is to be deduced from the surface features of language, the intention and importance of an act of communication, must be considered in terms of the social context. So, we have also laid great stress on the child's language experience. The child's knowledge of what language *does* will later be applied to encounters with language in books. In the same way that a child actively learns to negotiate meaning in conversations with adults, so too, there must be purposeful interaction with print. As a language activity, then, reading encompasses a broad spectrum of linguistic achievements, insights and experiences.

It is sometimes argued that reading itself provides the child with insights about how language is structured, what it means and what it does. For children with poor language skills, reading is put forward as a compensation, or a 'way in'. There is a certain appeal in the visual stability and permanence of written language for deaf children. After all, the child's biological capacity for learning a symbolic language is not affected by deafness. Is it, therefore, any more difficult for a child to grasp a visual symbol than a spoken symbol, if the two are linked with a meaningful experience? A familiar illustration is that reading provides a 'window into knowledge', a key to knowledge and to learning. In some people's minds reading may also be the 'window into *linguistic* knowledge', the key to language.

Hearing children, certainly, have access to information, are able to refine and deepen their linguistic concepts, and gain a medium for reflective, abstract thinking, in fluent reading. Children learn new vocabulary and language forms through reading complex written structures which are never spoken. One of the distinctions we have drawn between spoken and written language is that print is less context-bound and may demand reflective or disembedded thinking. In fact, children learn to use a range of sophisticated linguistic patterns which are specific to writing and which outstrip the capacity of spoken language for handling complex ideas. But can reading give a child the very first linguistic insights?

Some writers have said 'yes' to this last question. In an article on the teaching of early reading skills to deaf children, Söderbergh (1985) feels that reading can enrich the child's total language capacity. This is irrespective of the method of communication, speech or sign, used in face-to-face interaction with the child. According to Söderbergh, reading instruction should be started as early as possible in order to compensate for linguistic handicap. The child learns how to read and learns language, at one and the same time. Söderbergh describes a whole-word approach whereby written words are illustrated by being tied directly to their referents or by being acted out. Deaf children in this Swedish study appeared to have few problems in learning to read the names of relevant and meaningful objects, such as 'pyjamas', 'ice-cream', 'granny'. Children having difficulty with words like 'slowly' or 'quickly', played a running and walking game which tied the symbols directly to the child's experience, and subsequently learnt the words. Söderbergh's recipe is to present words, sentences and stories linked through pictures, spoken words or signs, to real life situations. Through this method the child breaks into the meaning of written language and 'cracks' the code.

There are some important ideas in this work for the early intro-
duction of reading to deaf children, and we shall be reiterating
them later on in the chapter. Unfortunately, the Swedish projects
did not last long enough for the children to be studied as fluent
readers. It will be recalled from Chapter 5, when the strengths
and weaknesses of hearing-impaired children were considered,
that there are usually no problems in associating words and
referents together. Kyle's studies (1980b) show no particular
difficulties in learning sight vocabulary. Reading difficulties begin
as soon as the deaf child tries to understand more complex text:
the point at which the reading skills of the deaf are said to plateau.
The gap which has to be bridged is where mastery of complex
syntax and discourse features in written language are necessary to
deduce meaning. This is the point at which text becomes decontextualized, released from the concrete 'here and now'; the point
at which the ties with concrete reality are transcended, where
ideas are pursued without a social context.

The weight of opinion, in the absence of any firm evidence,
suggests that progress in reading depends upon *prior* (or perhaps,
parallel) developments in the child's understanding and use of
language in communication. In other words, most children need
to discover what language is and what it does, in a spoken
context, before learning to read. It may be possible to build up a
first reading vocabulary as words enter the child's experience. But
only later, when both the language and reading processes are well
under way, can reading begin to extend the child's competence as
a language user. Where a child has not mastered the basic grammatical structures of English it is hard to see how sense can be
made of print, when the written language structures are far more
complex than the child's own. The child's expectations of how
language is organized will be so different from the patterns of
text, that comprehension founders. As a first step, then, teachers
need to ensure that they are providing optimum opportunities for
the child to develop primary communication skills.

Language and listening

It would, of course, be the subject of another book to address this question fully, and many competent efforts have been made to discuss methods of fostering language with the hearing impaired (Quigley and Paul, 1984; Kretschmer and Kretschmer, 1978; Quigley and Kretschmer, 1982). It should be said that no one particular philosophy or methodology, speech, sign or combination of approaches, can be *guaranteed* to give the child a better knowledge of English language. However, it would be remiss not to mention some of the major principles, particularly for non-specialist teachers, which have emerged from recent research.

Wherever a specialist teacher of the deaf is asked to visit a hearing-impaired child in an ordinary school setting, the first concern usually lies with the auditory environment. It was pointed out in Chapter 3 that children with mild conductive hearing losses are likely to have their listening difficulties highlighted in noisy conditions. When a child is expected to listen for long periods and where there are competing sound stimuli, such as in a busy class of thirty primary children, then a child with difficulties in discriminating sounds, comprehending speech and using language, is likely to be further disadvantaged. For the more severely hearing-impaired child dependent on hearing-aids, listening conditions are perhaps more important. There are very few deaf children who derive no benefit, and some who gain a great deal, from wearing hearing-aids. Early diagnosis and intervention is the best way to reduce the impact of deafness on the child at source, by making use of the child's residual hearing as soon as possible through amplification. However, traditional hearing-aids do not select the sounds which are most helpful to the child: they magnify all sounds, irrespective of their relevance. The noisier the environment, the more likely it is that unwanted sounds will be amplified, at the expense of more important auditory input, such as the teacher's voice. Radio aids (see Chapter 2) were designed to get over some of the problems associated with conventional hearing-aids in poor acoustic conditions. However, it is of the utmost importance to children with any degree of hearing loss, that the listening environment is as good as can be.

There are three factors to consider in the acoustic environment. First, keeping unwanted sound *out*. Rooms which are regularly invaded by the noise of road traffic, the workshop next door, voices and running feet going past, and where there is no door to close on outside activities, are going to make for listening difficulties. Secondly, reducing sound sources *in* the listening situation. Rooms with hard floors, ceramic surfaces, wooden cladding and concrete pillars, reverberate sound and therefore prolong unwanted sound interference. Speech perception will improve where walls have acoustic tiles, floor are carpeted, cork and other soft absorbent materials are used, for example on table tops, and where curtains and blinds are provided. Classes for young children often do have quiet carpeted areas for story time and other sections for more boisterous or messy play. The teacher needs to be alert to the increased listening demands made of the child in positions near to well-used areas such as a store-cupboard or passage way; in the gym, hall or workshop; and generally where there is a lot of reverberant noise.

The third, most important consideration, is the sound-level at the child's ear. If the child needs to listen to the teacher's voice but there is a nearer and louder competing sound source, the teacher's voice will not be heard, unless the child is wearing a radio aid. With conventional hearing-aids the child's ability to hear what is said depends on distance from the speaker. As a general rule of thumb, the teacher should not expect the child wearing aids to hear clearly, at distances of more than 2 metres (6 feet) away from the speaker. The implications of this for classroom practice are that the child should be positioned away from noise sources and distracting views, and not too far away from the teacher. In order to see and hear contributions from other children, positions to the side and a few rows from the front are generally best in mainstream classes. These issues are discussed in greater detail in the book by Webster and Ellwood (1985).

In this last reference too, the authors discuss a range of 'enabling strategies': how to help the hearing-impaired child participate in the learning experience. Teacher strategies for communication include lip-reading, full use of gesture and facial expression, gaining the child's attention and establishing eye contact by calling the child's name or a nudge from a neighbour, before giving the child the message. Speech input to the child needs to be clear, not 'mouthed' with exaggerated lip patterns, but using simple sentences rather than convoluted ones. Where a concept is difficult to grasp, paraphrase rather than repetition is better. Open-ended conversation without a social context may pose problems for mutual understanding, depending on the child's receptivity to speech and oral intelligibility. Conversation may therefore be easier around a specific topic, task, materials or a shared experience. This is in no sense undervaluing the importance of open-ended, free-ranging discussion for children with hearing and language difficulties. In fact, later on in this chapter we shall be discussing the likely ways in which children acquire grammatical knowledge through using language forms and having their ideas about syntax challenged. But where communication is a problem the teacher needs to get to know the level of sentence complexity that the child can handle confidently, be careful about the context of a discussion, and engage the child in a dialogue with some real purpose and intention to communicate.

Strategies for the mainstream group situation include clear setting of teaching objectives, co-ordinating any support work from specialist teachers through lesson plans and profiles of lesson content, using written summaries and highlighting new, technical or subject vocabulary. Multiple ways of presenting information using picture illustrations, charts, graphs, television and overhead projectors, are a useful adjunct to 'hands-on' learning experiences. Strategies such as peer-adoption, whereby a hearing child cues-in his neighbour to lesson changes, topic breaks, announcements and other important variations in procedure, are also helpful. Group discussions are always difficult to follow for hearing-impaired people. The teacher may need to identify the speaker, paraphrase what is being said, and check comprehension. Teachers with little specialist knowledge will need to become expert in managing hearing-aids effectively, and using radio aids appropriately. For example, not everything that the teacher says will be relevant to a hearing-impaired child and other people's contributions need to be transmitted via the microphone. Teachers need to switch off their transmitters, particularly if they are prone to let things slip in the staffroom at break! Fuller treatment of the efficient use of hearing-aids in the ordinary school is given in Webster and Ellwood (1985) and, for specialists, Tucker and Nolan (1984).

Lessons from mainstream language research

A great deal has been written about the role of adults in fostering early language growth, and there is a wide diversity of opinion. At one end of the spectrum some authorities believe that children with language delay should be prescribed an intensively structured programme. The teacher may be asked to drill the child, or work on specific aspects of phrase or clause structure. There is a wealth of material available commercially, which focuses on the early production and comprehension of specific language forms. This kind of systematic teaching of language might be appropriate for some children in certain contexts, such as the speech therapy clinic. For most schoolteachers there are practical limitations on the amount of time which can be spent with individual children. Some thought needs to be given also, to the kinds of objections to language remediation programmes registered by Harris (1984). In his review of twenty-four language-training programmes Harris argues that language cannot be dispensed bit-by-bit from a teaching package. According to this view it is the quality of the child's language interactions with others which is the most effective teaching tool, and that cannot be taught in a package.

In Chapter 3 a model of the language-learning process was put forward in which the child acquires language through negotiating meaning in conversations with adults. Conversation requires a social context. Both listener and speaker are actively engaged in creating and searching the context for communication clues. Communication also requires purpose. The speaker has an intention: something to pass on to and share with the listener. Adults seem to be especially tuned into the child's needs as a language novice. They make a range of adjustments when talking to children which hold the child's attention, simplify and clarify what is being talked about. For example, adults often respond to a child's utterance by expanding what the child says, restating and interpreting the intended meaning. The child is not overwhelmed by a barrage of complex language because the adult gauges the child's level of understanding and tunes the level of sentence complexity to the child's own.

Lessons from mother/baby talk are discussed in the work by

Snow and Ferguson (1977). Some intuitive capability is suggested in the skills which adults display in talking to children. It may be that what occurs spontaneously in the normal language interactions between adult and child, will also provide the foundations for language development in the hearing-impaired. This approach to children with special needs in speech and language has been discussed in depth by Webster and McConnell (in press). It is a view which emphasizes the normal strategies of adult–child interaction. The child learns from an experience of language in use. The adult facilitates and nurtures, but does not teach language. We have argued that these broad, pragmatic experiences of language being used to communicate, are also necessary for the child's later encounters with reading.

Unfortunately, severe deafness seems to interfere both with the social context in which language is learned, and with the natural strategies of adults as language partners. The first shared dialogues between mother and infant may be interfered with, such as turn-taking and mother–infant voicing. Parents may contrive to bring new vocabulary to the child, and to teach new language forms. One of the secondary effects of deafness we have considered is that teachers also feel they should work directly on language activities. The child is usually put in the position of being a passive assimilator of language. The child may be asked to imitate an adult model or to rehearse a 'correct' sentence. The teacher may be looking for grammatical correctness in the child's speech at the expense of disrupting conversation. Examples from Brennan (1976), McNeill (1966) and Van Uden (1977), given in Chapter 3, suggest that the teacher's aims in working with language-delayed children, run counter to the spontaneous processes observed in normal adult–child interactions. To sum up neatly, when a hearing child comes in from play and announces: 'I rode my bike', Dad is much more likely to ask the child where she got to, rather than insisting on a grammatical correction.

The lessons from mainstream language research can be summarized as follows. It is the quality of the adult's interactions with the child which is the most effective teaching tool. Good teachers provide opportunities and experiences which stimulate the child's interest. The responsive teacher elaborates and expands upon what the child initiates through the opportunities which arise for adult–child exchanges. The complexity of the adult's speech is tuned appropriately to the child's own. The adult may want to take up the child's utterance, restate, bring in additional information and make explicit the intended meaning. Language, therefore, needs to be linked with a shared and purposeful experience. Children and adults normally converse about things which are real and which matter to them. To begin with, the flow of talk surrounds mundane contexts, such as washing-up, going to the shops, or suppertime. The adult gives the child time to respond and does not talk *for* the child. Correction of verbal mistakes is avoided, since it is the child's meaning which is central. The child is allowed to enter a dialogue on equal terms with the adult, each making a contribution, with no attempt to control. Strategies such as imitation, rehearsal and repetition of language forms, do not occur in normal language development.

What emerges as good practice for hearing children learning language also turns out to be most effective with the hearing-impaired. On the basis of earlier work with hearing pre-schoolers, Wood and Wood (1984) have looked at the effects on conversation which different strategies have. Teachers were asked to change their conversational styles with hearing-impaired children and measures were taken of the child's contributions: how often an initiative was taken to speak and how much was said. It was hypothesized that the greater the degree of control the teacher exerted, the more limited would be the child's participation. Strategies with high control include enforced repetition: asking the child to repeat a corrected utterance; together with forced choice questions and 'What', 'Why', 'When' type questioning. Strategies with low control include the adult giving personal contributions ('It was my birthday, yesterday') and phatic responses or social oil ('Ooh, that sounds nice'). As teachers changed their style towards low control, the child in turn would contribute more frequently and more substantially.

Early reading experience

In just the same way as ideas about child language development have changed course in the last decade or so, opinions about the teaching of reading have also been revised. The major rethinking in child language acquisition concerns the active, central role of the child in discovering the rules of the system in a meaningful social context. The adult's role is as facilitator: providing the right opportunities, immersing the child in relevant language and giving appropriate feedback. In a recent article, Moon (in press) highlights the important features of the present position: oral language is mastered by the child's own efforts, rather than as a result of direct teaching. It is the *conditions* which facilitate such learning which are important. Reading and writing should not be considered as isolated phenomena. Hearing children bring the same impulses to written language as they bring to spoken language. Their experiences as language-learners are also brought to bear upon literacy. It follows that the same conditions which help children make sense of oral interactions with adults should also help children make sense of print.

What might these conditions be, and do they have relevance for the young hearing-impaired child? Let us begin with the principle of immersion. Children are said to be immersed in a rich bath of oral language: adults use it as an integral part of every shared experience. So too, in a literate society, reading and writing surround the child and become a part of everyday life. In Söderbergh's (1985) natural reading method, the deaf child is not presented with rules or systematic repetition. Written words are given to the children to accompany their immediate experiences. Words reflect the child's interests and involvements. Important names are written out for the child, together with familiar objects, activities, places and feelings. As the child sees, touches or experiences something, the appropriate word is spoken or signed together with its written form. Where the meaning of a specific word is elusive, the child may be asked to act out what is referred to. There is no specific programme or plan, and the child is said to acquire written forms in the same way as spoken or signed forms, so long as the words are tied directly to a real-life situation.

A second condition which facilitates learning involves expectancy. When children are introduced to written materials in books the language used should be compatible with the expectations of the child. This is one reason why children are often encouraged to write their own first 'books', relating a story to the teacher, which is then written down. The language of print is then bound to reflect the interests and expectations of the child as a language user. 'Breakthrough' materials also utilize this principle (Mackay *et al.*, 1970). The child has a bank of vocabulary: a personal store of printed words relating to family, self, interests; together with action words such as 'jump' and function words such as 'to'. The child composes sentences on a special frame which holds the cards on which individual words are printed. Later, these may be written into the child's book. In the early stages of learning to read, for both hearing and hearing-impaired children, it makes sense to use materials written around the child's experience and linguistic competence. Plenty of opportunity should be given to discuss the topic and any new vocabulary that the child is likely to meet in print.

This view that reading should reflect the child's own concerns and level of linguistic competence has not informed many of the reading schemes which are often used to introduce written material to infants. Reading schemes usually sacrifice most aspects of real literature: recognizable language patterns, emotional involvement, dramatic plot, identifiable characters and lifestyles, in order to grade vocabulary and control its repetition. As Crystal (1976) points out in his discussion of language in the classroom, many infant schemes immediately confront the child with an *alien* pattern of language, far removed from what might be expected on the basis of the child's own experience. Structures such as the following:

> Up and down, up and down, up and
> down we go.

actually prevent the child from making use of the predictable features of familiar language. The idea is fostered that print is quite unrelated to other forms of language activity.

Teaching 'bottom-up' skills

In Chapter 4 we discussed one model of the reading process which views reading as a hierarchy of subskills. There is some difference of opinion over the insights which children require about language and its written forms in order to read. Some researchers believe the basic building-blocks are visual and the child needs to establish distinctive letter or whole word shapes. Others believe that the child needs to learn a set of rules which relates the spelling patterns of print to the sound patterns of speech. 'Bottom-up' skills may undoubtedly provide some useful information as the child tries to work out what text means. We have implicated 'bottom-up' skills in a multifactorial approach to reading whereby the reader utilizes several parallel sources of information during reading. These include letters, sounds, whole words, sentences, context, as well as the reader's hypotheses about text. In terms of the study of language, sound and spelling features are peripheral aspects, far less important than the organizing principles of grammar. Without grammar, sounds and words are isolated elements, devoid of meaning.

It is surprising to find that a great deal of time has been spent in arguing the respective merits of 'phonic' versus 'whole-word' approaches in the teaching of reading. These two methods have greatly influenced the form of early infant reading schemes. Traditionally, such schemes are built around repetition: the rote learning of selected vocabulary, perhaps reinforced by flashcards; or the repeated exposure to letter-sound associations of the 'pat a fat rat' variety. Subskill learning, drill activities, repetition and rote memorization of rules, all run contrary to the view of reading as a natural language process rooted in the child's social experience of communication.

For the hearing-impaired child any approach to reading which starts with 'phonics' or sound blending, may be very confusing. Even children with very minor conductive hearing losses are likely to have some difficulty in discriminating speech sounds. So, a reading scheme or rote learning activity designed to teach letter–sound correspondences is likely to highlight one of the poorest aspects of the child's emerging language skills. Some teachers have used this as an argument *in favour* of working on 'phonic' skills. The only logical reason for doing this, is to accept that letter–sound awareness is a necessary pre-condition of reading. Given that fact, there would be no escaping the need for every child to have these skills. However, it was pointed out in our review of the literature that there is much disagreement over the significance of phonic awareness for reading. Insights about the phonic structure of words may in fact reflect a child's growing experience of print. Encounters with words in books may well lead the child to uncover many of the alphabetic regularities and spelling-to-sound patterns. But to teach phonic correspondences as pre-reading skills, and more so, to assess the child's progress in letter–sound awareness, attaches a lot of importance to what might be a secondary skill.

Teaching word-attack skills such as phonics to children is usually defended on the grounds that good readers seem much more aware of these rules than poor readers in nonsense words (Snowling, 1980). Also, good auditory discrimination and having an ear for sounds, alliteration and rhymes, seem good predictors of children who learn to read early and well (Clark, 1976; Bradley, 1980). When different treatment strategies for poor readers are compared, remedial programmes which emphasize phonic skills are claimed to be more effective (Gittleman and Feingold, 1983). A well-considered view of this compounded area of research has been given by Briggs (1983) who says that very young children do pay attention to phonic clues, until the point at which they become printborne. Thereafter, good readers have more rapid, direct visual access to word meanings and do not rely on phonic clues. In other words, they have automatic 'bottom-up' skills and are able to focus their attention on 'higher' aspects of text, such as relating new information to old. There is a certain irony then, in teaching poor readers what only good readers appear to do well: 'bottom-up' skills. At the same time, we often ask good readers to emulate the strategies of the least able: paying attention to alternative routes to meaning, such as making predictions from context. The fact remains, however, that children may only achieve efficient 'bottom-up' skills through reading.

Some recent evidence has been reported which supports the argument that in order to learn to read, you have to read. To put this another way, there is no novice or practice stage in which subskills must be learnt, before the whole act can be accomplished. Sometimes the analogy of learning to ride a bicycle, or learning to swim is used. Children must be able to discover something of the whole experience for themselves, however imperfectly, in order to learn. Having done that, children develop and refine their expertise. In the study by Backman (1983) of children who learned to read before going to school, skills such as sound-blending, auditory discrimination and segmenting speech into separate phonemes, were tested. Backman was interested in whether any of these skills were more evident in early readers than in a matched control group of non-readers. Were these skills prerequisite to reading, did they facilitate reading, were they a consequence of reading, or nothing to do with reading? The results of this study suggest that precocity in reading is not made possible by sound segmentation, blending or discrimination, since some of the non-readers were just as good at these tasks as the early readers. What these test findings did show was that children use a wide variety of strategies, and that there are no true prerequisite reading skills.

In another study by Meyer (1982) the effects of two procedures for correcting oral reading errors were looked at, in a group of 58 remedial readers. Meyer gave one group intensive phonic training over a four-month period, which her pupils were encouraged to use when they came across a word they did not know as they read aloud. A second group were simply told the correct word when they made an error. The relative impact of the two methods was evaluated using a battery of reading tests at the end of the teaching programme. The word-attack, phonic analysis approach, despite its expense in terms of teacher-time, was no more effective than the word-supply strategy. One can describe the latter as a meaning-oriented approach, which simply enables the child to sustain the reading flow.

What implications do these findings from mainstream research hold for the teacher working with hearing-impaired children? Two things should be borne in mind. First, that for normal readers, direct teaching of subskills such as phonics may be secondary to the business of reading for meaning. Out of this latter philosophy has arisen the view that children learn to read by being immersed in reading. They discover the rules of reading, in the same way as they discover the rules of spoken language, by experiencing language in use. The teacher's job is to provide the right conditions for learning. Second, that for hearing-impaired children, teaching phonic attack skills is teaching from the child's weakness, not the child's strength. At the beginning of this chapter a wish was expressed not to be didactic. There are several good resource books on phonic skills training, such as Gregory (1982) or Herbert and Davies-Jones (1977). This book should have provided a perspective, a language model, within which the function of 'bottom-up' skills can be located. What the likely effects of such training might be for the hearing-impaired child learning to read, should be apparent.

Sharing books

As we have said, a contrasting view of the normal reading process suggests that what children have to do in order to learn to read, is to read. Children learn how the written system works by discovery. Rules are unearthed and then pieced together as the child reads for meaning. There is no necessity to practise a set of subskills beforehand. Reading, then, is an active process which is acquired in the same way as spoken language, through an experience of language in use. Other parallels can be drawn between the special skills of adult caretakers in the primary language-learning situation, and the help that seems to nurture early reading. The most important learning context for reading is provided by adults who share books with the child.

Here too, there may be differences in the effectiveness of adults and in the perceived intentions served by reading with the child. When studies have been made of adults reading with deaf children (Wood *et al.*, in press), it is usually observed that the experience has a different function than it might otherwise have. The adult may use the occasion to teach the child, to draw attention to new vocabulary or the correct pronunciation of a word. The adult may 'step in' to the reading activity more often to test understanding or make a point to the child. As a consequence, story continuity may suffer and the overall meaning of a piece may be more elusive. These changes in adult–child interactions have been observed in spoken language situations. Deafness appears to evoke more directive, questioning and didactive behaviour from adults, even though there are good reasons to believe that these strategies are less helpful to language-learning.

How, then, may adults share books with hearing-impaired children in a way which is more facilitative? This is something of a current issue in mainstream primary schools and there are some useful accounts of parent–teacher ventures to encourage children's reading with the focus on regular book sharing at home (Griffiths and Hamilton, 1984). Important ingredients of these schemes are short, frequent reading sessions of say, 15 minutes, three times a week. The sessions must be friendly, in the sense that the child and adult want to take part and would not be rather doing something else at the time. Praise and encouragement are essential. A quiet, relaxed part of the day should be chosen. The emphasis is upon enjoying books together, not working at them.

Books must be chosen with care, perhaps with the help of teachers or library staff. A record is kept of books read with comments which go backwards and forwards betwen home and school. Initially, and particularly for hearing-impaired children, books written around the child's interests and experiences, with good illustrations, are preferable. Some children's books are visually appealing but have very complex language. Some teachers feel they can adjust the language patterns to make them more natural, and provide an overlay for the text. There is a danger, and this is an issue we shall be addressing in some detail later in this chapter, that modifying language patterns too much reduces the information available to the child. A certain amount of commonsense is required in this respect.

Essentially, shared reading activities should encourage children to use whatever clues they can to discover the meaning of text. This will include an awareness of where to begin; which direction across the page to move; using headings, page numbers, and index. To begin with, the adult may want to read the story to the child as the pictures are followed. Children will naturally want to talk about the illustrations and the story experience. For the older hearing-impaired child with more limited language under control, it is important to select book material with sophisticated conceptual interest, even though the language patterns may need to be less demanding. Meek (1982), whose basic philosophy is that reading cannot be taught apart from what is to be read, gives a comprehensive review of book materials appropriate to a wide range of levels and abilities.

When children have begun to identify words and can tackle simple materials, parents and teachers usually want to know what they should do when the child gets stuck on a word. The key here is to be flexible, bearing in mind that the whole point of the exercise is to help the child discover meaning. A number of strategies are given below:

1 Guessing from the sentence, paragraph or story context, perhaps by reading onwards.
2 Using the illustration for clues to meaning.
3 Predicting what is likely to happen from experience of other stories, or in reality.
4 Use any other cues in the text, such as letter shapes and sounds.
5 Tell the child the word if the thread of the story is likely to be lost.
6 Correct the child's reading errors only when the meaning is likely to be misinterpreted.
7 Good guesswork should be praised by confirming and restating what the child has discovered.

Reading and syntax

> . . . grammar is the central organizing principle or structuring process in language, without which sounds, no matter how well spelled, and words, no matter how well recognized, remain isolated units, a disorganized juxtaposition of noises and ideas.
>
> (Crystal, 1976, p. 61)

By the age of 3 or 4 years most hearing children have already mastered the main elements of grammar in spoken language. The way in which sounds and words are interrelated in a sentence determines meaning. We look to the social context of communication to discover how children and adults negotiate meaning with each other. In hearing-impaired children these processes may be disrupted at the very earliest stages. Even children with very mild conductive losses are likely to be delayed in their acquisition of sentence structures. Children with more severe hearing-impairments are unlikely to master complex syntax and may depend on immature strategies, such as assuming that all sentences follow a Subject-Verb-Object pattern. A supportive sign-language system used alongside spoken language, or a combination of sign language, finger spelling and gestural clues, is usually justified in terms of helping the child to grasp grammar. However, as we have said previously, there is no one method of communication which can guarantee the deaf person an adequate control of English language syntax.

One of the central problems which teachers of the deaf have to face is how to foster the child's experience and mastery of syntax. In Chapter 3 we drew attention to the fact that deafness may evoke strategies from adults and teachers which in themselves are not very helpful to language learning, because language is least effectively acquired through direct teaching. Normally-hearing children, at each stage of syntax acquisition, generate their own rules about the language system. By a process of trial and error, hearing words used in different ways in different contexts, discovering how words modify each other in sentence forms, and relating the surface structure of sentence patterns to the deeper intended meanings, hearing children make successive approximations to the adult system. To do so requires a rich experience of language in use.

Having a 3-year-old child at home is living testimony of the untiring energy required in order to make sense of situations through language. Very little of what the child says is commentary. Almost every utterance demands a response: affirmation, restatement, further information, or clarification. Even as relative language novices, hearing infants are using language to predict and anticipate events, to report on things that have happened and to project themselves into imaginary experiences. We have mentioned the moves of the language game around a triangle, involving the speaker's intention, how the message relates to the context, and what interpretation is made. One of the conditions for learning which the adult seems so adept in providing as part of this language triangle is just sufficient challenge to the child's emerging grasp of rules. Processes of paraphrase and expansion do just that, by extending and providing a more adult model of what the child wishes to say. With the deaf child, because of the constraints on interactive conversation, the adult may make fewer demands on the child, challenging the rule system much less. In the book by Wood *et al.* (in press) it is suggested that the deaf child's syntax may be limited because there is less exposure to complex registers of speech. The adult rarely moves beyond the concrete, simple 'here and now', to abstract ideas involved in prediction, projection and imaginary experience.

It could be anticipated that where there is a large gap between the grammatical complexity of reading materials and the deaf child's own control of syntax, then the child might have a serious reading problem on the basis of grammar alone. If we add to this other potential problems of vocabulary and concepts, together with limitations in experience, then it is not surprising that reading fluency is difficult to achieve. In this book we have also put forward other potential sources of difficulty. These include thinking *about* language structures. The child who does not use inner speech coding may be unable to hold information in working memory. Complex syntactic patterns require verbal material to be held in short-term store for comprehension to take place. Deaf children may not have developed the cognitive framework (their working memories) to cope with complex syntax.

Given such obstacles in mastering syntax, researchers have thought up ways of teaching grammar through the written word. These methods are sometimes referred to as the 'structural' teaching of language. They consist of grammatical principles learned by drill and through textbook exercises. Some kind of key or coding system might be taught which indicates parts of speech. Coded parts of speech are sequenced together by the child to construct correct sentence patterns. Some teachers denote the separate word classes in a written sentence by using different colours: red for nouns, blue for verbs, green for adjectives, and so on. There are several variations on this theme. Other teachers have tried to mark parts of speech through shapes. Nouns might be written in a diamond shape, verbs in a circle and definite articles in a square. The child might be asked to organize a sequence of words with the possibility of seeing the grammar expressed as a series of geometric shapes.

Shapes and colours may help to reinforce a child's sense of grammatical structure in the early stages. It is difficult to know how far one can go with this approach since grammar quickly becomes too complex to describe visually. The underlying objection to these methods is that the main ingredients of normal language-learning contexts are missing. Language may not be tied to a direct and meaningful experience. There is little sense of interaction, whereby different language structures are experienced as conversation is passed backwards and forwards. The child may be asked to make strictly grammatical decisions on written material. Yet we know that this kind of thinking about language may not be possible until much later in the child's development as a language user. To put this in terms which we have already discussed: the child is expected to proceed to an explicit awareness of the syntax of language, before developing proficiency at the implicit level, where the child simply uses the language without knowing how it is put together.

Occasionally, what have been described as more 'natural' teaching approaches turn out to be thinly disguised structural methods where the child is attempting to learn grammar by rote. Many of Van Uden's 'reflective exercises' require the child to solve precise syntactic questions on written materials devoid of any social context or function:

Which underlined verb is an infinitive form? A participle form? A progressive form? A finite form?
Example: 'Where _are_ you going?'. 'There and back again to _see_ how far it _is_. I never _have_ _been_ there.'

(Van Uden, 1977, p. 237)

It goes without saying that this kind of language activity does not reflect the normal language-learning process. Nevertheless, the difficulties experienced by deaf children in learning language through the normal processes of interactive communication have justified the use of structured programmes and special materials.

Teachers who are tempted to use these methods for children who are stuck at the early stages of learning syntax, should be aware of the shortcomings and be careful to evaluate whether they work. For further discussion about structural approaches, a review is given in Quigley and Paul (1984).

Modifying reading materials

At the beginning of this chapter one of the conditions for learning felt to be facilitative, is the principle of expectancy. Children should not be confronted with alien patterns of language or vocabulary in print, otherwise they will be unable to benefit from the predictable features of familiar language. There is something of a cul-de-sac here in that if deaf children's linguistic experiences leave them with a restricted set of grammatical rules, they will never be familiar with the language of most book materials, because the patterns of language will be much more sophisticated than the children's own. In response to this dilemma, some authors (Quigley *et al.*, 1976) have consciously tailored written materials to suit the grammatical level of the hearing-impaired child. In the United Kingdom, Williams and Dennis (1979) have devised special teaching materials with deliberately restricted syntactic patterns. The question remains: How will the child ever learn to read texts which contain more complex structures unless asked to attempt them?

In order to respond to this question we need to consult the model of the reading process presented in Chapter 4. The interactive view is a particularly useful way of accommodating 'bottom-up' and 'top-down' processes in reading. Children may gather information from letter–sound correspondences, whole words, grammar, meaning, or cue-sources beyond the text, such as knowledge of stories and how they are usually put together. The child searches actively for cues, checks one against another, and often has a very rich and diverse range of sources to draw upon. The problem for the deaf child, of course, is that the child's past experience of language and reading brings a more limited knowledge-base to the task. Whilst good readers appear to make very efficient use of cues for word identification, the slower reader has to compensate by drawing on broader sources of information from different cue-levels.

A number of experiments reported in this book, such as the Wide-span, Southgate and Hamp studies, give some insights into what children do when they are faced with reading materials which overwhelm them linguistically. The short answer is that they continue to tackle the reading materials, but in a different way to hearing children. They use alternative test strategies, such as using word-association, picture saliency or spatial information, in order to solve the linguistic puzzles presented. Similarly, the diagnostic reading battery was designed specifically to look at what deaf children attempt to do with a controlled reading task. This study gave insights of direct importance to the principle of reducing the linguistic mismatch between written and spoken language. To summarize this piece of research, it was wrongly assumed that a sentence-reading task would be made easier for the child by reducing the richness of information available. Children were helped in searching for the critical features of print if there were more, rather than fewer to choose from. Consistent errors occurred in this reading task when children themselves over-simplified the number of features amongst which they had to choose.

The collected evidence of this research data suggests that deaf children see reading as a decision-making process which utilizes information from a number of levels in text. This approach may indeed be necessary when the reader is inexperienced, inefficient, or has to compensate for gaps in knowledge (in this case un-doubtedly, syntactic). The implications of this view are far-reaching for teachers. Should we reduce the linguistic complexity and information content of text material presented to the child, if to do so makes it more difficult to read for meaning? The commonsense view is a middle-of-the-road one. Totally unfam-iliar and linguistically overwhelming materials will result in the child's expectations about what will be found in text miscarrying. On the other hand, deliberately restricted language materials run the risk of losing some of the information content which the child could respond to.

There is supportive evidence, apart from our own, that reading comprehension can occur well beyond the level at which children can express themselves. In one study, Ewoldt (1981) looked at the reading comprehension of deaf children aged 7 to 17 years. She analysed the 'retellings' of twenty-five stories by her deaf subjects using sign language. The children were asked to read and then interpret the stories, which were video-taped. Ewoldt used the miscue analysis framework described in Chapter 4, which allowed her to see whether the deaf children were responding to the meaning and grammar of the sentence material. Whilst many of the children did make syntactic errors in the story 'retellings', they demonstrated that they did understand the content of the stories and were able to make inferences about the text. Ewoldt's view is that deaf students can read for meaning by using predictions about the schema of the story, cause and effect, plot, likely relationships between setting, beginning and ending, together with the cohesive ties between ideas in sentences. The syntactic complexity of the material is, in a sense, by-passed. The deaf child takes an alternative route to the meaning of a story which is not wholly dependent on grammar. Ewoldt has come out strongly against the use of modified or rewritten materials with deaf students because in revision most texts lose their literary qualities and may become harder to read (Ewoldt, 1984).

In another experiment, Cumming *et al.* (1985) wanted to find out whether reading comprehension was made easier by: simplifying the syntax of a passage (breaking relative clauses into simple sentences); changing the information content (on a scale from concrete to abstract); reorganizing the layout on the page; or providing extra notes to help with harder vocabulary. One might have predicted that passages high in syntax complexity and abstractness would have produced lower comprehension scores. However, for deaf 12- to 16-year-olds, comprehension was unaffected by syntax or meaning difficulty. These authors conclude that when short stories or passages are used the cues available for meaning in the context are much more powerful than any of the modifications made to text.

Modifying the reader

One productive approach for the teacher to adopt may be to attempt to modify the reader rather than the text. We may need to accept that hearing-impaired children will rarely achieve the kind of underlying linguistic mastery and sophistication enjoyed by hearing counterparts. Reading may never become a process of direct transduction from print to meaning, where print is derived from spoken language structures in the first place. We may have to agree that the deaf child will depend more heavily upon alternative strategies and cue sources. In other words, the deaf child is a more active 'top-downer'. The next logical step is to help the child make more efficient use of indirect routes to meaning.

This kind of approach has been advocated for hearing children in mainstream schools who find reading comprehension difficult. Two publications stemming from a Schools Council Project: *The Effective Use of Reading* (Lunzer and Gardner, 1979) and *Learning from the Written Word* (Lunzer and Gardner, 1984) are especially relevant. These authors take the view that many children fail to understand because they have not grasped the function of reading. We said earlier that one of the dangers of teaching and testing reading as a decoding skill, going from print to spoken sounds, is that children may be led to believe that reading entails no more than this. To read for meaning requires reflection: making sense of what is said and relating what is read to what is known already. When children take it for granted that all they have to do is to recognize the words, then they are falling short of the active effort required to establish the overall sense and coherence of the material.

One of the first findings of the Schools Council enquiry was that teachers were unused to showing children how to learn from their reading. Attempts to use comprehension exercises, of the kind found in English workbooks and reading laboratories, typically do not require reflective reading. Traditional comprehension exercises usually test factual recall, are highly predictable and do not involve much interpretation or analysis of the text. The project developed a range of techniques and strategies which encourage reading for learning and these are collectively known as

'Directed Activities Related to Texts', or DARTs. Some important principles of DARTs are that activities are rooted in areas of
the curriculum such as geography, history or science; they are not
separate. The children are encouraged to learn from each other in
small discussion groups and to test out their ideas against one
another. The whole point of 'text-based' lessons is that children
are learning how to learn in a topic area; discovering the right
kind of questions to ask in reading; recognizing and recording the
information they derive; and checking back to their original questions to see whether the text has provided the answers. In contrast
to the 'continuous' read appropriate to some fiction, DARTs
encourages a 'broken' read, an integral part of which is cross-
reference, deciding beforehand what one is trying to find out,
what purpose is served, and whether having read, these functions
are satisfied.

In one variety of DART task whole extracts from texts are
used and the children are helped to penetrate beyond the surface
sentences, to discover the critical features and their interrelation-
ships. They may be asked to locate specific information in the
text, such as underlining the words which describe the subject of
the story, place or time. They may be asked to find the phrases
which give particular insights or meanings. They may be asked to
label a diagram by reading a passage; to set out the sequence of
events in a story; to complete a table of information derived from
a text under specific headings; and to reorganize information
according to different schemata. The exercises move beyond
literal questions to inference, interrogation and qualitative judgement. The whole point of these search-for-meaning activities is to
sharpen the child's existing reading skills, to develop strategies
which make greater use of the cues which are already there, but
may be missed. Analysing text content in different ways, reorganizing information in a variety of forms (tables, diagrams and
charts), and highlighting the parts of text which reveal important
ideas, are all designed to help children make sense of reading
materials which would overwhelm them in some respects, such as
syntax.

An example of material used for DART activities, taken from
the work of a group of 10-year-old hearing-impaired children, is

given in Figure 6.1. The 'captain's log' was written as part of a sequence of lessons around the theme of treasure islands. In pairs, children were asked to work on the story by underlining any reference to the sea monster in blue, things 'heard' in the story in red, and anything felt to be frightening in yellow. They were then

---

November 19th, 1834

After the dreadful storm, we are glad to have calm sailing for five days.

Yesterday, I saw some orange dolphin-like animals jumping through the smooth emerald water and flying fish.

An hour ago, one sailor spotted a strange sea monster like an enormous snake. Through the telescope, I was amazed to see that it had hundreds of spikes down its back, blue and red fins on its side and an enormous tail like a fish. Its four scaly arms had claws the size of swords. I was terrified to see two fire-breathing heads with horrible, purple eyes and rows of dagger-like teeth.

Shaking with fear, I shouted that the wheel must be turned east – we would have to go another way. Late this afternoon, we sailed past a small group of islands just like the ones drawn in the corner of the map.

I feel sure we are getting nearer Shipwreck Island.

November 20th, 1834

Last night, an awful roaring noise woke me up. Looking out of my port hole, I was scared out of my wits. The same monster that we spotted yesterday had followed us!

I heard a terrified scream and saw the creature reach out and grab a sailor. Then, it ate him alive. I shouted instructions to the crew to set off the cannons.

Several cannonballs exploded out at the monster, just bouncing off its scales, all except one. This hit the beast in the eye and it gave a dreadful cry of pain, breathing out boiling flames. I instructed the cannons to shoot again, at the animal's heads.

Figure 6.1 Story used for DART activities with 10-year-old hearing-impaired children

asked to collect together all the information which describes the monster's appearance under the headings: 'head', 'tail', 'claws' and 'body', and to draw its protrait. The children were asked to list the four most dangerous aspects of the monster in order of merit, and to write down the phrases in the story which give particular meanings, such as 'the sea was green and calm', 'the claws were sharp'. Together with these locating and collating activities, children were also asked to predict the outcome, and to imagine the feelings of those involved.

In a second variety of DARTs activities, modified text is used. The teacher deliberately alters the form of a text, which is then given to children in one of two main ways. In the first method, words or phrases are deleted from a passage and replaced with a line. The puzzle is to complete the gaps, using the passage for clues. There are some similarities with cloze procedures, although the point of deletions in DARTs is to select words which will encourage discussion and reflection. So, the technique is not to delete every nth word, but to focus the child's attention on

---

There are two major types of DARTs: those which can be carried out using modified texts and those using unmodified texts. Unmodified DARTs include underlining or highlighting the main ideas in a text, labelling, or constructing diagrams and tables using the main ideas identified.

_____ text DARTs include deleting words which are important to _____ of the text and this is an _____ of a _____ DART. You will notice that there is an introductory passage which _____ the style and _____ of the prose. Approximately _____ deletions should be _____.

Another type of _____ text DART is called sequencing or _____. A _____ which develops in a logical _____ is selected and scrambled into 6 to 8 sections. Each section is _____ onto cards of uniform size and pupils are asked to _____ them in a _____ sequence.

Figure 6.2   Example of modified text: a completion DART

relevant information in the text, in order to fill in the gaps. More than 1 in 5 deletions will probably leave insufficient clues in the passage to make the exercise soluble. Usually, an adequate run-in passage needs to be given which establishes the style and content before any deletions are made. There are no absolutely correct answers to deletions, which leaves room for discussion. An example of a completion DART is given in Figure 6.2.

A second method of modifying text is to choose a passage with a fairly logical presentation of ideas in a relevant topic area. The passage is reproduced, cut up into about six to eight sections and mounted on card. The cards are jumbled and the child is asked, with a partner, to restore them to a logical sequence. The puzzle for the child then is to think carefully about the concepts and information in the material, in order to discover the sequence in which the ideas develop. For some hearing-impaired children, sequencing can be difficult if there are no other clues apart from the written word. It might be more helpful in that case to turn some of the child's own writing or reading materials into a sequencing exercise, or to add picture illustrations to the sections.

Teaching study skills

The principle of helping the child to be more effective in encounters with written material can be applied in other ways. Children can be shown how to use reference books more efficiently, how to use chapter summaries, the contents page and index, how to locate a name or topic, and how to read a passage to seek out specific details by skimming or scanning. Children can be helped to find their way about a dictionary, Yellow Pages, newspaper, holiday brochure, shopping catalogue, gas bill, train timetable or price list. Practice can be given in summarizing content, isolating the sequence of events in a story and recalling them, predicting appropriate outcomes from unfinished sentences or stories, and making appropriate judgements about an author's intention to amuse, sell or persuade. One of the points made by *The Bullock Report* (DES, 1975) was that many normally-hearing youngsters are unable to read purposefully in order to make notes, follow instructions, summarize, digest and make judgements about what they read. An additional problem, faced particularly by older hearing-impaired students at the secondary level of schooling, is an increased emphasis on textbook learning, where the level of textbook language is more complex than the conceptual level of the material it presents. The whole point, then, of this work is to use the existing skills of the child more productively, draw attention to the accessible features of texts which give relevant information, and foster independent learning.

The direct teaching of study skills should accompany more specialized subject work, especially in an examination-oriented curriculum. We mention here some of the ideas developed in Webster and Ellwood (1985) in helping older hearing-impaired children cope with the academic demands of a mainstream school. Lesson summaries, plans of subject content and the critical information to be learned, should be highlighted by the teacher, before the lesson if possible. Then, when the student is presented with a textbook or has to listen to an oral lesson for long periods, there is a framework for reference. Pupils read and listen for information more effectively when they have a knowledge base, and know what they are reading or listening out for. Any technical or specialized jargon, specific to a subject area, can be given further explanation. Misunderstandings often arise in the language of direction: 'rank the following in order of merit', 'define briefly', 'encircle', 'cross out which does not apply', 'represent in a diagram', 'tabulate', or 'describe the relative contributions made by'. The hearing-impaired child may benefit from a careful spelling out of the tasks demanded in study.

It is often said that hearing-impaired youngsters are discriminated against by public examination procedures. This is usually because the carrier language of test questions outstrips the concepts being assessed. Some examination boards are becoming aware that instructions should be given in uncomplicated terms so that pupils can display their true grasp of the subject area. If the purpose of an exam is to assess mathematical, scientific or practical skills, it is senseless to present questions in such a way that the major demands are made upon the students' comprehension of the written language of instruction. Nevertheless, since less enlightened boards feel that competing on equal terms implies that any modifications are unacceptable, it is just as well to teach examination skills too. Direct tutoring in making notes, distilling key facts, memorizing information, revising past work and checking recall, are very relevant. Some authors, such as Hamblin (1981), believe that all children benefit from practising exam techniques, such as allocating time appropriately to the various sections of a test, careful reading, tackling all questions set, checking over answers, setting work out clearly and writing legibly.

Helping the child to write

Writing is one aspect of a richly interwoven tapestry of language skills. As Griffiths (1983) has shown, reading, speaking and writing are closely interrelated and a child who has achieved well in one area, is likely to have good achievements in the others. Like reading, writing depends on the child's grasp of vocabulary, an underlying control of the organizing principles of grammar, and an awareness of intention: conveying meaning to the reader. Where a hearing loss has disrupted a child's experience of language in use, the child will be less well prepared for writing. If a child has had a limited exposure to patterns of spoken language and has not internalized the rules of the system, it will be difficult to generate written sentence structures.

One of the characteristics of the writing of many severely hearing-impaired children which we have drawn attention to is that the pressure of what children want to express, bursts out of the language patterns at their disposal. The written language of the deaf is also often typified by simpler, shorter, more rigid sentence structures; more errors and non-standard usages; more 'content' words such as nouns and verbs; with fewer function words such as prepositions and conjunctions (Cooper and Rosenstein, 1966). The qualities which we admire in fluent writing, such as extending and co-ordinating clauses, linking sentences together, and creating a cohesive passage, may pose special difficulties for the hearing-impaired, perhaps because of limitations in working memory.

Many normally-hearing children have problems in writing, and some of these difficulties arise from the features which distinguish writing from reading, and reading from speech. Spoken language has a social context from which meaning is interpreted. Written language requires disembedded thinking, an explicit awareness of how the language system works. The practised writer has mastered the techniques of sustaining a dialogue with an imaginary audience. Professional writers usually agree on three separate stages of creating text. The first stage involves listening to one's inner thoughts prior to writing. The second stage requires ideas to be translated into formal sentences. The third and final stage is one of review: having committed pen to paper, sentences can be inspected and related one to another. Without the final stage of reappraisal it is difficult to see how a writer could develop cross-reference, conjoin sentences and create a cohesive whole.

Let us begin with the early stages: how best to introduce writing to a hearing-impaired child. All children write more easily about what they have recently experienced as exciting events, in stimulating stories, or through doing and seeing important and relevant things. Like the first words introduced in reading, the child needs to attempt to write words tied to immediate experience. The child with good motor skills and pencil control can be asked to trace over the teacher's caption on a drawing or painting. The writing is an integral part of a whole: touching, feeling, doing, talking, drawing or making, and then encapsulating the experience in a written word or phrase. The principles of immersion and expectancy are as applicable to writing as they are to reading. Children's attention can be drawn to print which surrounds them, and they will want to try and write about the familiar and the important from their own view of the world.

Most children spend a long time practising and copying words before they are able to write them from memory. That is why infant classroom walls appear like word-banks with clear labels and sentences pinned to everyday objects and functions. Children also often have personal word banks which they can refer to. The 'Breakthrough' approach incorporates reading and writing activities related to the child's own spoken language use. Having constructed a sentence on a word-frame using a word store, a subsequent step might be to copy this into an exercise book and illustrate it with a picture. The child's personal writing may grow less quickly than reading skill because of the mechanical demands on hand–eye co-ordination and constraints upon visual memory. However, there is no particular reason why a hearing-impaired child should have difficulties in recalling the written symbols for words. As we pointed out in the section on spelling, deaf children are more likely to adopt a visual strategy in which the shapes are more salient than the sounds of letters. Much more important is the need to relate what the child writes to the predictable and the familiar, generated by the child's own impulse to communicate. Drilling and repeating alien vocabulary and sentence patterns in reading may be unprofitable. For the same reason, the copying and repetition of isolated letters and words not rooted in experience may be less effective. At this early stage of writing it is important to foster the notion that writing, reading and speaking, have the same purpose.

Inevitably, the child's grasp of sentence structure in the primary mode of communication, speech or sign, will determine early written attempts. Beard (1984) suggests that many young hearing children are confused about what a written sentence looks like. Speech is made up of loosely 'chained' clauses, and children at first produce written sentences which either fit the line, or simply run into one another. The textual unit of a written sentence must be learned formally. What is clear is that the child's prior experience of listening to stories, sharing books with adults, together with a wider store of experience of what language is and does, inform the child's writing efforts. Most children appear to internalize story-structure by school age: beginnings, central character, sequence of events, reported speech, and appropriate endings. So, in this respect, like all other aspects of language, the child appears to discover the rules of the game from the experiences which adults provide.

For the hearing-impaired child, specific difficulties in writing may arise at any one of the three stages of the writing process described earlier. At the first stage the child may be unable to think about content. One teaching strategy which might help here is 'brainstorming'. This involves talking with a child or group before writing, around the topic of interest. Lists of important or relevant ideas, vocabulary and information are drawn up. Basically, the technique asks children to say what they know about the subject before writing about it. Children rarely utilize all that they know when they write.

At the second stage, when ideas have to be translated into sentence patterns, hearing-impaired children are likely to need a lot of help. At the simplest level the teacher could discuss what the child would like to say, write a sentence down using the child's own structures, and the child simply has to transfer print from one place to another. Completion techniques, such as those used in DARTs activities, can be used to stimulate children's discussion about appropriate choices to complete a sentence. Children may be given key words to use in a new sentence or a series of stem sentences can be given, which the child has to finish off. An important part of these exercises is that alternative choices are tried out and tested, with opinions offered by the children themselves about suitability.

In our discussion of the theoretical models of reading in Chapter 3, reference was made to the notion of a lexicon: the inner dictionary of words, their meanings and functions. This inner store is also thought to house selectional restrictions: the rules which modify the forms words take in use with one another. The writing of severely hearing-impaired children sometimes shows very little awareness of the constraints which exist in English grammar on word selections ('we was enjoyed ourself'). Whilst there is some controversy about how much language can be acquired as a pencil-and-paper exercise, some teachers do advocate replacement exercises to give written practice with syntax and word forms. In replacement exercises children are given whole sentences, but asked to change an element, such as a verb from past to present, a noun from plural to singular, replace an adjective with a synonym, or spot a deliberate error. In all of these techniques, of course, most of the grammatical material is given and the child's writing task is one of selection or reorganization.

Independent writing can sometimes be encouraged by joint composition between teacher and child. Openings and endings can be discussed together with sentence structure. Alternative ways of organizing sentences can be put forward and talked about. This kind of drafting and revision at the point of writing fosters the approach of self-monitoring and self-correction, so important in reading. Where a child does tend to stick to rigid sentence patterns, more flexible ways of presenting things can be experimented with. Joint writing can also be the occasion to show how punctuation is used correctly to amplify meaning, where full stops, speech marks and commas are rightly introduced and why.

Perhaps the two greatest concerns have been expressed about the deaf child's inability to extend sentence sequences and poor sense of discourse. The first results in simple sentences without co-ordination or subordination. The second results in lack of connection between sentences in a passage: sentence-by-sentence writing. Limited exposure to the function words of language in conversation offers some explanation for this. The words which enable a child to connect and extend clauses, may have only weak and fleeting stress in speech. These devices are late to appear in normal development anyway, and may not have been experienced in conversation beforehand. Added to this, handling long sequences of verbal material may require a working memory facility not possessed by many deaf people who lack inner speech. Is it possible to teach these discourse features to children?

The cohesion of written language has only very recently come to prominence as a field of study in its own right (Halliday and Hasan, 1976; Chapman, 1983). We can study cohesion by looking at the ways in which sentences are tied together in a text, and which otherwise would appear as a haphazard jumble. One common kind of cohesive tie is the use of a pronoun substitution which refers the reader back to words used earlier on.

> Alice liked animals and (her) parents
> said (she) could have a pet:
> '(You)'ll have to look after (it) yourself'
> (they) told (her)

In this exercise used with hearing-impaired primary children attention is drawn to the words which are ringed and the words which are substituted. Similarly, when cohesion is achieved by cross-reference, the important words can be highlighted and discussed:

Goats were kept for their skins. (These) were
later made into coats.

Yet another kind of cohesive device is ellipsis. Here a word or phrase is omitted but has to be assumed:

Joe wanted sausages. There weren't any. O

Other forms of cohesion identified by Halliday and Hasan (1976) include conjunctives: *causal,* such as 'therefore', 'so'; *temporal,* such as 'then', 'afterwards'; *additive,* such as 'also', 'and'; and lastly, *adversative,* such as 'however', or 'but'. There is a danger of children attempting to use cohesive devices mechanically and without real understanding. However, teachers should be able to centre discussion around appropriate choice of cohesive ties in order to avoid writing sentence-by-sentence.

Spelling strategies

It has been argued that hearing-impaired children have few problems in spelling because, of all the routes a child might take to storing and retrieving the spelling patterns of words, deaf children choose the most effective. In hearing children, proficient spellers tend to make greater use of visual patterns. They may start out by trying to spell a word phonically, using the sound–letter correspondences. However, a shift in strategies usually occurs so that good spellers recall words by analogy with related words which they know, and eventually by building up a visual store. That is the most convincing explanation of why, when adults face a word they are uncertain about spelling, most people want to write it down, to see if it 'looks right'.

There are some important principles for teaching and correcting children's spelling which apply equally well to hearing and hearing-impaired children. The first of these is that any attempt to teach spelling should centre around words which are meaningful and relevant to the child and which the child wishes to use. Spelling, like most other aspects of language skill addressed in this book, will be learned least effectively in the abstract, without a context or purpose. So, learning words from spelling lists is unlikely to help children become better spellers. Secondly, if children produce a wealth of spelling mistakes in their written work it is advisable to pick three or four important, frequently occurring words, rather than marking every error. Confidence is easily lost otherwise. Draw attention to words which need correcting rather than inserting letters in a word which is wrong. Paying attention to spelling should not divert the teacher's attention away from what it is the child wants to convey; and for a hearing-impaired child, the more important discussion points may relate to the grammatical structure of the child's writing.

However, where the teacher feels a child really needs to master the spelling patterns of some key writing vocabulary, the most effective strategy is this:

1 Write the word for the child.
2 Ask the child to read the word.
3 Cover the word or turn the page over.
4 The child now writes the word from memory.
5 Check accuracy and repeat steps 2–5 if necessary.

The key aspect of this strategy is that the child is not copying letter-for-letter, but learning visual wholes. This can be combined with activities which draw attention to the internal structure of words by grouping them into families. Children can, from an early stage, keep their own spelling books as a reference source. For older children, learning how to use a dictionary is an important part of a child's reference and study skills. For some further practical ideas, see Torbe (1977).

Computer-assisted learning

This survey of teaching approaches to literacy would be incomplete without some reference to micro-computers in the classroom. In the not too far-distant future most primary and secondary schools will have access to micro-technology. The advantages of computer-assisted learning have important implications for children with special needs generally, and hearing-impaired children in particular. Most children find micro-computers stimulating and highly motivating. A teaching program usually presents individually-paced learning steps which are controlled by the pupil. Children have immediate feedback to their responses which is, of course, an efficient learning principle. But perhaps the most important point for a hearing-impaired child is the visual presentation of the material and potential for overcoming many of the obstacles to communication which the child may experience in other areas of learning. It should be said that computer-assisted learning is not an end in itself and needs to be used selectively to support the teacher's work. As Ward *et al.* (1985) have pointed out in a review of software programs for the hearing-impaired, computers in the classroom do not create extra time for the teacher.

For teachers who specialize in working with the hearing-impaired there are some interesting devices available commercially. One piece of equipment displays the sound spectrum of speech on a television monitor to give visual feedback of speech input. This is to help a child monitor speech production visually where there is poor auditory feedback. There are several devices which have a wider application in providing language enrichment activities. Programs have been produced to teach the vocabulary of mathematical shapes: words are exposed along with the corresponding shape, such as hexagon. When the child punches the correct word into the keyboard, this is rewarded by some kind of musical or visual treat on the screen. Some programs allow the child to interact with the computer by animating written commands and illustrating concepts entered into the keyboard by the child. There are several alternative keyboards, some with words, symbols or pictures, which engage the child in matching and selection games.

Software has been devised to help children write and spell. In one program a child's written work is scanned and any spelling mistakes are highlighted. Spelling games present words which then have to be reproduced by the child. Any incorrect entries are dealt with, in one instance by a 'gremlin' digging out the wrong letters and burying them in a hole; unfortunately, correct entries are less spectacularly rewarded. A computerized thesaurus has been produced which suggests alternative words to those given by the child in composing a sentence, akin to the 'brainstorming' technique suggested earlier. Perhaps most serviceable are text-editing facilities which enable children to see and amend their sentences before they are printed out. This would be an extremely useful way of putting into practice some of the ideas for writing presented earlier: joint composition, trying out different cohesive ties, experimenting with discourse features such as story beginnings and endings. A very useful handbook on the role of micro-computers for children with special needs has been written by Hogg (1984).

An assessment profile

There is no reading test in the United Kingdom designed specifically for hearing-impaired children, nor would such a test be desirable. There are some glaring pitfalls in using traditional standardized yardsticks of reading. Tests usually reflect a particular model of the reading process and make many assumptions about what is important in learning to read. We still do not know exactly what the child requires in order to read. What is more, there can be a wide gap between what researchers think tests measure, and what they actually reveal. In Chapter 4 we looked in some depth at the respective test responses of deaf and hearing children on standardized test materials. There can be no doubt that tests tap different reading processes in different populations. The summary reading age or quotient may tell us very little about children's reading skills: their strengths and weaknesses. It is also true that if we set about testing reading in a particular way, such as phonic knowledge, we may adversely influence the strategies children believe they must bring to the reading task.

For reasons such as these some teachers want to move away from the pass/fail model of assessing reading, in order to make more detailed observations of what the child actually does when reading. The kind of assessment framework recommended in this book is one which a teacher uses as part of an ongoing process of setting objectives for the child and evaluating the outcomes of the

Table 6.1   Literacy profile of the hearing-impaired

Early skills
Looks at picture books with an adult
Listens to a story and can identify pictures
Predicts a story sequence: notices any changes
Points to where book begins
Locates starting-point and direction for reading print
Matches a word with a picture
Matches word pairs together
Chooses own books and likes to take them home
Spends time looking at books other than when asked
Reads aloud own name
Asks what labels and signs mean
Scribbles for 'own' writing
Traces over large model of name
Copies a few letters of name
Writes own name without model
Copies words accurately

'Bottom-up' skills
Attempts a few familiar words
Reads aloud individual letter sounds
Reads aloud and blends simple Consonant-Vowel-Consonant words,
    such as 'pot'
Guesses from the first letters in a word e.g. 'garage' for 'green'
Guesses a word which looks similar e.g. 'three' for 'there'
Uses letter names to sound out words
Reads aloud words with initial consonant blends,
    e.g. fl_____, bl_____, sw_____, gr_____, pr_____
Reads aloud final consonant blends,
    e.g. _____ft, _____nd, _____mp, _____st, _____rd
Reads letter combinations,
    e.g. oo, ee, ch, ay, th, sh
Has a sight vocabulary of a few familiar words
Reads aloud 10, 20, 30 plus sight words
Writes letters when given letter sounds,
    e.g. m, p, r, e, o
Writes regular, predictable words,
    e.g. cat, put, in, tip
Writes irregular words,
    e.g. their, said, the, school

(continued)

Table 6.1—continued

Will persevere in correcting a word and check it looks right
Writes 10, 20, 30 plus words from memory.

'Top-down' skills
Uses picture clues to guess a word
Will re-read a sentence to guess a word which fits the syntax
Looks for key words and then guesses the rest
Guesses a word which means the same, e.g. 'boy' for 'brother'
Uses knowledge of world to predict a word, or events in a story
Uses story context to read unfamiliar words
Monitors own errors in reading and self-corrects
Enjoys simple readers and can retell the story sequence
Talks about stories or books read
Can take in a paragraph and answer comprehension questions
Locates a point of information or main idea in a passage
Needs help with complex syntax
Retells a longer story and retains the sense
Able to use content, index, headings and summaries to gain information
Reads for information using reference books, tables, maps, dictionaries, directories
Reads independently with understanding books which are age appropriate
Seeks out information by scanning or skimming
Summarizes and makes notes on passage
Can assume mastery of complex language in reading
Copies captions and simple sentences
Can use a word folder to construct and then copy out own sentences
Completes a stem sentence with an appropriate word
Fills in a cloze task with words of good fit
Needs most of the sentence frame and vocabulary to be given
Generates own sentences but needs help to correct
Writes a short sequence of ideas
Locates words and spellings in a dictionary
Creates own stories
Expresses own feelings and opinions in print
Uses complex sentences in writing including function words such as 'and', 'but'
Re-inspects own writing to correct
Few grammatical errors: has learned most of the selectional restrictions
Ties sentences together using pronouns, cross-reference, conjunctives ('so', 'but', 'then', 'next')

child's learning experience. An informal profile approach incorporates whatever skills the teacher feels are important for the child
to acquire. These are usually set down in a logical sequence and are
written in such a way that they are easily observable and not open
to interpretation. Such a framework can be used to plan learning
steps for a child, to identify any gaps in skills, and to record
progress over time. A literacy profile for hearing-impaired
children has been prepared as an example. This is not exhaustive
and the purpose of the exercise is to show teachers how they can
shape their own observations and construct a profile related to
their own personal objectives.

Chapter summary

1   Teachers need a perspective: an awareness of the skills they
are working towards and the likely effects of their teaching on the
child. Reading is intimately related to a broad spectrum of
language skills but the extent to which reading can *teach* language
is under dispute. Some researchers (Söderbergh, 1985) believe the
written word should be tied early to the child's experience.
Others feel that the child's comprehension of more complex
language in books depends on the prior mastery of spoken
language.

2   The major principles of fostering language with the hearing-impaired are briefly mentioned, such as providing a good
listening/acoustic environment. Enabling strategies in mainstream schools are discussed, such as ways of presenting information and proper use of hearing-aids. Lessons from language
research show that *conditions* for learning are more important than
drilling, rehearsing and contriving to teach language directly. The
quality of language interactions is perhaps the most effective
teaching tool. The principles of immersion and expectancy,
important to first language learning, are also applicable to early
reading experience.

3   Teachers should know which level of the reading process
they are tackling. Working on subskills such as phonics attaches a
lot of importance to what might be a secondary skill for the
normally-hearing. There is evidence that children learn to read by
reading and may not require a practice phase. Efforts to teach

syntax are more clearly justified because of the central importance of grammar to reading for meaning. However, *special* materials and strategies must be considered suspect if they are not part of the normal developmental process.

4   Modifying reading materials to match the child's grammatical control is one approach. Unfortunately, rewriting and simplifying text tends to reduce information content and cue sources and makes text harder to read for meaning (Ewoldt, 1984). Modifying the reader may be a more productive approach. Accepting the linguistic limitations of deaf children inspires an approach whereby more efficient, active questioning of text is encouraged. Attention is directed to the important features of text. Several exercises from DARTs materials are presented such as underlining, completion and sequencing. The principle of helping the child to study more effectively has a wider application to aspects such as note-taking, using reference books and training examination techniques.

5   The development of writing is considered from the earliest efforts at copying captions, to discovering the rules of story structure. At the first stage of pre-writing, 'brainstorming' vocabulary and ideas may help. At the second stage of composing a sentence, discussion, joint writing and replacement exercises are useful. The greatest concern is usually felt over extending sentence sequences and connecting sentences together in a passage. The teaching of various kinds of cohesive ties is discussed, such as substitution, ellipsis and conjunctives (Halliday and Hasan, 1976).

6   Spelling may not be a problem for a hearing-impaired child because a visual route (chosen by proficient hearing children) is preferred in recalling word patterns. However, a read, cover, write, check procedure is advocated and suggestions are made for marking spelling errors. Computer-assisted techniques are now available for practising spelling, illustrating the speech spectrum, manipulating language forms and teaching concepts.

7   Finally, an informal reading inventory is advocated rather than traditional tests, for setting teaching objectives, highlighting learning steps and monitoring individual progress. Such a literacy profile should reflect the teacher's own philosophy and priorities, whilst providing a useful framework of observation.

7

OVERVIEW

No one with an interest in the way children learn, having spent time in a school for the hearing-impaired, could fail to be grabbed by the experience and not wish to know more. This has been a book of explorations, beginning with the very first questions: 'How is deafness caused?' 'How identified?', and 'What are the parameters used to define it?'. The significance of a hearing loss for the individual varies enormously, not least of all in relation to its severity and permanence. From the very outset, however, we have been cautious in avoiding the deficit-model approach, which stresses difficulties, not achievements. We have preferred to locate the child's problems in the environment or with adult caretakers, rather than *within* the child. It is unfortunately true that almost everything which has been written about deaf children has been in the deficit mould.

The first strand of exploration concerned the impact of deafness on the social context of child development. Particular emphasis was given to the emergence of a wide spectrum of language skills within a social framework. The model of language study from Crystal (1976) gives a useful breakdown into the areas of sound, syntax and meaning. Prominent in this model is the *active* role of the child in mastering the structural principles of the language system, providing the conditions are right. Most adults seem especially geared to facilitate and negotiate meaningful language interactions with their children.

The literature which describes the impact of even very mild conductive hearing losses on child development seems to point in one direction only. Early hearing loss is associated with delays in development, speech and language immaturity, together with subsequent school and behavioural difficulties. Some problems of interpretation were pointed out, for example, the notion of specific auditory processing deficits, when a hearing loss occurs at a critical period. There are high *associations* of developmental delay with early middle-ear disease, but no straightforward *causal* links. Hearing loss is often compounded by a nexus of social, physical and environmental factors, all of which create obstacles to learning in themselves. There is some evidence that children may later overcome the effects of an early hearing loss, but the ongoing presence of even a mild impairment is a significant hindrance to learning in school. One very popular idea has arisen that mild hearing losses are a direct cause of reading failure. Here too, a single-factor explanation of reading disability seems unlikely, but there may well be a more diffuse relationship between conductive hearing loss and a broad range of verbally-dependent skills, such as reading.

The impact of more severe, sensori-neural hearing losses on development can be devastating. The fact that some deaf children achieve just as well as their hearing peers encourages us to look at the quality of the child's interactions with others, and conditions in the teaching environment. Severe deafness does not simply restrict what the child can hear, it also disrupts the social-interactive processes important for language growth. There may be secondary effects of deafness on the behaviour of adults and teachers, evoking more directive, controlling and questioning strategies. The child may be discouraged from being an active user of language, to become a passive assimilator. The child may have to learn *how to learn from language.* Whatever the reasons and whatever the mode of communication used, hearing-impaired children throughout their lives generally compare poorly with hearing peers in all areas of the language model outlined. Most important perhaps is the less-flexible grasp of the rules of syntax. Studies of reading have been mainly evaluative, content to demonstrate the limited achievements of deaf children on standardized tests: a plateau around a reading age of 9 years, beyond which few progress. Studies of writing too, have described the poor organization of language, proliferation of errors and non-standard usages, together with a kind of sentence-by-sentence effect.

The second strand of exploration considered what we know of the normal reading process. Reading was described as finding information in print. However, there is much disagreement about the skills children need in order to read, and how reading is learned. Certainly, reading is a complex perceptual, thinking and reasoning process, and no *single* factor has the power to explain how it is achieved or why it goes wrong. Two models of reading were presented. The first, a view of reading as information-processing, taking cues from the 'bottom-up' sources in text, such as letter-shapes, sounds or word-shapes. The second model considers the reader to be an active language user, and the insights gained by the child in mastering spoken language are later applied to reading. There is purpose, expectation and meaning in text; the child's job is to predict what these might be by sampling the written material. As a compromise, elements of both models can be incorporated into an 'interactive' view of reading where the reader is sensitive to many cue-levels in text, 'bottom-up' and 'top-down'. Interestingly, very good readers are thought to be using direct visual access to meaning in print: they are 'bottom-uppers', which leaves more available thinking space. These different reading routes can be aligned roughly with the different areas of language outlined earlier. Sound/letter features occupy the periphery, with grammar as the central organizing principle, relating sounds to meaning.

The assessment of reading suffers from the lack of an underlying theory. Reading tests often sample aspects of behaviour which bear little relation to what children do when they read.

Tests over-simplify reading, tell us little about the learning process and often lack validity: a measure of how well a test measures what it purports to. We argued that teachers need to know the scope, status and limitations of test findings. Teachers should always ask themselves why they want to test a child, what skills they would like to reveal, and whether more informal observations of children as they read authentic materials will do the job just as effectively as a standardized test. Those who have attempted to test the reading achievements of deaf children have been caught by almost all of the snares in traditional yardsticks. In fact, looking at *how* deaf children tackle reading tests rather than their respective test scores, tells us a great deal about the strategies they do use in reading. It seems likely that the notion of a 'plateau' is an artefact of test materials which simply overwhelm the child linguistically. More finely detailed observations of deaf children reading are likely to provide the key to understanding.

At this point the two strands of exploration were brought together. What strengths and weaknesses, particularly in the three areas of our language model, do hearing-impaired children bring to reading? What does the reading task demand of the child? The areas of linguistic delay which mildly hearing-impaired children bring to reading are felt to be broad-based and affect the whole spectrum of language-related skills, including auditory processing, vocabulary, grammar, together with less-effective strategies for learning. Whichever model of the reading process is accepted, a mild hearing loss may be disruptive because both low-level and larger units in print are unfamiliar and inaccessible. The child's linguistic experience, at all levels, shows discrepancies with the task.

For the severely hearing-impaired child the picture is more complicated. Reading problems arise in the comprehension of text, not in learning sight vocabulary or decoding letters into sounds (Conrad, 1979). True, a child with limited control of syntax has to face complex structures in print. But the problem is more than one of a mismatch between reader and text. We suggested that inner speech coding provides the major tool for thinking and reading. Working memory stores complex verbal sequences just long enough to work out the meaning. If working memory depends on inner speech, we have an explanation of why extended sentence structures are problematical for deaf people. For similar reasons the act of writing is more hazardous. Stages of pre-writing, composition and review, seem highly dependent on working memory and inner speech. The 'invisible ink' experiment was very successful at disrupting the hearing child's writing by simply removing feedback.

The several experimental studies presented have important implications for teaching strategies. The reading battery we devised shows that deaf children utilize alternative information sources in text and use 'top-down' strategies with a heavy pragmatic basis. Given that, teachers may wish to develop 'reading for learning' as a priority, helping children to use their existing skills more efficiently. That might be a better long-term plan than modifying materials and teaching 'bottom-up' skills. In the final analysis teachers must judge for themselves, what and how they teach. This book will have succeeded in its aims if it provides a working perspective which informs what teachers do.

The last exploration in this book was not intended to be didactic, but to give some useful suggestions. Areas covered include: early reading experience; creating optimum conditions for listening and language interaction; important principles from mainstream language research, such as immersion and expectancy; sharing books; reading for meaning; study skills; ideas for introducing writing and developing cohesive styles; together with some brief notes about spelling, computer-assisted learning, and an assessment profile. Inevitably, and with no apology, the many ideas discussed in this book will have raised more questions than provided answers. The sincere hope, then, is that the next exploration will be the teacher's own!

REFERENCES

Ainscow, M. and Tweddle, D. M. (1979) *Preventing Classroom Failure: an Objectives Approach*, London, Wiley & Sons.

Allington, R. L. (1978) 'Sensitivity to orthographic structure as a function of grade and reading ability', *Journal of Reading Behaviour*, 10, 437–9

Ames, T. (1980) *Diagnostic Reading Pack*, London, Macmillan.

Arnold, H. (1982) *Listening to Children Reading*, Sevenoaks, Hodder & Stoughton.

Backman, J. (1983) 'The role of psycholinguistic skills in reading acquisition: a look at early readers', *Reading Research Quarterly*, 18 (4), 466–79.

Baddeley, A. D. (1976) *The Psychology of Memory*, London, Harper & Row.

Baddeley, A. D. (1979) 'Working Memory and Reading', in Kolers, P. A., Wrolstad, N. E. and Bouma, H. (eds) *The Processing of Visible Language*, I, New York, Plenum Press.

Bamford, J. M. and Saunders, E. (1985) *Hearing-impairment, Auditory Perception and Language Disability*, London, Edward Arnold.

Baron, J. (1973) 'Phonemic stage not necessary for reading', *Quarterly Journal of Experimental Psychology*, 25, 241–6.

Baron, J. and Strawson, C. (1976) 'Use of orthographic and word-specific knowledge in reading words aloud', *Journal of Experimental Psychology: Human Perception and Performance*, 2, 386–93.

Bax, M., Hart, H. and Jenkins, S. (1983) 'The behaviour, development and health of the young child: implications for care', *British Medical Journal*, 286, 1793–6.

Beard, R. (1984) *Children's Writing in the Primary School*, Sevenoaks, Hodder & Stoughton.

Beggs, W. D. A. and Breslaw, P. I. B. (1982) 'Reading retardation or linguistic deficit? III: a further examination of response strategies in a reading test completed by hearing-impaired children', *Journal of Research in Reading*, 6 (1), 19–28.

Bench, J. and Bamford, J. (eds) (1979) *Speech-Hearing Tests and the Spoken Language of Hearing-impaired Children*, London, Academic Press.

Bishop, D. V. M. (1983) 'Comprehension of English syntax by profoundly deaf children', *Journal of Child Psychology and Psychiatry*, 24 (3), 415–35.

Bookbinder, G. E. (1976) *Salford Sentence Reading Test*, London, Hodder & Stoughton.

Bradley, L. (1980) *Assessing Reading Difficulties: a Diagnostic and Remedial Approach*, London, Macmillan.

Bradley, L. and Bryant, P. (1979) 'Independence of reading and spelling in backward and normal readers', *Developmental Medicine and Child Neurology*, 21, 504–14.

Brandes, P. J. and Ehinger, D. M. (1981) 'The effects of early middle ear pathology on auditory perception and academic achievement', *Journal of Speech and Hearing Disorders*, 46, 301–7.

Brennan, M. (1976) 'Can deaf children acquire language? An evaluation of linguistic principles in deaf education', supplement to *The British Deaf News*, February, Carlisle, The British Deaf Association.

Briggs, P. (1983) 'Phonological coding in good and poor readers', unpublished doctoral dissertation, University of Nottingham.

Brimer, A. (1972) *Wide-span Reading Test*, London, Nelson.

Brimer, A. and Raban, B. (1979) *Infant Reading Tests*, Newnham, Gloucestershire, Education Evaluation Enterprises.

British Association of Teachers of the Deaf (1981) 'Audiological definitions and forms for recording audiometric information', *Journal of the British Association of Teachers of the Deaf*, (5) 3, 83–7.

Brooks, P. H. (1978) 'Some speculations concerning deafness and learning to read', in Liben, L. S. (ed.) *Deaf Children: Developmental Perspectives*, 87–101, New York, Academic Press.

Bruner, J. S. (1975) 'The ontogenesis of speech acts', *Journal of Child Language*, 2, 1–19.

Burgener, G. W. and Mouw, J. T. (1982) 'Minimal hearing loss effect on academic/intellectual performance of children', part 1, study 1, *Hearing Instruments*, 33 (6), 7–8; part 2 *Hearing Instruments*, 33 (8), 14–15.

Burt, C. (1921) *Mental and Scholastic Tests*, London, King.

Chapman, J. (1983) *Reading Development and Cohesion*, London, Heinemann.

Chen, K. (1976) 'Acoustic image in visual detection for deaf and hearing college students', *Journal of General Psychology*, 94, 243–6.

Clark, E. V. (1978) 'From gesture to word: on the natural history of deixis in language', in Bruner, J. S. and Garton, A. (eds) *Human Growth and Development*, Oxford, Oxford University Press.

Clark, M. M. (1976) *Young Fluent Readers*, London, Heinemann.

Clark, M. M. (1980) 'Difficulties in reading and writing in schools: another perspective', in Clark, M. M. and Glynn, T. (eds) *Reading and Writing for the Child with Difficulties*, University of Birmingham, Educational Review: Occasional Publications, no. 8, 80–6.

Clay, M. M. (1968) 'A syntactic analysis of reading errors', *Journal of Verbal Learning and Verbal Behaviour*, 7, 434–8.

Clay, M. M. (1977) *Reading: the Patterning of Complex Behaviour*, London, Heinemann.

Clay, M. (1979) *The Early Detection of Reading Difficulties*, London, Heinemann.

Collins-Ahlgren, M. (1975) 'Language development of two deaf children', *American Annals of the Deaf*, 120, 524–39.

Commission of the European Community (1979) *Childhood Deafness in the European Community*, Luxembourg, CEC, ESSC-NE-EAEC.

Conrad, R. (1979) *The Deaf School Child*, London, Harper & Row.

Cooper, R. and Rosenstein, J. (1966) 'Language acquisition of deaf children', *Volta Review*, 68, 58–67.

Crystal, D. (1976) *Child Language, Learning and Linguistics*, London, Edward Arnold.

Crystal, D. (1979) *Working with LARSP*, London, Edward Arnold.

Crystal, D., Fletcher, P. and Garman, M. (1976) *The Grammatical Analysis of Language Disability*, London, Edward Arnold.

Cumming, C., Grove, C. and Rodda, M. (1985) 'A note on reading comprehension in hearing-impaired adolescents', *Journal of the British British Association of Teachers of the Deaf*, 9 (3), 57–60.

Dale, P. S. (1976) *Language Development: Structure and Function*, 2nd edn, New York, Holt, Rinehart & Winston.

Dalzell, J. and Owrid, H. L. (1976) 'Children with conductive deafness: a follow-up study', *British Journal of Audiology*, 10, 87–90.

Davis, J. (1974) 'Performance of young hearing-impaired children on a test of basic concepts', *Journal of Speech and Hearing Research*, 17, 342–51.

DES (1967) *Units for Partially Hearing Children*, Education Survey, no. 1, London, HMSO.

DES (1975) *A Language for Life* ('The Bullock Report'), London, HMSO.

DES (1983) Tabulation of returns on forms 21M and 7 (schools) at table 1 of consultative document SH (82) 3, 'The need for rationalisation of special school provision for the hearing-impaired', June 1982, and statistics from the same sources for 1982 and 1983.

de Villiers, J. G. and de Villiers, P. A. (1978) *Language Acquisition*, Cambridge, Massachusetts, Harvard University Press.

DHSS (1981) Advisory committee on services for hearing-impaired people, final report of the sub-committee appointed to consider services for hearing-impaired children.

Di Francesca, S. (1972) *Academic Achievement Test Results of a National Testing Program for Hearing-Impaired Students, Spring 1971*, series D, no. 9, Washington, DC, Gallaudet College, Office of Demographic Studies.

Djupesland, G., Nicklasson, B., Helland, S. and Hemsen, E. (1981) 'Hearing threshold level and middle ear pressure in children with phonetic/phoneme disability', *Scandinavian Audiology*, supplement 16, 73–9.

Dodd, B. (1976) 'The phonological systems of deaf children', *Journal of Speech and Hearing Disorders*, 41, 185–98.

Dodd, B. (1980) 'The spelling abilities of profoundly pre-lingually deaf children', in Frith, U. (ed.) *Cognitive Processes in Spelling*, 423–40, London, Academic Press.

Dodd, B. and Hermelin, B. (1977) 'Phonological coding by the pre-linguistically deaf', *Perception and Psychophysics*, 21, 413–17.

Donaldson, M. (1978) *Children's Minds*, London, Fontana.

Downing, J., Ayers, D. and Schaefer, B. (1983) *Linguistic Awareness in Reading Readiness (LARR) Test*, Windsor, NFER-Nelson.

Downs, M. P. (1977) 'The expanding imperatives of early identification', in Bess, F. (ed) *Childhood Deafness: Causation, Assessment and Management*, 95–106, New York, Grune & Stratton.

Ewing, I. R. and Ewing, A. W. G. (1944) 'The ascertainment of deafness in infancy and early childhood', *Journal of Laryngology and Otology*, 59, 309.

Ewoldt, C. K. (1981) 'A psycholinguistic description of selected deaf children reading in sign language', *Reading Research Quarterly*, 17, 58–89.

Ewoldt, C. K. (1984) 'Problems with rewritten materials, as examplified by "to build a fire"', *American Annals of the Deaf*, 129 (1) 23–8.

Ferrier, L. J. (1978) 'Some observations of error in context', in Waterson, N. and Snow, C. E. (eds) *The Development of Communication*, Chichester, Wiley.

France, N. (1979) *Primary Reading Test*, London, Nelson.

Freeman, B. A. and Parkins, C. (1979) 'The prevalence of middle ear disease among learning impaired children', *Clinical Pediatrics*, 18, 205–10.

Frith, U. (ed.) (1980) *Cognitive Processes in Spelling*, London, Academic Press.

Fundudis, T., Kolvin, I. and Garside, R. (eds) (1979) *Speech Retarded and Deaf Children: Their Psychological Development*, London, Academic Press.

Fusfeld, I. (1955) 'The academic program of schools for the deaf', *Volta Review*, 57, 63–70.

Geers, A. and Moog, J. (1978) 'Syntactic maturity of spontaneous speech and elicited imitations of hearing-impaired children', *Journal of Speech and Hearing Disorders*, 43, 380–91.

Gibson, E. J. and Levin, H. (1975) *The Psychology of Reading*, Cambridge, Massachusetts, MIT Press.

Gittleman, R. and Feingold, I. (1983) 'Children with reading disorders I: Efficacy of reading remediation', *Journal of Child Psychology and Psychiatry*, 24, 167–91.

Glass, R. (1981) 'The association of middle ear effusion and auditory learning disabilities in children', *Rehabilitation Literature*, 42 (3–4), 81–5.

Goodman, K. S. (1969), 'Analysis of oral reading miscues: applied psycholinguistics', *Reading Research Quarterly*, 5, 9–30.

Goodman, K. S. (1976) 'Reading: a psycholinguistic guessing game,' in Singer, H. and Ruddell, R. (eds) *Theoretical Models and Processes of Reading*, 2nd edn, Newark, Del., International Reading Association.

Gottlieb, M. I., Zinkus, P. W. and Thompson, A. (1980) 'Chronic middle ear disease and auditory perceptual deficits', *Clinical Pediatrics*, 18, 725–32.

Gregory, J. (1982) *Phonics: a Resource Bank and Teacher's Guide*, London, John Murray.

Gregory, S. (1983) 'The development of communication skills in young deaf children: delayed or deviant?', paper presented to the Child Language Seminar, University of Strathclyde, March 1983.

Gregory, S. and Mogford, K. (1981) 'Early language development in deaf children', in Woll, B., Kyle, J. and Deuchar, M. (eds) *Perspectives on British Sign Language and Deafness*, London, Croom Helm.

Griffiths, A. J. (1983) 'The linguistic competence of deaf primary school children', unpublished doctoral dissertation, University of Nottingham.

Griffiths, A. and Hamilton, D. (1984) *Parent, Teacher, Child*, London, Methuen.

Halliday, M. A. K. (1973) *Explorations in the Functions of Language*, London, Edward Arnold.

Halliday, M. A. K. and Hasan, R. (1976) *Cohesion in English*, London, Longman.

Hamblin, D. H. (1981) *Teaching Study Skills*, Oxford, Basil Blackwell.

Hamilton, P. and Owrid, H. L. (1974) 'Comparisons of hearing-impairment and socio-cultural disadvantages in relation to verbal retardation', *British Journal of Audiology*, 8, 27–32.

Hamp, H. W. (1972) 'Reading attainment and some associated factors in deaf and partially hearing children', *The Teacher of the Deaf*, 70, 203–15.

Hamp, H. W. (1975) *The Picture Aided Reading Test*, Northampton, Hamp.

Harris, J. (1984) 'Early language intervention programmes: an update', *Association for Child Psychology and Psychiatry Newsletter*, 6 (2), 2–20.

Herbert, D. and Davies-Jones, G. (1977) *A Classroom Index of Phonic Resources*, Stafford, National Association for Remedial Education.

Hirsh-Pasek, K. and Treiman, R. (1982) 'Recoding in silent reading: can the deaf child translate print into a more manageable form?', *Volta Review*, 84, 71–82.

Hogg, B. (1984) *Microcomputers and Special Educational Needs: a Guide to Good Practice*, Stratford-upon-Avon, National Council for Special Education.

Holm, V. A. and Kunze, L. H. (1969) 'Effect of chronic otitis media on language and speech development', *Pediatrics*, 43, 833–9.

Howie, V. M., Jensen, N. J., Fleming, J. W., Peeler, M. B. and Meigs, S. (1979) 'The effect of early onset of otitis media on educational achievement', *International Journal of Pediatric Otorhinolaryngology*, 1, 151–5.

Ingram, D. (1976) 'Phonological disability in children', *Studies in Language Disability and Remediation II*, London, Edward Arnold.

Ivimey, G. (1976) 'The written syntax of an English deaf child: an exploration in method', *British Journal of Disorders in Communication*, 11, 103–120.

Jackson, S. (1971) *Phonic Skills Test*, Glasgow, Gibson.

Jensema, C. J. (1975) *The Relationship Between Academic Achievement and the Demographic Characteristics of Hearing-Impaired Children and Youth*, series R, no. 2, Washington, DC, Gallaudet College, Office of Demographic Studies.

Jorm, A. F. (1977) 'Parietal lobe function in developmental dyslexia', *Neuropsychologia*, 15, 841–4.

Juel, D. (1980) 'Comparison of word identification strategies with varying context, word type and reader skill', *Reading Research Quarterly*, 3, 358–76.

Kaplan, G. J., Fleshman, J. K., Bonder, T. R., Baum, C. and Clark, P. S. (1973) 'Long term effects of otitis media: a ten year cohort study of Alaskan Eskimo children', *Pediatrics*, 52, 577–85.

Karmiloff-Smith, A. (1978) 'The interplay between syntax, semantics and phonology in language processes', in Campbell, R. N. and Smith, P. T. (eds) *Recent Advances in the Psychology of Language*, New York, Plenum Press.

Kolers, P. A. (1973) 'Three stages of reading', in Smith, F. (ed.) *Psycholinguistics and Reading*, New York, Holt, Rinehart & Winston.

Kretschmer, R. R. (1978) 'Comparison of the spontaneous written language of hearing and deaf children', in Kretschmer, R. R. and Kretschmer, L. W. (eds) *Language Development and Intervention with the Hearing-Impaired*, 120–1, Baltimore, University Park Press.

Kretschmer, R. R. and Kretschmer, L. W. (eds) (1978) *Language Development and Intervention with the Hearing-Impaired*, Baltimore, University Park Press.

Kyle, J. G. (1980a) 'Measuring the intelligence of deaf children', *Bulletin of the British Psychological Society*, 33, 54–7.

Kyle, J. G. (1980b) 'Reading development of deaf children', *Journal of Research in Reading*, 3, 86–97.

Lake, D. (1978) 'Syntax and sequential memory in hearing-impaired children, in Reynolds, H. and Williams, C. (eds) *Proceedings of the*

Gallaudet Conference on Reading in Relation to Deafness, Washington, DC, Gallaudet College.

Lehmann, M. D., Charron, K., Kummer, A. and Keith, R. W. (1979) 'The effect of chronic middle ear effusion on speech and language development: a descriptive study', *International Journal of Paediatric Otorhinolaryngology*, 1, 137–44.

Lewis, N. (1976) 'Otitis media and linguistic incompetence', *Annals of Otology*, 102, 387–90.

Liberman, I., Shankweiler, D., Fischer, F. and Carter, B. (1974) 'Reading and the awareness of linguistic segments', *Journal of Experimental Psychology*, 18, 201–12.

Locke, J. and Locke, V. (1971) 'Deaf children's phonetic, visual, and dactylic coding in a grapheme recall task', *Journal of Experimental Psychology*, 89, 142–6.

Lunzer, E. and Gardner, K. (eds) (1979) *The Effective Use of Reading*, London, Heinemann, for Schools Council.

Lunzer, E. and Gardner, K. (1984) *Learning from the Written Word*, Edinburgh, Oliver & Boyd, for the Schools Council.

Mackay, D., Thompson, B. and Schaub, P. (1970) *Breakthrough to Literacy*, London, Longman.

McLeod, J. and Atkinson, J. (1972) *Domain Phonic Test*, Edinburgh, Oliver & Boyd.

McNeill, D. (1966) 'Developmental linguistics', in Smith, F. and Miller, G. A. (eds) *The Genesis of Language*, 15–84, Cambridge, Massachusetts, MIT Press.

Maliphant, R., Supramaniam, S. and Saraga, E. (1974) 'Acquiring skill in reading: a review of experimental research', *Journal of Child Psychology and Psychiatry*, 15, 175–85.

Markides, A. (1970) 'The speech of deaf and partially hearing children with special reference to factors affecting intelligibility', *British Journal of Disorders of Communication*, 5, 126–40.

Marsh, G., Friedman, M., Welch, V. and Desberg, P. (1980) 'The development of strategies in spelling', in Frith, U. (ed.) *Cognitive Processes in Spelling*, 339–53, London, Academic Press.

Martin, F. N. (ed.) (1978) *Pediatric Audiology*, New Jersey, Prentice-Hall.

Masters, L. and Marsh, G. E., (1978) 'Middle ear pathology as a factor in learning disabilities', *Journal of Learning Disabilities*, 11 (2), 54–7.

Meadow, K. P. (1980) *Deafness and Child Development*, London, Edward Arnold.

Meek, M. (1982) *Learning to Read*, London, The Bodley Head.

Meyer, L. A. (1982) 'The relative effects of word-analysis and word-supply correction procedures with poor readers during word-attack training', *Reading Research Quarterly*, 17 (4), 544–55.

Mindel, E. D. and Vernon, M. (1971) *They Grow in Silence*, Silver Spring, Maryland, National Association of the Deaf.

Mitchell, D. C. (1982) *The Process of Reading*, Chichester, John Wiley & Sons.

Mitchell, D. C. and Green, D. W. (1978) 'The effects of context and content on immediate processing in reading', *Quarterly Journal of Experimental Psychology*, 30, 609–36.

Moon, C. (in press) 'Reading: where are we now?', in Meek, M. and Mills, C. (eds) *Language and Literacy in the Primary School*, London, Falmer Press.

Murdoch, H. (1984) 'Maternal rubella: the implications', *Journal of the Association of Educational Psychologists*, 6 (5), 3–6.

Murphy, K. P. (1976) 'Communication for the hearing-impaired in the United Kingdom and the Republic of Ireland', in Oyer, H. H. (ed.), *Communication for the Hearing Handicapped*, 155–222, Baltimore, University Park Press.

Myklebust, H. R. (1964) *The Psychology of Deafness*, 2nd edn, New York, Grune & Stratton.

National Deaf Children's Society (1983) *Discovering Deafness*, London, NDCS.

Neale, M. D. (1958) *The Neale Analysis of Reading Ability*, London, Macmillan.

Needleman, H. (1977) 'Effects of hearing loss from early recurrent otitis media on speech and language development', in Jaffe, B. (ed.) *Hearing Loss in Children*, 640–9, Baltimore, University Park Press.

Neville, M. H. and Pugh, A. K. (1976–7) 'Context in reading and listening: variations in approach to cloze tasks', *Reading Research Quarterly*, 12, 13–31.

Nordén, K. (1975) *Psychological Studies of Deaf Adolescents*, Lund, C. W. K. Gleerup.

Nowell, H. and Eaton, D. M. (1982) *Reading disability and middle ear pathology*, unpublished manuscript, London, St Mary's Hospital.

O'Hagan, F. and Swanson, I. (1984) 'Special education: which way forward?', *Special Education: Forward Trends*, 11 (2), 6–8.

Pikulski, J. (1978) 'A critical review: informal reading inventories', in Chapman, L. J. and Czerniewska, P. (eds) *Reading: From Process to Practice*, 352–66, London, Routledge & Kegan Paul.

Pintner, R. and Patterson, D. (1916) 'A measurement of the language ability of deaf children', *Psychological Review* , 23, 413–36.

Pugh, G. (1946) 'Summaries from appraisal of the silent reading abilities of acoustically handicapped children', *American Annals of the Deaf*, 91, 331–49.

Quigley, S. P. (1978) 'Effects of early hearing-impairment on normal language development', in Martin, F. N. (ed.) *Pediatric Audiology*, 35–60, New Jersey, Prentice-Hall.

Quigley, S. P. and Kretschmer, R. E. (1982) *The Education of Deaf Children: Issues, Theory and Practice*, London, Edward Arnold.

Quigley, S. P. and Paul, P. V. (1984) *Language and Deafness*, London, Croom Helm.

Quigley, S. P., Wilbur, R., Power, D., Montanelli, D. and Steinkamp, M. (1976) *Syntactic Structures in the Language of Deaf Children*, Urbana, Illinois, Institute for Child Behavior and Development.

Raban, B. (1983) *Guides to Assessment in Education: Reading*, London, Macmillan.

Rapin, E. (1979) 'Conductive hearing loss: effects on children's language and scholastic skills; a review of the literature', *Annals of Otology*, 88, 3–12.

Redgate, G. W. (1972) *The Teaching of Reading to Deaf Children*, Manchester, University of Manchester.

Reich, P. A. and Reich, C. M. (1974) *A Follow-up Study of the Deaf*, Toronto, Ontario, Toronto Board of Educational Research Report.

Reichman, J. and Healey, W. C. (1983) 'Learning disabilities and conductive hearing loss involving otitis media', *Journal of Learning Disabilities*, 16 (5), 171–8.

Richards, S. H., Kilby, D., and Shaw, I. D. (1971) 'Grommets and glue ears: a clinical trial', *Journal of Laryngology and Otolaryngology*, 83, 17–22.

Richman, N., Stevenson, J. E. and Graham, P. J. (1982) *Pre-school to school: a behevioural study*, London, Academic Press.

Rozin, P., Poritsky, S. and Sotsky, R. (1971) 'American children with reading problems can easily learn to read English represented by Chinese characters', *Science*, 171, 1264–7.

Russell, G. (1982) 'Impairment of phonetic reading in dyslexia and its persistence beyond childhood: research note,' *Journal of Child Psychology and Psychiatry*, 23, 459–75.

Sak, R. and Ruben, R. J. (1981) 'Recurrent middle ear effusion in childhood: implication of temporary auditory deprivation for language learning', *Annals of Otology, Rhinology and Laryngology*, 89, 303–11.

Schaffer, H. R. (ed.) (1977) *Studies in Mother–Infant Interaction*, New York, Academic Press.

Schlesinger, H. S. and Meadow, K. P. (1972) *Sound and Sign: Childhood Deafness and Mental Health*, Berkeley, University of California Press.

Schonell, F. J. (1942) *Backwardness in the Basic Subjects*, Edinburgh, Oliver & Boyd.

Schulze, G. (1965) 'An evaluation of vocabulary development by 32 deaf children over a 3-year-period', *American Annals of the Deaf*, 110, 424–35.

Shah, N. (1981) 'Middle ear effusion – glue ear', in Beagley, H. A. (ed.) *Audiology and Audiological Medicine*, 2, 699, Oxford, Oxford University Press.

Silva, P. A. Kirkland, C., Simpson, A., Stewart, I. A. and Williams, S. M. (1983) 'Some developmental and behavioural problems associated with bilateral otitis media with effusion', *Journal of Learning Disabilities*, 15, 417–21.

Simmons, A. (1962) 'A comparison of the type–token ratio of spoken and written language of deaf and hearing children', *Volta Review*, 64, 117–21.

Smith, F. (ed.) (1973) *Psycholinguistics and Reading*, New York, Holt, Rinehart & Winston.

Smith, F. (1978) *Reading*, Cambridge, Cambridge University Press.

Smith, F. (1982) *Writing and the Writer*, London, Heinemann.

Smyth, G. D. L. and Hall, S. (1983) 'Aetiology and treatment of persistent middle-ear effusion', *Journal of Laryngology and Otology*, December, 97, 1085–9.

Snow, C. E. and Ferguson, C. A. (eds) (1977) *Talking to Children: Language Input and Acquisition*, Cambridge, Cambridge University Press.

Snowling, M. (1980) 'The development of grapheme–phoneme correspondence in normal and dyslexic readers', *Journal of Experimental Child Psychology*, 29, 294–305.

Söderbergh, R. (1985) 'Early reading with deaf children', *Prospects*, XV (1), 77–85.

Sokolov, A. N. (1972) *Inner Speech and Thought*, New York, Plenum Press.

Southgate, V. (1962) *Group Reading Test (Test 2, Form A – Sentence Completion)*, Sevenoaks, Hodder & Stoughton.

Stanovich, K. E. (1980) 'Towards an interactive – compensatory model of individual differences in the development of reading fluency', *Reading Research Quarterly*, 16, 32–71.

Stanovich, K. E. and West, R. F. (1979) 'The effect of orthographic structure on the word search performance of good and poor readers', *Journal of Experimental Child Psychology*, 28, 258–67.

Start, K. B. and Wells, B. K. (1972) *The Trend of Reading Standards*, Slough, NFER.

Streng, A. (1965) *Reading for Deaf Children*, Washington, DC, Alexander Graham Bell Association for the Deaf.

Torbe, M. (1977) *Teaching Spelling*, London, Ward Lock.

Tucker, I. and Nolan, M. (1984) *Educational Audiology*, Beckenham, Kent, Croom Helm.

Tweedie, J. K. (1983) 'Hearing loss and academic failure', *Public Health*, 97, 136–8.

Van Uden, A. (1977) *A World of Language for Deaf Children, Part I: Basic Principles; a Maternal Reflective Method*, The Netherlands, Swets & Zeitlinger.

Vellutino, F. R. (1979) *Dyslexia: Theory and Research*, Cambridge, Massachusetts, MIT Press.

Vernon, P. E. (1938) *A Standardisation of a Graded Word Reading Test*, London, University of London Press.

Ward, R., Lindley, P., Rostron, A., Sewell, D. and Cubie, R. (1985) 'Computer-assisted learning and deaf children's language: using the language and thought software in a hearing-impaired unit', *Journal of the British Association of Teachers of the Deaf*, 9 (3), 61–6.

Watts, A. F. (1980) *The Holborn Reading Scale*, London, Harrap.

Webster, A. (1983) *Reading and Writing in Severely Hearing-impaired Children*, unpublished PhD thesis, University of Nottingham.

Webster, A. and Bamford, J. M. (in press) Royal Berkshire Hospital Study.

Webster, A. and Ellwood, J. (1985) *The Hearing-impaired Child in the Ordinary School*, Beckenham, Kent, Croom Helm.

Webster, A. and McConnell, C. (in press) *Speech and Language Difficulties in Childhood: a Teacher's Guide*, Eastbourne, Holt-Saunders.

Webster, A., Saunders, E. and Bamford, J. M. (1984) 'Fluctuating conductive hearing-impairment, *Journal of the Association of Educational Psychologists*, 6 (5), 6–19.

Webster, A., Scanlon, P. and Bown, E. (1985) 'Meeting the needs of hearing-impaired children within a local education authority', *Journal of Association of Educational Psychologists*, supplement to 6 (5), 2–10.

Webster, A., Wood, D. J. and Griffiths, A. J. (1981) 'Reading retardation or linguistic deficit? I: interpreting reading test performances of hearing-impaired adolescents', *Journal of Research in Reading*, 4 (2), 136–47.

Webster, D. B. and Webster, M. A. (1979) 'Effects of neonatal conductive hearing loss on brainstem auditory nuclei', *Annals of Otology*, 88, 684–8.

Wells, G. (1981) *Learning through Interaction*, Cambridge, Cambridge University Press.

Wepman, J. M. (1958) *Auditory Discrimination Test*, Windsor, NFER.

Wilbur, R. B. (1977) 'An explanation of deaf children's difficulty with certain syntactic structures in English', *Volta Review*, 79, 85–92.

Williams, P., Congdon, P., Holder, M. and Sims, N. (1971) *Swansea Test of Phonic Skills*, Oxford, Basil Blackwell, for the Schools Council.

Williams, J. E. and Dennis, D. B. (1979) 'LARSP in clinical settings: a partially-hearing unit', in Crystal, D. (ed.) *Working with LARSP*, 214–41, London, Edward Arnold.

Wolff, J. G. (1973) *Language, Brain and Hearing*, London, Methuen.

Wood, D. J. (1984) 'The assessment of linguistic and intellectual abilities of hearing-impaired school children', *Journal of the Association of Educational Psychologists*, 6 (5), 31–9.

Wood, D. J., Griffiths, A. J. and Webster, A. (1981) 'Reading retardation or linguistic deficit, II: test-answering strategies in hearing and hearing-impaired school children', *Journal of Research in Reading*, 4 (2), 148–57.

Wood, D. J., Howarth, C. I., Wood, H. A. and Griffiths, A. J. (in press) *Teaching and Talking with the Deaf Child*, London, Wiley.

Wood, D. J., McMahon, L. and Cranstoun, Y. (1980) *Working with Under Fives*, London, Grant McIntyre.

Wood, H. A. and Wood, D. J. (1984) 'An experimental evaluation of the effects of five styles of teacher conversation on the language of hearing-impaired children', *Journal of Child Psychology and Psychiatry*, 25, 45–62.

Wrightstone, J., Aronow, M. and Moskowitz, S. (1963) 'Developing reading test norms for deaf children', *American Annals of the Deaf*, 108, 311–16.

Young, D. (1982) *The Cloze Reading Tests*, Sevenoaks, Hodder & Stoughton.

Zinkus, P. W., Gottleib, M. I. and Schapiro, M. (1978) 'Developmental and psycho-educational sequelae of chronic otitis media', *American Journal of Diseases of Children*, 132, 1100–4.

INDEX